When Faith
Meets Reason

When Faith Meets Reason

Religion Scholars Reflect on Their Spiritual Journeys

Edited by Charles W. Hedrick

POLEBRIDGE PRESS
Santa Rosa, California

Cover and interior design by Robaire Ream

Library of Congress Cataloging-in-Publication Data
When faith meets reason : religion scholars reflect on their spiritual
journeys / edited by Charles W. Hedrick.
      p. cm.
Includes index.
ISBN 978-1-59815-010-0
1. Christian biography. 2. College teachers--Religious life. 3. Faith
and reason. I. Hedrick, Charles W.
BR1700.3.W44 2008
277.3'0830922--dc22
                                                        2008034626

For Robert W. Funk

Whose faith journey led him, and finally us, into public conversations about private matters of personal faith.

Table of Contents

Contributors

Susan M. (Elli) Elliott (Ph.D., Loyola University, Chicago) is an independent scholar living in Red Lodge, Montana. Her first book was *Cutting Too Close for Comfort: Paul's Letter to the Galatians in Its Anatolian Cultic Context* (2003). The working title of her current book project is "Whose Family Values?—Early Christians Re-Envision the Family, the World, and Everything."

† **Robert W. Funk** (Ph.D., Vanderbilt University) was Director of the Westar Institute and founder of the Jesus Seminar. A Guggenheim Fellow and Senior Fulbright Scholar, his many books and articles include *The Five Gospels* (1993, with the Jesus Seminar), *Honest to Jesus* (1996) and *A Credible Jesus* (2002).

David Galston (Ph.D., McGill University, Montreal) is the former Principal of Iona College, University of Windsor, and a co-founder of Canada's SnowStar Institute of Religion. In 2001 he left the University to become the Director of the Eternal Spring Learning Centre in Hamilton, Ontario, where he teaches theology and is Minister to a historical Jesus church community.

Charles W. Hedrick (Ph.D., Claremont Graduate University) is Emeritus Distinguished Professor of Religious Studies at Missouri State University. His books include *When History and Faith Collide* (1999) and *Many Things in Parables: Jesus and His Modern Critics* (2004).

Glenna S. Jackson (Ph.D., Marquette University) is Professor in the Department of Religion and Philosophy at Otterbein College. Her publications include *"Have Mercy On Me": The Story of the Canaanite Woman in Matthew 15:21–28* (2002) and many articles on women in the first century as well as African parable parallels.

Paul Alan Laughlin (Ph.D., Emory University) is Professor of Religion and Philosophy at Otterbein College in Ohio. His books include *Remedial Christianity: What Every Believer Should Know about the Faith, but Probably Doesn't* (2000) and *Getting Oriented: What Every Christian Should Know about Eastern Religions, but Probably Doesn't* (2005).

Nigel Leaves (Ph.D., Murdock University, Australia) is Director and Dean of Studies at the John Wollaston Anglican Theological College,

Perth, Western Australia. His books include *Odyssey on the Sea of Faith: the life and writings of Don Cupitt* (2004) and *The God Problem: Alternatives to Fundamentalism* (2006).

Darren J. N. Middleton (Ph.D., University of Glasgow, Scotland) is Associate Professor of Literature and Theology at Texas Christian University. He has published five books. And his sixth, *Theology after Reading: Christian Imagination and the Power of Fiction*, will be released in 2008.

Robert M. Price (Ph.D., Drew University) is Professor of Theology and Scriptural Studies at the Johnnie Colemon Theological Seminary and the author of *The Widow Traditions in Luke-Acts* (1997) and *The Incredible Shrinking Son of Man* (2004).

James M. Robinson (D.Th., University of Basel, Switzerland, and Ph.D., Princeton Theological Seminary) is Professor of Religion Emeritus, Claremont Graduate University, and Director Emeritus, Institute for Antiquity and Christianity. Author of *The Gospel of Jesus* (2006) and *The Secrets of Judas* (2006).

Mahlon H. Smith (M.S.L., Pontifical Institute of Medieval Studies, Toronto) is Professor Emeritus of Religion and former Chair of the Department of Religion at Rutgers University in New Brunswick, NJ. He co-authored *The Gospel of Mark: Red Letter Edition* and is editor of *Forum*.

Hal Taussig (Ph.D., The Union Institute) is Visiting Professor of New Testament at Union Theological Seminary in New York, Professor of Early Christianity at the Reconstructionist Rabbinical College, and co-pastor at Chestnut Hill United Methodist Church. His several books include *Jesus Before God* (1999) and *A New Spiritual Home* (2006).

Theodore J. Weeden, Sr. (Ph.D., Claremont Graduate University) is a retired minister of the United Methodist Church, and has also taught in various undergraduate and graduate academic institutions. Widely known for his *Mark-Traditions in Conflict* (1971), he has authored articles on Christian faith and New Testament issues.

Walter Wink (Th.D., Union Theological Seminary, New York) is Professor Emeritus at Auburn Theological Seminary and author of *Engaging the Powers: Discernment and Resistance in a World of Domination* (1992) and *The Human Being: Jesus and the Enigma of the Son of the Man* (2000).

Preface

Robert W. Funk

The exchange among the Westar Leaders in April 2005 about Easter and the resurrection burrows into the heart of our problem: at what point does the discrepancy between what I know, or think I know (I like to add that important qualification) and what I am willing to say publicly become so acute that my personal integrity is at stake? The breaking point came fairly early for me. I decided for the academic world because I thought I could maintain my integrity longer there than in the parish ministry. Then the seminary became a threat to that integrity and again I sought relief by moving to a secular university. But there is no escape if you wish to be true to yourself.

I finally realized that Westar Institute and the Jesus Seminar lay in my future because only in that context could I hope to recover any modicum of personal integrity. I worried initially because I feared I was the only one who had secretly been on this pilgrimage to discover the historical truth. How surprised I was to learn that many other scholars were on the very same trek. At the same time, I began to realize that the historical truth is not the fundamental issue. The fundamental issue is the nature of faith itself. So I longed to embark on the second big phase of the seminar and take up what has been called a "Second Nicea."

I have often asked myself how I got to the first stage—the desire to determine and articulate the historical truth. And the answer I always get is this: I was learning things about my own tradition that undermined the original affirmations I had inherited from my predecessors. Why had I not thought to share those things, one at a time, with people in my church? Instead I do what many clergy do and that is dissemble. And I dissembled as much by what I didn't say as by what I did say.

And now we have Associates in Westar who are convinced that we should stop with the historical Jesus, and perhaps the historical Paul, and rest our oars. There is of course wisdom in the suggestion that we should pass on the fragments of truth we gained from our intense studies to those who haven't been let in on the secret as yet. And that would be sufficient. In other words, go back into the education business and simply transmit what we now know, or think we know, about the gospels, and the Bible, and let it go at that.

But that won't do. And the reason is that personal integrity is still at stake—for me at least. If it is the case that we live by faith—by trust—I want to know what that means for me. So exploration of the future of the faith is inevitable—for me.

In the Westar Institute and the Jesus Seminar I have come to think that our collective or group integrity is now at stake (it has been all along, in fact), if we break off now and be satisfied with what we have done.

Or so it seems to me.

—Robert W. Funk
April 2005

Introduction
Making Personal Sense of Ancient Religion in the Modern World

Charles W. Hedrick

In the Beginning, Diversity

There never has been a "right" way of viewing Jesus—or God for that matter. The Bible does not attest a single view of God. Rather, one finds in its pages multiple views—for example, the capricious God of Job, the unconscionable God of 1 Samuel 15 who ordered the annihilation of the Amalekites, and the ethical God of the Hebrew prophets. The same is true of Jesus. In the earliest texts about Jesus, enough diversity of perspective exists to astonish an average reader whose religious life has been nourished by the traditional creeds of Christian faith. Consider, for example, these statements that describe three different moments at which Jesus became the divine son of God:

> From a human perspective, he [Jesus] was descended from David, yet by his resurrection from the dead he was appointed son of God with power (Rom 1:3–4).

> A holy spirit will come upon you [i.e., Mary] and the highest power will overshadow you. Therefore the one born will be called holy, son of God (Luke 1:35).

> The word was at the beginning, and the word was with God, and the word was God. This [word] was at the beginning with God (John 1:1–2).

Did Jesus become God at his resurrection, at his birth, or was he always the son of God? The truth is this: given the nature of the sources, many images of Jesus may be developed from the gospel narratives about him.

At the beginning Jesus, his friends, associates, and acquaintances were not yet called "Christians." In those early days, they were only slender threads woven into the fabric of Judaism. Later, in the period following Jesus' crucifixion, his "followers" conceived of him as Messiah and the Son of God. He was, in Matthew's words, "Jesus the Anointed, son of David, son of Abraham" (Matt 1:1), "God's son" (Matt 16:16), and his earliest friends and associates were remembered as his "disciples."

The early gospels offer varied portrayals of both him and his career, the variety growing, in part, out of the individuality of each author's personal faith. The sharpest disjunction occurs between the Gospels of Mark and John. These two gospels differ so much that if their authors had met by chance in an out of the way wine bar in Rome or Ephesus, neither would have recognized the story about Jesus in the other's gospel as the same story. The differences among the several gospel narratives sparked multiple responses in ancient auditors and readers, and that in turn led to a variety of movements tracing themselves back to Jesus as their originator. Some of the best known of the movements can be identified by the different religious perspectives surviving in the literature the church later collected: the view inherent in Paul's letters, the "synoptic" understanding of Jesus (found in Matthew, Mark, and Luke), John's idiosyncratic vision, and the conservative stance of Paul's opponents in Galatians (the "circumcision party"), and second Corinthians (the "superlative apostles"). Then the Deutero-Pauline and Pastoral letters reflect Pauline disciples who understand their teacher in somewhat different ways, and the later followers of Peter are represented by First and Second Peter. Other ways of understanding Jesus and his sayings are only briefly hinted at here and there in the early literature: for example, one finds Hymenaeus and Philetus (2 Tim 2:16–18), who said that the resurrection was already past as well as those whom the author of the Johannine letters described as denying that Jesus had come "in the flesh" (2 John 7). Still later in the first century, Cerinthus of Asia Minor was said to have taught that God did not create the world and that Jesus was the natural son of Mary and Joseph. To judge from those esoteric groups that emerged in Alexandria in the early second century—people like the Valentinians and Basilideans, for example—no doubt many more similarly diverse movements existed, of which no record survives.

Creeds and Confessions

For the first three centuries of the Common Era no generally accepted standards defined the "right way" to be a follower of Jesus—or even whether a "right way" could be identified among all the different views about him. Diversity of perspective was the rule. The claim that the "faith once delivered to the saints" (Jude 3) was the "true" faith was only one claim for authority among the many competing claims that emerged in the early period.

In the western part of the Roman Empire during the second century, one wing of these competing movements defined itself as the true descendant of the original apostles of Jesus and set itself apart from the rest by promoting its own belief system as the "true" faith and libeling all others as "heretical." Late in that century Irenaeus, Bishop of Lyons, refuted the views of those not subscribing to the Rule of Faith taught by his church, which he described as a "universal" church. By the fourth century this so-called "universal" (catholic) church had developed a "canon" of writings that they described as "God-inspired Scripture" and discredited the literature of their competitors as "not genuine" and "heretical." In the fourth and fifth centuries the "universal" wing of these competing movements called for creedal councils in an effort to define precisely what constituted "true faith." These two developments (canon and creeds) aimed at promoting what the "universal church" regarded as the "true faith" in order to marginalize, discredit, and eliminate other forms of what was by then generally known as "Christianity." Nevertheless, religious writings other than those specified in the canon of the "one holy, Catholic and Apostolic Church" (as these believers called themselves) were not completely eradicated and indeed continued to be used. Some of these so-called "heretical" texts survive today—discovered in such ancient trash dumps as Oxyrhynchus in Egypt, where Greek fragments of the Gospel of Thomas were found, or rediscovered in modern libraries and museums, where they had lain for centuries without their significance being recognized. Despite the best efforts of the champions of "orthodoxy," the creeds of the fourth and fifth centuries failed to consolidate under one authority all those who claimed the name Christian; Coptic churches in the east, for instance, withdrew and rejected the decisions of the councils.

Nevertheless, these two initiatives (canon and creeds) by the catholic churches eventually prevailed, their dominance spread a thin religious veneer over the Roman west, and certain political decisions by the fourth-century Roman Emperor, Constantine gave the catholic churches a political advantage in the Empire. The result was that what the catholic churches defined as "orthodoxy" (right belief) became the state religion. The years that followed saw a consolidation of the political and religious influence of the catholic churches, the disestablishment of the old religions of the Roman Empire, and the political recognition of western "orthodoxy" (as opposed to Orthodoxy in the east) as the only way to be "Christian." This one-sided decision had the effect of driving underground those movements that held different visions of what it meant to be "Christian."

Further Fragmentation

For one thousand years Christianity remained divided between the Roman Catholic Church in the west, Coptic Christianity in Egypt, and

Eastern Orthodoxy in the east. Even today they remain three fundamentally different ways of being Christian. In the sixteenth century further divisions occurred. The hegemony of the church in the west was shattered by "protest" movements that led to the formation of still other ways of conceiving what it meant to be Christian. The Protestant Reformation saw the establishment of such distinct types of "protest" church groups as Lutheran, Calvinist, and Anabaptist. These faith communities formed around different ideas about what it meant to be a follower of Jesus than those espoused by Roman Catholicism. Nevertheless, the fourth and fifth-century constructs of canon and creed have, in the main, survived from that time as the "accepted" place to begin answering the question, "What does it mean to be a follower of Jesus?"

The Challenge of Renaissance and Enlightenment

The two foundations of modern Christendom (canon and creeds) were challenged in the fourteenth through seventeenth century by the intellectual rediscovery of the past known as the Renaissance, a series of movements in Europe that revived interest in the classical learning of ancient Greece and Rome. And in the following century they were seriously undermined by the Enlightenment, a movement in Europe and America that witnessed the birth of the critical method, the rejection of the hegemony of Christian belief, and an increasing reliance on human reason for addressing humanity's place in the universe. The ancient Christian creedal synthesis was further weakened by the subsequent and ongoing discoveries of modern science, and particularly by the rediscovery of some of the repressed texts of the early competitors of orthodoxy. The discovery of the Nag Hammadi Library, the Gospel of Judas, and other texts, has opened a window to the past by bringing to public attention some of the amazing religious diversity of the early period of Christian origins. These texts, suppressed by the winners of the debates between early orthodoxy and its competitors, have cast a spotlight on the ideas of the losers, and further undermined the assertion that only one true faith existed in the period of origins. Since the Enlightenment, critical thought and human reason applied to the biblical texts have continued to erode their authority as a special revelation from God. Modern science has revealed the Bible's worldview to be antique and mythical—particularly, for example, as a description of how the world came to be (cf. Genesis 1–3).

The old creedal edifices have proven inadequate for expressing the faith of modern human beings who are children of the Renaissance and Enlightenment. No longer do these traditional formulae command unquestioning assent; indeed, they raise more questions than they resolve. In particular, like the New Testament they assume the ancient Near Eastern view of a three-tiered universe: God resides "in the heavens," human beings live on the surface of a flat earth, and beneath the surface of the earth lies the abode of the dead. The image of God sitting on a throne high in the heavens to which Jesus ascends after the resurrection and from which he will come to judge the world, if taken literally, is completely inadequate to explain the data that junior high school children of today learn from their study of geology, astronomy, and physics.

The Challenge of Human Reason and Modern Science

Since the eighteenth century, scholars who have completed terminal degrees (the Ph.D. or its equivalent) in the critical study of religion—even scholars closely identifying themselves with traditional forms of reformation Christianity—can scarcely help being influenced by Renaissance and Enlightenment thinking, since so much of their work involves logic, human reason, and critical methodology. What happens to traditional faith when the old creeds and confessions can no longer be squared with an empirical worldview? The contributors to this volume have faced that question and found ways to accommodate faith, human reason, and modern science. Their views have changed over a lifetime of critical study into the roots of the Christian tradition.

In principle, the same four general options were available to them that are open to anyone who faces the modern challenges to traditional faith. (1) They could simply have jettisoned the entire religious enterprise, given up faith altogether, and found some other line of work less intellectually demanding than that of being a professional thinker about religion. Not a single one of them selected that option. (2) They might simply have denied what their reason told them and looked for ways to rationalize the data. In this way they could remain a confessing member of the faith community and a critical member of the community of scholars. Not one of them chose that option. (3) They could have chosen to conceal what they really thought by not addressing the issues and avoided answering questions about their own personal religious faith. In this way they would never have to "go public" with what they really believed. None took that option. (4) A final choice, not generally practiced in the academic guild, is simply to say what they really think about their religious faith, and explain how they have gone about making modern religious meaning for themselves. The contributors to this volume have chosen this last option.

How This Volume Came About

Three years ago (2005), I sent invitations to all Fellows of the Jesus Seminar inviting them to describe how they went about making religious meaning for themselves in the modern world. Twenty-three Fellows expressed an interest in submitting a paper for inclusion in the volume. Ten Fellows had actually submitted papers by August of 2007. The reader should understand that publishing such a paper is not without its risks for a scholar. Nearly all religious groups have community creeds and confessions by which they identify themselves. If scholars violate the confessions of faith of their religious communities, they may endanger their careers—particularly those who are employed by academic institutions aligned with religious denominations. By speaking one's mind in such circumstances, one risks termination of an academic position or clerical ordination—and even expulsion from a religious community. In the history of the Jesus Seminar at least two Fellows have been fired from academic positions for participation in the deliberations of the Seminar, and others pressured with either overt or subtle threats.

When I spoke to Robert Funk, the Director of the Westar Institute, about asking the Fellows of the Jesus Seminar to go public with what they believed "in their heart of hearts," he was not sure it would be possible. There were good reasons to think that it might not be. "Confessions" have never been part of the modern academic study of religion, since they fall outside the purview of the objectivity demanded by critical studies. That said, however, even the most critical scholar among us has found ways to reconcile at least to some extent personal religious beliefs with the scholarship he or she practices in the guild. Scholars tend, however, not to share those personal views in a public forum and will generally avoid such subjective personal reflections for a wide variety of reasons, not the least of which is an inability to resolve some of the basic questions for themselves. At some point, I suspect, all scholars find themselves in the same situation as the non-professional in not being able to answer certain basic questions of faith.

Being honest about what one thinks has always mattered in critical scholarship. Along with the independence and integrity of a scholar's research and the logic of the scholar's results, candidness is a highly regarded virtue in our guild. But how one creates religious meaning from the results of critical study has never been highly valued. Whether or not one is religious has never been a requirement for participation in the academic fellowship—perhaps because scholars are critical thinkers, and critical thinkers can never really be satisfied with a consensus, which is the real function of confessions and creeds.

When I wrote to the Fellows in October of 2005, here is the way I pitched the volume to them:

Aim at avoiding all insider language in your essay. You are not writing for the academy, but rather for the general public. Write about how *you yourself* are making religious sense in your life in the 21st century, rather than suggesting potential ways *the reader* might go about making sense of *their* faith. In other words, what you write is a personal statement describing your own personal faith and ideas, which will then be one model among the others we will have in the book. The task is not to produce an objective analysis of your religious odyssey, but rather a personal statement of "where you are now" based on your scholarship and whatever else you use to "make sense of things" for yourself.

Making Sense of Religion

I suppose in one sense it really doesn't matter what any one else believes about religion; for in the final analysis, whether we work things out for ourselves or simply accept the solutions of others, we all must make our own religious meaning. Nevertheless, seeing how critical scholars have created meaning for themselves does have value: each of these essays is an example of a conclusion reached by someone who has given due consideration to the problems and possibilities for arriving at a sustainable personal religious synthesis in the modern world.

Like the diversity of views represented in the prior collection *Profiles of Jesus*, the views represented in this volume are scarcely uniform. They begin at different points. Robert Price begins with the Christian community. Nigel Leaves, Elli Elliott, David Galston, and I begin with the religious traditions of our youth. Hal Taussig and Darren Middleton begin with a divine presence evident in the world of nature. James Robinson, Theodore Weeden, Mahlon Smith, and Walter Wink focus their remarks on Jesus. Paul Alan Laughlin begins with Eastern mysticism, and Glenna Jackson begins with Africa.

Darren Middleton's primary spiritual concern is God, whom Middleton describes as "evolving" by "interconnectedness with our emerging world." He rejects the "strangely unmovable God" of classical Christian theology. Hal Taussig affirms a "personalized universe" and describes encounter with "God" as participation in the universe's central dynamic. As a child Elli Elliott discovered that the image of God as a grand old man in the sky was inadequate and found instead that God was a divine Listening Presence.

James Robinson, Mahlon Smith, Theodore Weeden, and Walter Wink focus their essays principally on Jesus of Nazareth. Robinson rejects antiquity's structure of belief as thoroughly inadequate for modern life. For Robinson, Jesus' words mediate God more than his deeds: Jesus' parables, he submits, are "God happening." Mahlon Smith asserts that nothing has been more influential in shaping his life than Jesus of Nazareth, a Jewish man, who is present to him in his words and the ancient stories about him. Theodore Weeden, after having served in parish ministry for thirty-six years, describes his current views under three rubrics: Jesus; God; the church and its Bible. Walter Wink, on the other hand, looks to the gospels for that which "Jesus revealed." "The gospels continue to feed me, as does all of Scripture, . . ." he says.

Nigel Leaves is deeply rooted in the Anglican tradition but found his ideas changing over the years because of the situations in which he practiced his ministry. For my own part, I believe in God, because I "cannot explain why there is nothing at all." I take the world as my point of departure for thinking about God. Robert Price sees himself as a near "secular humanist" who finds the universe "neutral and empty of any personal God pulling the strings." In short, he is "a religion-loving atheist." Glenna Jackson describes losing her "faith in Hippo, North Africa," when she found herself in strong disagreement with the early Christian theologian, Augustine, whose theological writings provided the basis for modern Orthodoxy. In his youth Paul Alan Laughlin became disillusioned with the evangelical faith of his childhood, but rediscovered a mystical Christian faith in the academic study of religion, and in particular, Eastern faiths and philosophies. David Galston calls himself a "fallen theologian" in describing his move from neo-orthodox faith into a kind of Christian atheism, which he sees as "Jesus following." It is a kind of humanism that results from taking Jesus resolutely as a human being.

What strikes me as interesting is that all these Fellows began their spiritual odyssey within some aspect of traditional Christianity—Baptist, United Methodist, Presbyterian, United Church of Christ, Anglican—but have ended up, not unlike the earliest followers of Jesus, following their reason as well as their spirit to very divergent positions. Yet they still identify themselves in some way, however tenuous, with traditional communities of faith. One can only wonder what other scholars have come to believe, should they offer candid statements of their own personal religious faith.

Works Consulted

Bainton, Roland H. *The Age of the Reformation*. Princeton: D. Van Nostrand Company, 1956.

Bettenson, Henry and Chris Maunder, eds. *Documents of the Christian Church*. 3d ed. Oxford: Oxford University Press, 1999.

Bultmann, Rudolph. "New Testament and Mythology." Pp. 1–44 in *Kerygma and Myth. A Theological Debate*. Ed. Hans Werner Bartsch. New York: Harper & Row, 1961.

Gay, Peter, ed. *The Enlightenment. A Comprehensive Anthology*. New York: Simon and Schuster, 1973.

Hedrick, Charles W. "The Four/Thirty-Four Gospels. Diversity and Division among the Earliest Christians." *Bible Review*18.3 (June 2002) 20–31, 46–47.

_____. "What is Christian? Competing Visions in the First Century. *The Fourth R* 19.4 (July-August 2006) 3–8, 22.

Hill, Charles E. "Cerinthus, Gnostic or Chiliast? A New Solution to an Old Problem." *Journal of Early Christian Studies* 8.2 (2000) 135–72.

Hoover, Roy W., ed. *Profiles of Jesus*. Santa Rosa, CA: Polebridge Press, 2002.

Kasser, Rodolphe, Gregor Wurst, Marvin Meyer, Francois Gaudard, eds. *The Gospel of Judas Together with the Letter of Peter to Philip, James, and a Book of Allogenes from Codex Tchacos*. Washington, DC: National Geographic, 2007.

Mates, Julian and Eugene Cantelupe, eds. *Renaissance Culture. A New Sense of Order*. New York: George Braziller, 1966. (A collection of readings from the period).

Mazzeo, Joseph Anthony. *Renaissance and Revolution. Remaking of European Thought*. New York: Pantheon Books, 1965. (esp. pp. 3–68).

Meyer, Marvin, ed. *The Nag Hammadi Scriptures. The International Edition*. New York: HarperCollins, 2007.

Polk, Brayton and Bernard Zelechow, eds. *The Intellectual Adventure of Man to 1600*. Vol. 1 of *Readings in Western Civilization*. Toronto: York University, 1970. (A collection of readings).

Robinson, John A. T. *Honest to God*. Philadelphia: Westminster Press, 1963.

From Hippo to Hippos
Being on the Edge of Smash in Africa

Glenna S. Jackson

Africa on My Mind

"Tili pamadzi ndipo boti latifela. Malo lafelawo ndi owopsya chifuk-wa tazungulilidwa ndi mvuu. Tumizani boti lina mwansanga chifukwa chilichonse chingathe kuchitika." These words were whispered hurriedly in the Chechewa language through a walkie-talkie by the guide I was with in a small motor-boat on Lake Malawi. Just a few minutes earlier and out of curiosity, I had asked the guide why we were able to motor smack dab through the middle of the hippo pools since anytime I had been near hippo pools on the Zambezi River in Zimbabwe, we had stayed very far away. He answered that hippopotami are afraid of the sound of motors and we were in no danger. Fifteen minutes later, the motor conked out. The guide radioed back the message and motioned for us to be absolutely still and make no noises, even with the camera. I whispered, "Hippos are vegetarian, right?" He nodded yes. So I thought, "Cool—stuck in the middle of a hippo pool—how many times can that happen in one's lifetime?" I have to admit that when we were rescued forty-five minutes later by two other boats (one for us and one for the ailing vessel), I was disappointed: I was having a good time watching the hippos watch us and being close enough to touch and be touched by them in return. At supper that night with my Africa University traveling companions from Malawi, Mike Mwali and Justice Khimbi, I asked what the guide had said when he radioed back. They howled with laughter as Justice translated, "We're on water and the boat has broken down at a dangerous place because we're surrounded by hippos. Send another boat quickly because anything can happen. We are really at the edge of smash!!" Since Mike and Justice are always hedging their bets during our travels together, Mike decided that the odds had been about "fifty-fifty that the hippos didn't destroy us."[1]

A second edge of smash occurred when our son Thad and I were on safari in South Africa and we inadvertently got caught with a very large elephant herd in front of us and a lone male calf behind us; the incredibly huge matriarch of the herd was not happy and began chasing our Land Rover as we drove backward to (unsuccessfully) get out of her way. At one point, the second largest female of the herd joined her in the chase. Just as I had come to terms with the fact that our lives were probably over, the young bull trumpeted loudly and ran past our vehicle toward the matriarch rather than further behind us. We were lucky—we were no longer an imminent threat to the calf or the herd, but didn't dare try to approach that elephant herd for the remainder of our trip.

Africa has been on my mind since I was a child in a Methodist Church in southwestern Wisconsin listening to the missionary parents of our pastor. Their pictures and stories left three indelible imprints on me: the first included the smiles on everyone's face in the pictures; the second was the passion with which the missionaries spoke; and the third was a puzzle—why would we want to introduce people to Jesus if they would end up in Hell for not following Christianity "correctly"? Even at a very young age it seemed to me that ignorance might be bliss, especially in this case. After all, God couldn't possibly hold people accountable if they didn't know the "right" things in the first place. Thus the seeds were sown for one of my biggest problems with the Christian tradition: the missionary enterprise—and my first theological "edge of smash."

My Story

As I was struggling with this missionary conundrum, I was also growing to love the biblical story. Grandma Penniston, a self-taught biblical enthusiast who challenged her pastors at every level, urged her grandchildren to question religious authority. Simultaneously, she insisted that we know the story. She took great pleasure in cutting out pictures of biblical characters and scenery and used a flannel board to teach us the tales. Looking back on it, I think that she took most stories literally—except for Job. Since she had lost a five-year-old daughter to appendicitis, she knew that children could not be replaced and so refused to take the ending of Job's story seriously. And so I realized at a young age that it is at the point of personal experience that something does or does not make sense. And, here's where my African journey will come into play: it will make sense of my religious odyssey.

I grew up in the small town of Darlington, Wisconsin. My mother, three siblings and I were expected by my father to go to church and Sunday school, even though he had decided he "didn't need it." While my brother and sisters had various responses to that upbringing, I thrived on it. I was an enthusiastic Sunday school student, always winning at the races to find biblical passages or to name a certain biblical character. I relished giving the "sermon" at Methodist Youth Fellowship and was its president at least two different times. My other grandmother lived in a village seven miles from our home, and I would often go to the early worship service and Sunday school at my own church and then get dropped off at hers while

Dad went fishing in a local lake. Grandma White was the pianist, and my dream was to be able to play the hymns well enough that I could take her place occasionally at this little church of fewer than one hundred members. I pursued the dream with piano and organ lessons and, at the age of twelve, began playing the organ for worship at my own church. I did the 8:00 AM. service because it was mostly "old" people who got up and worshiped at that hour—or retired people who didn't have to milk the cows before going to church. "Real" church with the robed choir was held at 10:30. One of my grandfathers went to the "early" service and took great pride in his somewhat off-key tenor voice and would tell me, "The best way to sing in church is to be a half a beat ahead of the organist." I have to say that I do play hymns quicker than most as a result of trying to keep up with Grandpa Penniston. When I was fourteen, the "real" organist tried to burn the church down and so I was conscripted into service as the "real" organist. By the way, one knowledgeable writer on the subject has written that "it might appear peculiar to the average lay[person], but it is a fact that insanity prevails among the church organists. I do not know what the cause is, but figures show that in nearly all institutions for the insane many patients are organists. The only cause I can assign for it is that they as a rule devote all their time to religious matters."[2]

At the same time I began as an organist, I decided that I would go into the ministry. Two of the greatest influences on my life, other than family, were my piano-organ teacher, Marian, and her husband, Warren, who was in seminary. He graduated and they moved to Minnesota when I was in the seventh grade. Knowing that my parents could not afford to send me elsewhere for music lessons, Marian invited me to live with them during that summer. She gave me a year's worth of lessons; I practiced six hours a day and helped care for their brand new baby boy. I continued doing that for three more summers and each time they added a new baby boy to the family. When I told them that I had decided to go into the ministry, Warren said, "Men go into ministry; women go into Christian education." And so I did—without even so much as questioning the wisdom or the choice. This was an invisible edge of smash that I did not recognize.

During my college career, I did not go through any faith crises with the academic study of religion. What my grandmother had imbued in me went along well with college classes. I did continue to struggle with sexism, however: I tried to take a Greek grammar class that I knew other undergraduates were allowed to take in the seminary on campus. The registrar called me into his office and said, "Aha, I *thought* you were a girl." I looked bewildered as he continued, "Greek is needed only by men going into ministry; girls have no need for it. You can't take Greek." This time I questioned the wisdom and the decision, but to no avail; this was an edge of smash that I recognized, but couldn't do anything about. I graduated from the University of Dubuque with a major in Christian education and a minor in music, organ as applied instrument. I had to wait seventeen years—when I began graduate school—to take Greek.

Immediately following graduation from college, Gary and I married and moved to Los Angeles, the other end of the earth as far as we could tell, where he went to graduate school and I was hired as a director of Christian education in a Methodist Church in El Segundo. At the ripe-old age of twenty-two, and as I was chairing a Sunday school teachers' meeting, I made the comment that I wouldn't care if my (as yet unborn) children didn't know who Jesus was. What would be important to me was that they know what love is all about. What the teachers didn't let me finish saying before questioning my employment by the church was this: "and I wouldn't know how to teach them about love without talking about Jesus." Of course I came to question the wisdom of making such a statement, but the thought never left me—was it only the notion of relationships and social responsibility that I thought was important? If so, how could I call myself a Christian? Was I not "just" a humanist? What else do I or don't I believe?

Excursus: An Edge of Smash
from North Africa

If one takes as a norm for Christianity Augustine, Bishop of North Africa in Hippo in the fourth and fifth centuries, how do my beliefs measure up to his standards? Many of his ideas were reflected in Methodist catechism class. Do I believe in the literalness of the Bible and explain differences between the gospel writers with the simple observation that "different eye-witnesses normally give different accounts of the same event"?[3] No. Can I defend the "just war" theory? No. Does God work miracles at the expense of natural law? No. Do I believe in the blood atonement? No. Do I believe in original sin? No. (And, therefore, baptism is not necessary—at least not for that reason.) Do I believe in predestination? No. Should clergy be married? My answer is yes, if she or he wants to be and, even more heretical to Augustine, to a person of either gender. Should there be a hierarchical ordering of the ministry? No. Is the pope infallible? Answering as a United Methodist, certainly not! Is God male? No. One of the few concepts I can take from Augustine is that the United States is as guilty as Augustine thought the Roman state was when, in their self-understanding, they "had grown great . . . to form the cadre of recruitment for the 'City of God.'"[4] In spite of my differences with Augustine and my later repudiation of affirmative answers to all questions asked of me at the Official Board Meeting determining whether or not I could be confirmed at age twelve, can I still call myself a Christian? Yes. How can that be? Here is my answer. I believe in Jesus' teachings and I attempt to follow them. In fact, I often disagree with our daughter Mandy, who is a pediatrician in clinics that serve the families of migrant workers near Salinas, California. She lives in a co-op that works with the homeless community. She claims to be an atheist. I claim she is a Christian. She would rather be called a Gandhian. But if Augustine of Hippo is a norm for Christianity, then I certainly lost my faith while "in" North Africa. That edge of smash could have been spiritually fatal.

My Story, Continued

Up to this point, religion for me was fairly academic. I had not had my faith tested with untimely deaths or fatal diseases. Life was not perfect, but neither did I somehow feel that I didn't have control. In fact, I had tremendous control: when Gary and I started dating in high school, I told him that I planned to go to college, get married at the age of twenty-two, give birth at age twenty-four, adopt a baby of the opposite gender at age twenty-six, give birth again at twenty-eight, and adopt another baby of the opposite gender at age thirty. In fact, I had my life divided into four very neatly packaged twenty-four-year periods: grow up until the age of twenty-four, create and raise a family until age forty-eight, go to graduate school and become a theologian until age seventy-two, retire and travel during the final twenty-four years of my life and die with a smile on my face at age ninety-six. Fortunately for me, Gary went along with the plan and life unfolded exactly as I anticipated—until I had cancer at age thirty-eight—a near fatal edge of smash that was definitely not a part of the plan. One day Gary came home from teaching and said, "I know you're not planning to go to graduate school for another nine years, but you need to go now—you're driving me crazy as you worry about leaving four young kids for me to raise alone. You need to get your brain occupied with something else." And so I began graduate classes at Marquette University a year later and completed my doctoral program at age forty-eight—the exact year I intended to begin. But even then religion was an academic exercise. All the while our four children were growing up, I worked hard as a volunteer Christian educator in our local church and I continued to hold the positions of organist, handbell leader, and director of music. Since my concern for social justice blended well with Jesus' teachings, I simply put doctrines and belief systems aside. (My love affair with Bach is tempered only by his seventeenth-eighteenth-centuries Lutheran theology, but his organ works have no texts!) When I began teaching at Otterbein College, my passion for all things academic continued with even greater fervor.

And then two things happened: Julian Hills, a Fellow of the Jesus Seminar, urged me to become a Fellow and, four years later, I went to the continent of Africa for the first time. The Jesus Seminar continues to be an invigorating path on a road that I was already on. Original sin doesn't matter, for example, but feeding the poor does. Predestination is beside the point, but loving our enemies is not. Being incapable of reconstructing a fool-proof Jesus is OK, but hitting people over the head (or bombing the "hell" out of complete societies) with absolute truths is not. And in spite of my chronological age (I'm old enough to retire), I'm just middle-aged in terms of the profession. My research interests were and continue to be women in first and second-century Judaism and Christianity, and the historical Jesus—topics that sometimes intersect, but not always. I like to discuss the anti-Jewish elements in the story of the hemorrhaging woman (Mark 5:24–34), or the call to unite the enemy tribes under the rubric of Judaism in the so-called Great Commission (Matt 28:16–20),[5] or Mel Gibson's apparent biblical illiteracy as seen in his movie *The Passion of the Christ*, or my favorite story—the Canaanite Woman (Mark 7:24–30 = Matt 15:21–28). But when I was teaching for the first time at Africa University in Mutare, Zimbabwe, I developed a third interest: the parables of Jesus. And at that point the notion that religion was merely academic immediately went out the window.

Sub-Saharan Africa

As I have often written and said, I discovered very quickly that Africans know far more and have much better insights into the practical, life-changing, and crisis-ridden study of the Bible than we privileged westerners could ever hope to achieve, and that is especially true of the parables, which are generally thought to derive from the historical Jesus. Many times I have been fortunate enough to return to various countries in Africa, to places like South Africa, Zimbabwe, Kenya, Malawi, Zambia, Mozambique, Egypt (in particular, the City of Garbage Pickers in Cairo), Tanzania, Burundi, and Rwanda. Many Africans continue to live in agrarian, technologically undeveloped rural areas and can therefore relate to an economically depressed, subsistence lifestyle of two thousand years ago. Sub-Saharan rural Africans, in my estimation, are living very much as first-century residents of Palestine likely were. The oral culture is still the means for transmitting stories and traditions from person to person, village to village, and generation to generation. Frankly, we in the West have no point of reference for understanding that kind of oral tradition. I can only imagine the "oral story" that must have evolved in Zimbabwe about the day that our daughter Wendy and I were having breakfast with Anglican nuns in the

Eastern Highland Mountains. We tried to keep a conversation going, but to no avail. We couldn't understand it: the sisters spoke very good English and were very friendly and attentive to our needs, but they simply would not converse with us. When we left with the priest, he wryly said, "Breakfast is usually taken in silence."

In addition to working on a parables project with former Africa University students, colleagues, and friends, I am excited every time I visit an African country to see for myself how the gospel plays out and how dynamic a two-thousand-year-old story can be. As far as I'm concerned, the best "modern" insights on ancient texts come from Africa where, contrary to the Western world (where books *about* the Bible have now exceeded the sale of Bibles, thus contributing to an ever-growing biblical illiteracy), the Bible itself is probably the most widely read book in Africa.

According to Fidon R. Mwombeki, the Bible in Africa is understood not just as a symbol of God's presence and protection, but also as a treasury for practical utilization—a source of comfort, instruction, exhortation, and even condemnation. He also observes that the Bible does not always have to be understood rationally, because African spiritualism supersedes intelligibility; but there are other occasions when settings do demand intelligibility. He discusses, for example, a seven-year-old boy, a firstborn child, asking why an angel from God would slaughter the firstborn child of every Egyptian family or why anyone would defend monogamy in the light of the stories about Abraham, David, Solomon, Elkanah, and many others. Mwombeki mentions a young intellectual who asks why Africans identify with Israel when they should be identifying with Egyptians, Jebusites, Philistines, and other peoples who were wiped out and driven out of their lands by the migrating Israelites. Mwombeki describes such parallel social arrangements of African and biblical cultures as lineage, age-grouping, the value of royalty, birthrights and inheritance laws, the value of the elderly, and emotional attachment to ancestral lands. I have seen first-hand the striking similarities between the religious and cultural context of the Bible and that of rural Africa: men going out to fish for that day's breakfast, women grinding maize for the day's meal, small boys catching mice and roasting them on sticks to eat and sell, beggars and prostitutes in the streets, demon-possession, women carrying babies on their backs and baskets on their heads, young men singing while riding in the back of a small pickup truck, a language created by light from oil and paraffin lamps on the roads at night that gives truck drivers information about pick-ups and deliveries, pottery being sculpted and then baked in the oven, neighbors going to ask for bread to feed an unexpected guest in the middle of the night (I was that unexpected guest on numerous occasions), and free "all-you-can-eat" weddings for entire villages. One of my favorite images is that of a completely bent-over old woman who stood up tall and danced the "old-fashioned" way when the music began during worship at a Roman Catholic church in Mutare and, when the music ended, went back to her head-to-feet posture.

Hilltop on My Mind

If I could move to Mutare, I would. On one of my recent spring breaks in Mutare, I worshiped at Hilltop United Methodist Church on Palm Sunday. Samuel Dzobo, the lead pastor was a former student of mine in a parables class at Africa University. Hilltop is located in the oldest, poorest part of the city of Mutare. More than 2,000 worshipers were gathered in a rela-tively small church sanctuary in a city where one-third of the people are dying of malaria, HIV/AIDS-related diseases, and schistosomiasis (a parasitic disease caused by flatworms). That fact did not keep a single one of them from waving palm branches, singing joyously, and proclaiming the gospel message. And what was the gospel message on that day? That if Jesus were a Mozambican who traveled over the Eastern Highland Mountains into Zimbabwe, he would see his people and know their need to be freed of political and economic oppression. And because of that, the Zimbabweans would greet him with palm branches, dancing, and singing. That sermon on a pre-election Sunday was not just powerful, but probably the only time that Palm Sunday has ever made any actual sense to me. And that strikes me as an amazing epiphany, since I've been a church organist for over fifty years and probably haven't missed a single Palm Sunday in all that time. At Hilltop I couldn't help but remember John Wesley's quadrilateral of scripture, tradition, experience, and reason: all four fit together beautifully that morning because when experience resonates with the story, that's where the dynamic of the historical Jesus is. Perhaps it is not surprising that Dzobo was eventually imprisoned for his preaching.

Hilltop United Methodist church is always on my mind. A casual observer would never imagine that it could possibly be related to any of the Jesus Seminar's findings, but I find it to be at the heart of what the histori-cal Jesus was about. Hilltop is all about heaven on earth, not heaven after death; Hilltop is about the salvation of the community, not the individual; Hilltop is about applauding the poor, but not poverty. Hilltop is about daily bread and forgiving one's economic debts as one's debts are also forgiven. Hilltop is about welcoming the stranger. Hilltop is about listening to the ancestors—Jesus, in particular. If I lost my faith in Hippo, North Africa, then I found it again in the biblical enactments of rural southern Africa. That edge of smash has been the best ever.

Another African understanding of Jesus' parables came from Sophirina Sign, also a student in the parables class at Africa University, who came to our home during Thanksgiving week and explained that it makes no sense to worry about the fourteen orphaned children she is raising by herself in Zimbabwe—no need to be concerned whether or not she is going to have food on the table for supper each night or if she is going to have enough funds to buy uniforms for them to go to school. Common sense tells her that she must have absolute trust like the lilies in the fields—and then she recited in the Shona language something that gets translated as: "Notice how the wild lilies grow: They don't slave and they never spin. Yet let me tell you, even Solomon at the height of his glory was never decked out like one of them" (Matt 6:26–29). I had taken Bob Funk's *A Credible Jesus* to Sophirina when it was first published, and it's possible that she had an "academic" context for the lilies of the field; but I know that she had a trust ethic long before Bob or any other scholar articulated it for her.

Volcanoes and Seas

A third animal-induced edge of smash occurred this past December when a colleague and I returned to Rwanda with twenty Otterbein College students. After climbing straight up into the mountains of *Parc National des Volcans* for what seemed to be an eternity, our guide finally motioned for us to be silent—the gorillas were just ahead. We were allowed to sit and observe them for an hour and I can tell you that when the silverback wants your spot in the trees, the silverback gets your spot in the trees. On our way up the volcano, I had asked to return to base camp three different times because it was becoming increasingly difficult to breathe in such thin air. The guide wasn't about to lose one of his clients, but when my body began to shake, my toes and fingers tingled, and I couldn't breathe in or out, he signaled my porter and all of a sudden, I was on the porter's back for the remainder of the trek—and I think he is older than I! Whenever I tell these stories, at least one person says assumingly that my prayers for survival in each case were obviously answered. And I retort, "I certainly wasn't praying; I was wondering where I had lost the common sense with which I was born." And this is my second largest problem with the Christian tradition—praying.

When Gary and I were awaiting the arrival of Adam from Vietnam in 1975, the plane he was to be on crashed in the South China Sea. As we waited all day to hear his fate, countless friends and relatives called to offer support with their prayers that our baby would be one of the survivors. I responded (too hastily, I'm sure) that they should not do that: why should God favor us over other families? This edge of smash was, quite literally, hurting many people the world over. My attitude didn't preclude my jumping up and down for joy when we received a call from Sen. Bill Proxmire's office that our baby was not on that ill-fated flight, but I have always struggled with the "omni-God." Why *do* bad things happen to good and innocent people if an omniscient, omnipresent, omnipotent, and omni-benevolent deity is on the throne of justice?

A Final Note on My Story

I don't have an answer to that question and the biggest edge of smash is in my own mind. I often tell my students that I don't expect or even want them to believe everything I tell them, but they do need to understand it because only when one can articulate other positions, especially those of the opposition, can one articulate one's own belief. I also warn them that when one studies academic religion, one must expect an edge of smash. I enjoy the smash, but for some of them it is devastating. The only idea I'm absolutely sure about is that we are to be working toward heaven on earth. I'm also sure that the way things are going, I'll not see it.

In the meantime, I'll continue to be a person who left Augustine and Hippo and North Africa long ago, and wound up among hippos in southern Africa—among whom I'll continue to play, even though that may yet again put me on the edge of smash.

Notes

1. A version of this story was printed earlier: Jackson, "Hippos are Vegetarians, Right?"

2. Price, "The Last Page," 128.

3. McManners, *Oxford History of Christianity*, 35.

4. McManners, *Oxford History of Christianity*, 2.

5. The "Great Commission" is all about who controls first-century Judaism, Pharisees or Matthew's community; see Jackson, "Are the 'Nations' Present in Matthew?"

Works Consulted

Funk, Robert W. *A Credible Jesus: Fragments of a Vision*. Santa Rosa, CA: Polebridge Press, 2002.

Jackson, Glenna S. "Are the 'Nations' Present in Matthew?"/"Is die 'nasies' teenwoordig in Matteus?" *Hervormde Teologiese Studies* 56 (November 2000) 935–48.

———. *"Have Mercy on Me": The Story of the Canaanite Woman in Matthew 15:21–28.* Journal for the Study of the New Testament Series 228. Copenhagen International Seminar 10. Sheffield, England: Sheffield Academic Press, 2002.

———. "'Hippos are Vegetarians, Right?': Teaching and Learning Parables in an African Context." *SBL Forum* (June 2004). An On-Line Electronic Publication. http://www.sbl-site.org/Article.aspx?ArticleId=281.

————. "Jesus as First-Century Feminist: Christian Anti-Judaism?" *Feminist Theology* 19 (September 1998) 85–98.

————. "Rebel Soldiers as Good Samaritans: New Testament Parables in an African Context." *Hervormde Teologiese Studies* 60 (March/June 2004) 239–47.

————. "Teaching the Parables of Jesus from an African Context." Pp. 300–2 in *Teaching the Bible: Practical Strategies for Classroom Instruction*. Eds. Mark Roncace and Patrick Gray. SBL Resources for Biblical Study 49. Atlanta: Society of Biblical Literature, 2005.

————. "The Complete Gospel: Jesus and Women via the Jesus Seminar." *Feminist Theology* 28 (September 2001) 27–39.

————. "The Jesus Seminar in Africa." Pp. 81–90 in *The Historical Jesus Goes to Church*. Santa Rosa, CA: Polebridge Press, 2004.

————. "The Trials of Jesus." Pp. 118–27 in *Jesus and Mel Gibson's The Passion of the Christ: The Film, the Gospels and the Claims of History*. Eds. Kathleen E. Corley and Robert L. Webb. New York: Continuum, 2004.

McManners, John, ed. *The Oxford History of Christianity*. Oxford: Oxford University Press, 1993.

Mwombeki, Fidon R. "Reading the Bible in Contemporary Africa." *Word & World* 21.2 (2001) 121–28.

Price, Susan A. "The Last Page: Organists Often Insane?" *The American Organist* (September 2005) 128. Reprint of a 1915 article.

Out of the Enchanted Forest
Christian Faith in an Age of Reason

Charles W. Hedrick

The "enchanted forest" is an imaginary setting where the folk tales and fairy tales of the eighteenth and nineteenth centuries take place. In such stories life is fancifully and naively portrayed without regard for the way things are generally thought to happen today. In the enchanted forest supernatural events are "natural" parts of the landscape. In my case it was the kind of religious environment in which I was reared—a Southern Baptist Church in Greenville, Mississippi located in the conservative religious climate of the Mississippi Delta in the late 1940s and early 50s. This setting was crucial in determining my future. What I learned in those environments shaped how I understood the world, and what it meant to be a religious human being. I was taught that the Bible was literally God's Holy Word, a divinely inspired guide for human life. As I look back, I am not surprised that the Bible would have become an iconic text for me. What does surprise me is that I eventually turned to the critical study of the Bible (to making judgments on the basis of evidence) and became a vocal critic of uncritical religious faith. The shift in understanding did not happen overnight, but was brought about over time by historical study of the Bible and reflection on the world around me. My change in thinking was fueled by the giant strides in science and the continuing challenge of human reason. As Gary Trudeau wrote in the comic strip, Doonesbury, "Once you make a concession to the empirical world, once you let reason rub against faith, there's no end to it. Reason's a bully."

At some point I came to two conclusions: religious faith cannot demand that I believe something I find to be patently false or only partly true, and faith must begin with the world rather than religious texts, because natural environment and human culture form a more certain basis for theorizing about religion. Religious texts are passed off as having some sort of divine "authorship" or authority, but their real uniqueness lies in their cultural roots and perspectives rather than in any putative divine origin.

What follows describes how I am making sense of religious faith today. It is, and always will be, a work in progress.

The Traditions and Memoirs of the Elders . . .

I begin where it began for me: the Baptist tradition. In the Baptist tradition the Bible is the only basis for religious faith and its worldview is how people of faith should view the world. For some Baptists it is *literally* the "Word of God." Today, however, after almost forty years in critical study of Christian origins, I know that the Bible is a human product—literally human words about God, the nature of religious life, and the early histories of two modern Western religions, Christianity and Judaism. Human beings wrote each individual text under the influence of their different situations in life, and over time other human beings gathered these ancient texts into a canon of sacred Scripture. The selection of these particular texts was made on the basis of certain agendas. The collection was an attempt to make sense of religion, world, and human life from particular human perspectives typical of the first few centuries of the Common Era. In reality the Bible does not reflect a unified perspective but rather a variety of perspectives representing both Jewish and Christian traditions extending over 1250 years.

On the other hand, I find that the authors of the biblical texts raise enduring existential issues that still resonate with the human spirit: guilt, fear of death, the problem of evil, human suffering, justice, a sense of human inadequacy and moral failure (in religious language, sin), acceptance (in religious language, forgiveness), wholeness (in religious language, salvation), and human purpose. For that reason—that is, because they grappled with issues many still find relevant in the twenty-first century— these ancient authors deserve a hearing. Some texts clearly connect with modern readers while others appear plodding and pedestrian. Some are even demonic: take for example the egregious character of Samuel (and Yahweh) portrayed in 1 Samuel 15, where Samuel says that God ordered the annihilation of the Amalekites. At times I find the Bible inspiring—even "inspired," but no more so than other texts that similarly touch my spirit and humanity in my personal quest for meaning in life. For many centuries this collection has been used to exclude religious quests by validating one religious perspective over others. Nevertheless, the religious diversity in the texts undermines all attempts to harmonize their differences so as to mask their diversity and silence the debates that implicitly rage between the texts themselves.

Meeting Jesus . . .

When I was sixteen (1950), I had a religious experience that is described in Baptist jargon as "conversion": a conscious act in which one "accepts the Lord Jesus Christ as savior," or "commits one's life to Christ." Over time I came to translate that jargon into "following Jesus." Do I now think I actually encountered something "Wholly Other," or was the experience the result of autosuggestion induced by my religious and cultural environments? Looking back, I have no idea; what I can say is that it became a defining moment in my life. The experience led me to a Southern Baptist college, ordination to "the gospel ministry," seminary, and into a Baptist pastorate. I began graduate study in New Testament and early Christian literature in 1965, and eventually became an academic—a university professor of religious studies—and finally a Founding Fellow of the Jesus Seminar. I have come to conceive of my personal and professional odyssey simply as "following Jesus."

Jesus was a Jewish man who (like Herakles, Asclepius, and others in Graeco-Roman antiquity[1]) was elevated to divine status within decades of his death and later was deified (cf. Col 1:15–20; Phil 2:5–11).[2] This was not an unusual turn of affairs, since even Roman emperors were deified and had temples dedicated to their worship. If Christianity was to be competitive as a religion in Hellenistic culture, Jesus had to be divinized. Early Christians were threatened by the great numbers of human beings who became divine in the Graeco-Roman world. They inadequately explained the similarity between Jesus' divinity and the Graeco-Roman demi-gods (human beings elevated to divinity) as the artifice of demons,[3] and never solved the problem that Jesus' deification came out of the spirit of the times and was dependent on the prior Graeco-Roman models.[4] Their claim that Jesus was the *only* Son of God was basically a refutation of claims of divinity made in behalf of the other sons of God in the Greek and Roman worlds. Careful readers of the New Testament can actually follow the logical progress of his status from human being to deity moving backward from the resurrection. In Paul's view he was declared (or appointed) son of God by virtue of his resurrection from the dead (Rom 1:3–4); in Mark a voice from the sky declares Jesus son of God at his baptism (Mark 1: 11); in Matthew and Luke he is son of God at his birth (Matt 1:20–23; Luke 1:34–35); while in John he was always son of God (John 1:1–18). In their birth narratives Matthew and Luke try to explain how it is that a human being became a divine son of God (Luke 1:35; Matt 1:20). John's problem, on the other hand, is to explain how a divine figure became human (John 1:14). In the later creeds of the church, however, Jesus' human life is virtually eclipsed, swallowed up by his later divinity: ". . . born of the Virgin Mary, [. . .], suffered under Pontius Pilate . . . ." The ellipsis in brackets is where a description of Jesus' public career should by rights have been included in the Apostles' Creed. In other words, Orthodox confessions virtually ignored Jesus' personal history.

In truth, the creeds were never very interesting to me. What did interest me was Jesus, and I continue to be interested in the human spirit of the man, the individual essence that survives in his words and to some extent in his deeds. His humanity and personal religious faith still live in his words that reach across the centuries being kept alive almost by accident in early Christian faith communities. We are related, he and I. For one thing, we both had to work out our faith in God and its implications for our lives, he in an ancient pre-scientific Jewish world under early Roman emperors and I in the modern scientific world of Western culture. For another, we share a fundamental human experience—the quest for meaning in life. Today, I find that his idiom, surviving in the fragments of his discourse, tells me far more about God and the nature of religious life than I can glean from what was done to his person (his crucifixion) and how Orthodoxy came to explain him and his death. In a sense, then, his religious experience is precursor of my own.

The canonical gospels and, for that matter, all the gospels of the first and second centuries—some thirty-four of which we know today—present Jesus from the diverse perspectives of early Christian faiths. Getting behind their theological categories and agendas has given rise to the two-hundred year "quest for the historical Jesus"—a phrase that simply refers to the search for what we can learn about this first-century Jewish man by using modern scientific historical methods. Because our sources contain no more than scattered fragments of his personal history—the very number and nature of which are debated—we will never achieve a definitive historical description of Jesus on which all will agree.

Indeed, what I am willing at this point to state about the historical Jesus amounts to little more than a profile. Here is what I think today: Jesus was a Jewish man. Without appealing to metaphysics and mythology he is most easily described as a social and religious critic of his own Jewish tradition; hence I find the idea that he perpetrated an incident in the Temple at Jerusalem quite plausible—it is at least consistent with his character as evidenced by his words. I find it plausible that he performed faith healings, if I may appeal to psychosomatic healing as a parallel (although Jesus would have conceived of it as reflecting God's power). It is also plausible that he performed what are described as exorcisms of demonic spirits. Even though demons (or angels, for that matter) do not exist, first-century people generally believed in them as firmly as they believed that the earth was the center of the universe. Cultural conditions were "right" for exorcisms in the first century. I find the nature miracles (Jesus walked on the water, turned water to wine, etc.) simply incredible. However we choose to describe him, Jesus was a human being and subject to the same human limitations as everyone. Human beings cannot walk on water—unless, of course, it is frozen.

Did Jesus rise from the dead? It depends on what one understands by "rising from the dead." If the resurrection is understood as a resuscitation of Jesus' physical body, the answer is "no." The credit for the earliest explanation of the resurrection goes to Paul, who understands the resurrection of Jesus as a "spiritual" event (1 Cor 15:35–55). Although Paul is quite specific that Jesus' physical body was not resuscitated, he never adequately explains exactly how a "spiritual" resurrection happens. Nonetheless, he states unambiguously that "flesh and blood cannot inherit the kingdom of God" (1 Cor 15:50; cf. verse 44). Later Christians apparently came to regard the resurrection of Jesus as a physical resuscitation (cf. Matt 28:9; Luke 24:39; John 20:27). Mark's empty tomb may likewise suggest a physical resuscitation in that Mark reports the body of Jesus missing (Mark 16:6).

What is important about the Jewish man is not what the early Christians thought about him, but what he said and did. His words and deeds constitute the primary basis in the Christian tradition for developing a faith for the twenty-first century. Knowledge of his faith in God provides a "staging area" for developing one's own views as a "follower" of Jesus.

His God didn't discriminate between insiders and outsiders and do good things to righteous people and bad things to evil people. Rather the benevolence of Jesus' God extends to all (Matt 5:45). The ethics of Jesus are based on love for others, principally toward those we might consider enemies (Matt 5:44 = Luke 6:27, 35). I take this to mean that love is to be extended to all, friend and foe alike. In the fragments of his discourse, Jesus actually talked more about human relationships than he did relationship with God. His parables are aimed at challenging human beings to reflect on proper human behavior and requiring them to resolve with little or no guidance the ethical issues arising from a dialogue with the story. He is portrayed in the gospels as consistently challenging his own religious tradition. Such family squabbles I find historically plausible, and they are the only way I can make sense of his crucifixion. The Romans killed him in large part because he was marked as a "trouble maker" who criticized Jewish religion and argued with Jewish teachers. His public career was viewed as threatening the peace of the Roman Province of Palestine. Hence his death, like that of Socrates, was punishment for undermining the "laws" and corrupting the minds of the people.[5] Putting his personal ethical behavior into practice is what I take as the meaning of "following Jesus." While I take love to be the basis of his ethical views, I find I am left without specific guidelines for practical application and must work out for myself the details of how the love ethic works in actual situations of daily life. This problem is due in part to the small number of historical fragments of his life that survive, but more to the fact that indirect discourse seems to have been his style.

Why would anyone continue to be interested in such an ancient figure so uncharacteristic of our age? Wilhelm Bousset said, "When we absorb ourselves in the contemplation of that figure we feel a great uprising of the spirit. For there we touch indeed upon the foundations of our own spiritual and personal existence."[6] I agree.

We Gather Together . . .

At its best the church is a community of similar minded individuals on a common ethical and religious journey; it is not a mythical organism, but is a historical phenomenon always situated in a particular geographic location. The community is characterized by equality, tolerance for one another, and acceptance of one another as valued members of the group. Members are not bound together by confessions and creeds, which at bottom tend to divide and exclude, but rather by a common goal: to give and receive encouragement in support of the search for religious meaning. The church does not possess the answers; each person in the community is seeking answers, and hence each member may learn from another. The real function of the church is community—and that is why I remain a member of a local Baptist church and am involved in its community to the extent that I am permitted and choose to participate. I have been a member of the First Baptist Church of Springfield, Missouri since 1980. For about a year I was an adult Sunday school teacher, and I still regularly participate in the same men's Bible class.

Like all human associations and endeavors, the church is imperfect, as are all who are associated with it. Nevertheless, I think of this association as the "embodiment" of the resurrected Jesus—in some ways as Paul conceived of it (1 Cor 12:4–27), but more so as Matthew did (Matt 18:20; 25:31–46; 10:40; 28:18–20). When human beings interact in certain kinds of ways, I am willing to say with Matthew that "Jesus lives" in those encounters—not in a mythical sense but rather in the practical day-to-day sense that his ideas and practice continue to survive in community. This idea leads me to think if God works in the world at all, it is in individual human beings and in certain kinds of human encounters. We have no way to quantify suprahistorical influences operating on the human psyche; what is regarded as divine influence may just as well be learned responses inculcated by our cultural and religious socialization.

Living "the Religious Life"

I have never worried much about nailing down a precise meaning for the mythical statement that human beings were created in the image of God

(Gen 1:26). Both creation accounts in the Bible affirm that God is responsible for the creation of a benign world (Gen 1:26–31). The second account explains that the benign world became hostile (Gen 3:1–24) through the sin of the first human beings, which fated them to a life of toil and eventual death. And this "original sin," according to the biblical writer, contaminated the whole of the human species in perpetuity, and that is why human beings obsolesce and die (Rom 5:12). Thus the writers of Genesis conclude that God did not originally create a flawed world. He created a perfect world (Gen 1:31) and humanity, not God, is at fault for the world's current flawed state (Gen 3:22–24). The ancient writers worked with a particular theological assumption: God is good and hence would not deliberately create an evil world. Therefore evil must have come about some other way. However, other writers in Hebrew Bible—the author of Job, for example—attributed both good and evil to the same God. If we begin with the world as it is experienced today without making theological assumptions, it appears that for whatever reason obsolescence and death are the natural order of things. It really doesn't matter why it is so; we cannot change it. In other words by beginning theological reflection with the world rather than the Bible, we discover that dying is built into our genes. While we may extend our lives by diet, exercise, and a bit of good luck perhaps, none of us will live for ever. Finding ways to harmonize preconceived assumptions about God with the natural system we know will not alter this inevitable course of all life in the universe. Human mortality is not the result of Adam's "original sin," and our inhumane obscenities toward one another are not excused by that explanation of the worst aspects of our human character.

Living religiously in a Christian community begins by keeping faith with the religious traditions of our Judeo-Christian past. "Keeping faith" means maintaining continuity with the traditions of the past, aiming to understand them, and identifying the best of what has been passed down to us. Of course, not everything passed down has the same value for life in the modern world, and we must discriminate. Every generation must work out its faith response to changing circumstances, just as those who preceded us were forced to do. The biblical texts are a record of their struggles to express their faith in their own changed historical circumstances. Thus, I am not bound to express my faith using their idiom, but am free to create a new modality appropriate for my changed situation, just as they did.

Following Jesus in the twenty-first century, means engaging the world rather than retreating from the world. "Jesus followers" must engage all aspects of modern culture in ways that allow them to raise their voices in social criticism, as Jesus did. I assume that associations of Jesus followers will be open associations engaged in learning of all kinds, not just the study of religion. The church (as well as college and seminary classrooms, for that matter) should not teach people how to be religious. That is a form of indoctrination ultimately seeking to control the nature of religious experience. People should be free to experience God in their own way.

Even though I do not think God is active in the world in any traditional sense, I occasionally engage in community worship, because sometimes (though not always) it has a positive effect. I seldom pray in the traditional sense, but when I do, I think of it not as influencing God, but as having an effect on me. I think of prayer and religious meditation as reflective introspection rather than "communication with God." In such activities I meet only my own thoughts and ideas, but such practice does help me clarify my situation in life. The only place I find a recognizable encounter with something "other" is in the context of human relationships. Jesus "comes alive" for me when I interact with others in certain ways. As I have stated in a discussion of Matthew's radical theology, I recapture his spirit by responding in love to others for whose sake I have freely given up my rights, and on whose behalf I gladly inconvenience myself. It is in the context of responding in love to another's need, or reaching out in need and being met by a neighbor's response of love that Jesus lives.

In the Beginning . . .

From my perspective God is cloaked in mystery. I have no direct personal knowledge of God. I can learn what others think of God from the study of religions and from the writings of those who claim to have experienced God, but they offer me radically conflicting reports.

Is there a God? The word "exist" is inappropriate since God is not a "being" and does not occupy space and time as humans do. In nearly all Western faith traditions, however, belief in God is basic to the entire enterprise of religion, and so from my perspective religion requires belief in some kind of higher Power. I believe in God, quite simply because I cannot explain to my satisfaction why there is nothing at all. The popular scientific view that the universe came into being through a great cosmic explosion is for me unsatisfactory, since to produce the explosion the necessary elements must have preexisted the "big bang." Where did those elements come from? Since science has not provided a satisfactory answer to that question, I have come to think the ultimate source of everything is God.

Nevertheless, I am not affirming God as "first cause," since I cannot even be sure that God *deliberately* "caused" the universe. God seems to show an amazing disinterest in the cosmic order. Human beings must cope with disease, hurricanes, tornadoes, earthquakes and other natural disasters. Through scientific analysis of such events, we now know they are an essential part of the world we experience, and hence we call them "natural disasters." In other words, we are asserting that they are not the result of off-stage divine manipulation of the elements, but are more reasonably explained as natural events. Appealing to divine machination to explain natural occurrences challenges the ethical character of God. In short, the cosmic order seems to lack *rational* or *purposive* control. God is not a nature God, like the ancient Canaanite Baal, the God of storms who ruled over wind and clouds and whose power was manifested in thunder and lightening. Such a God was thought to juggle the day-to-day routine of the natural order as a matter of course. The God of the Hebrew Bible, on the other hand, "earned his spurs" by controlling history and managing the religious welfare of the Israelites. It would be more appropriate to say that the Israelite God was believed to use the natural elements to reward or punish the Israelites for their religious and ethical behavior. The God described in Hebrew Bible is much less inclined than his ancient contemporaries to rely on "hands-on" day-to-day management of the natural processes. The more-or-less dependable regularity apparent in our world does not lead inevitably to the idea of a deliberate creator, a benevolent designer, or to the idea that God is running the world. Who in their right mind, for example, would deliberately design multiple types of cancer into the universe, or cause—or even permit—hurricanes? The problem in affirming an intelligent designer behind the universe is precisely how to distance the designer from the world we now experience.

I do not think God is coequal with nature (pantheism), and I do not find God *in* nature (panentheism). The natural order has neither conscience nor morals, so how can it "reflect" God? If I am wrong in the first statement (denying the identification of God with the cosmos), I must conclude that there is no God, since by my understanding "things" are not and, cannot be, gods. If I am wrong about the second (denying that God is involved in the natural order of things), I must conclude that God is incompetent, devious, or capricious in the management of the world, since no God can treat humankind in such a horribly capricious way and have an ethical character. Thus, while I come to believe in God because the universe exists, I find that I can learn very little about the nature or character of God from the natural world.

If God actually does have an ethical character, as I must believe, then I am forced to conclude that, for whatever reason, God has withdrawn from the world. In the 1960s some theologians described God's absence from the modern world as "the death of God," an evaluation based on the idea that God is not (any longer) active in the world. On the other hand, if God is still involved with the world in some way, I must conclude from my experience that God is limited, and doing the best that can be done. Hence God is not omnipotent, omnipresent, or omniscient. The idea that

God is limited has roots in the New Testament. Paul uses the odd word "weakness" (odd to us post-Nicene Christians) to describe God to the Corinthians: "For the foolishness of God is wiser than humankind and the weakness of God is stronger than humankind" (1 Cor 1:25). While Paul is making an ironic comparison between human and divine capabilities for effect, the very fact that he can use the word "weakness" undermines the notion of divine omnipotence. But the truth of the matter is that in our day God is clearly evident in weakness, rather than in the powerful deeds of the past as described in the Bible. Or as Paul claimed the Lord said to him while he was praying, "my grace is sufficient for you, for my power is made perfect in weakness" (2 Cor 12:9). From this perspective God's chosen locus of operations is not in nature but in human beings; for as Paul assured the Corinthians, although Christ was crucified in weakness, he is powerful in you (2 Cor 13:3–4). Or put in the words of Jesus: "the kingdom of God is within you" (Luke 17:21)—or those words Matthew attributes to him: "where two or three are gathered in my name, there I am in the midst of them" (Matt 18:20). In our day God is manifest, if at all, as much in human frailties as in our occasional nobleness.

What's Left?

If omnipotence, omnipresence, the trinity, the divinity of Jesus, the physical resurrection, the Bible as iconic object, etc. are gone, what's left to "faith"? To speak bluntly, all that is left is only what we had in the first place: hope—nothing more or less! As Paul put it, our aspiration for "surviving" death is a hope based on our trust in God. In my case, I share Paul's hope that God has not finished with the world and its creatures (Rom 8:19–25; 1 Cor 15:19). I regard my continued hope in God as my affirmation that God believes in me; in the meanwhile, as Paul said, I wait (Rom 8:25) and live by a faith that expects no assurances.

Or so I think today.

Notes

1. See Farnell, *Greek Hero Cults*, Herakles, pp. 95–145; Asclepius, pp. 234–79. In particular see Talbert, "Concept of Immortals," 419–36.

2. How easy it is to turn humans into Gods is shown by the fact that as late as the middle of the 20th century the Japanese Emperor, Hirohito, was considered divine. He was the 124th descendant of the Sun Goddess, and did not publicly deny his divinity until January 1, 1946. See Packard, *Sons of Heaven*, esp. 1, 12, 28–29, 296–97, 299, 303. For the Emperor's Imperial Rescript Denying his Divinity see *Political Reorientation of Japan*, 2.470 (Appendix B:3b).

3. Talbert, "Concept of Immortals," 432–33.

4. Talbert, "Concept of Immortals," 433–36.

5. Fowler, *Plato*, the trial of Socrates (Apology), pp. 61–145; the death of Socrates (Phaedo), pp. 193–403. See also Marchant and Todd, *Xenophon*, the Memorabilia, pp. 1–77.

6. Bousset, *Jesus*, 211.

Works Consulted

Altizer, Thomas J. J. *The Gospel of Christian Atheism*. Philadelphia: Westminster Press, 1966.

Bettenson, Henry and Chris Maunder, eds. *Documents of the Christian Church*. 3d ed. Oxford: Oxford University Press, 1999.

Bousset, Wilhelm. *Jesus*. Ed. W. D. Morrison. Trans. Janet Penrose Trevelyan. New York: G. P. Putnam's Sons, 1906.

Farnell, Lewis Richard. *Greek Hero Cults and Ideas of Immortality*. Oxford: Clarendon Press, 1921.

Fowler, Harold North. *Plato in Twelve Volumes*. Cambridge: Harvard University Press, 1977.

Fuller, Reginald H. *The Foundations of New Testament Christology*. New York: Charles Scribner's Sons, 1965.

Gaster, T. H. "Cosmogony." Pp. 702–9. Vol. 1 of *The Interpreter's Dictionary of the Bible: An Illustrated Encyclopedia*. Ed. George A. Buttrick. 4 vols. New York: Abingdon Press, 1962.

Guth, Alan. "A Golden Age of Cosmology." Pp. 285–96 in *The New Humanists: Science at the Edge*. Ed. John Brockman. New York: Barnes & Noble, 2003.

Harris, Stephen L. *The New Testament: A Student's Introduction*. 4th ed. Boston: McGraw Hill, 2002.

Hedrick, Charles W. "Jesus of Nazareth. A Profile under Construction." Pp. 65–72 in *Profiles of Jesus*. Ed. Roy W. Hoover. Santa Rosa, CA: Polebridge Press, 2002.

———. "Miracles in Mark: A Study in Markan Theology and Its Implications for Modern Religious Thought." *Perspectives in Religious Studies* 34.3 (2007) 277–93.

———. *Parables as Poetic Fictions: The Creative Voice of Jesus*. Peabody, MA: Hendrickson, 1994.

———. "Resurrection: Radical Theology in the Gospel of Matthew." *Lutheran Theological Quarterly* 14.3 (1979) 40–45.

———. "The Four/Thirty-Four Gospels." *Bible Review* 18.3 (June 2002): 20–31, 46–47.

———. "The 'Good News' about the Historical Jesus." Pp. 91–103 in *The Historical Jesus Goes to Church*. Santa Rosa, CA: Polebridge Press, 2004.

———. "What is Christian? Competing Visions in the First Century." *The Fourth R* 19.4 (2006) 3–8, 22.

———. *When History and Faith Collide: Studying Jesus*. Peabody, MA: Hendrickson, 1999.

Koester, Helmut. *History and Literature of Early Christianity*. Vol. 2 of *Introduction to the New Testament*. 2d ed. New York: Walter De Gruyter, 2000.

Lovell, A. C. B. "Theories of the Origin of the Universe. The Evolutionary Theory." Pp. 407–25 in *Exploring the Universe*. Ed. Louise B. Young. 2d ed. New York: Oxford University Press, 1971.

Marchant, E. C., and O. J. Todd. *Xenophon in Seven Volumes. Memorabilia and Oeconomicus; Symposium and Apology*. Vol. 4. Cambridge: Harvard University Press, 1979.

Meyer, Marvin, ed. *The Nag Hammadi Scriptures: The International Edition*. New York: HarperCollins, 2007.

Packard, Jerrod M. *Sons of Heaven: A Portrait of the Japanese Monarchy*. New York: Charles Scribner's Sons, 1987.

Political Reorientation of Japan, September 1945 to September 1948. 2 vols. Westport, CT: Greenwood, 1949.

Schweitzer, Albert. *The Quest of the Historical Jesus: A Critical Study of Its Progress from Reimarus to Wrede*. Trans. W. Montgomery. New York: Macmillan, 1968.

Talbert, Charles H. "The Concept of Immortals in Mediterranean Antiquity." *Journal of Biblical Literature* 94.3 (1975) 419–36.

Trudeau, Gary. "Doonesbury." *The Springfield News-Leader* (February 26, 2006) 2H.

Weaver, Walter P. *The Historical Jesus in the Twentieth Century 1900–1950*. Harrisburg, PA: Trinity Press International, 1999.

A Journey in Life

Nigel Leaves

All religions will pass, but this will remain:

Simply sitting in a chair and looking in the distance. [1]

My Personal Journey

I find it suggestive that Bishop Richard Holloway selected Vasilii Rozanov's aphorism to characterize his own spiritual journey. Holloway was a working-class child who discovered in Anglican Christianity an endless quest for meaning, became one of its official representatives and liberal spokesmen, took strong issue with its fundamentalist wing, and came at last to identify with those whose spirituality is no longer grounded in a particular religion or even a sense of God. I am intrigued because Rozanov's vision also resonates with me, and Holloway's pilgrimage has uncanny echoes of my own faith odyssey. And it is no exaggeration to say that similar paths have been trod by countless anonymous seekers who, lacking the inclination or the opportunity to put pen to paper, have quietly taken up membership in the "church alumni association." Many of these anonymous pilgrims can be found in networks like Sea of Faith and educational centers such as the Westar Institute and the Jefferson Center.

Yet differences are as noteworthy as the similarities: my own spiritual journey has been the product of a random and unique interplay of cultural and genetic elements. In this essay I will take a page from philosopher-theologian Don Cupitt's book *Life, Life* in expressing contentment with what my life has become—not in a passive or fatalistic way, but rather by way of affirming who or what I am at the present moment of this continuous process of change and exchange that is my life. It is this reflection of where life is for me *now* that forms the context for my profile of faith. What follows, then, is a very *selective* account of some the factors that have made me who I am and what I understand "being religious" to mean in a new millennium. In particular I will highlight some of the more contentious religious issues that I encountered on my journey and that are still being hotly debated today. So let me begin at where I am *now* on my faith adventure.

The Anglican Church

I have always been involved in the Anglican Christian tradition. I was born into an Anglican Church family, though my mother's roots had been in Welsh Calvinism, from whose strictures she had been more than happy to be rescued by marriage. One of my earliest memories is that of standing outside the ancient parish church counting the number of times the bell chimed to let us know how many years our new rector would stay. I counted up to twenty, but in fact he remained for much longer and finally died in office. My experience was traditional Church of England, revelling in the language of the Prayer Book of 1662 and firmly linked to the British monarchy symbolized by the rows of Union Jacks that hung from the rafters emblazoned with the names of local regiments and historic military campaigns. The church was also an integral part of the social fabric of the local community and I readily accepted its embrace by becoming an altar boy and joining the Sunday school and the church-sponsored scout group. I have remained within its walls from school days, through universities at Oxford and London, and on to a slow climb of the ecclesiastical ladder from deacon to priest to Dean of Studies. It has afforded me the privilege of travelling the world and has given me appointments in Papua New Guinea, The United Kingdom, Hong Kong and Australia.

Yet now I must admit to being deeply troubled by the conservative direction that my religious tradition and its leaders have taken. I find myself marginalized and increasingly alarmed by the claims of some of its adherents. When the titular head of my church (the Archbishop of Canterbury) proposes that homosexuals must change their sexuality if they are to be *welcomed* into the church, then I fear that the church has returned to the dark ages.[2] How can an allegedly enlightened thinker and former university professor ignore the scientific evidence of the discovery of gene Xq28 (the so-called: "gay gene") and refuse to acknowledge that homosexuality is a *biological* fact? How can I still belong to an organization that excludes one tenth of the adult population of the world on the basis of six verses of an ancient text? It is especially difficult because that text (Rom 1:22–27) was written by a first-century man who—as retired Episcopalian Bishop John Shelby Spong intimates, taking up an earlier suggestion by the distinguished Harvard classicist and theologian Arthur Darby Nock—might have been a repressed, self-loathing gay man.[3]

Whether Nock and Spong are correct in their evaluation of Saint Paul's sexual orientation is open to much conjecture: there is only circumstantial evidence from the scriptural texts to back up the claim that homosexuality was Paul's "thorn in the flesh." However, the fact remains that hostility towards gay people by Christians has been based on a worldview that has now been surpassed by modern science. I align myself with fellow Anglican

Bishop Desmond Tutu in being deeply ashamed of my homophobic church. The secular world has embraced the full sexual rights of gays and lesbians: it is time for all the churches to do the same.

So, what should I do? One option would be to take leave of my church and join a growing band of "freelance monotheists" led by people like the author and broadcaster Karen Armstrong, whose only test for the validity of a religious idea or doctrinal statement is that "it must lead directly to practical compassion."[4] If God is love, to put their case simply, then only those fragments of each religious tradition that promote a more loving, compassionate world are from God. The rest is bad theology and a departure from what God prescribes.

God

This brings me to my next difficulty—how does one talk about God in the twenty first century? I have discussed this at length in *The God Problem*. Here the reader may be expecting definitive answers to any number of burning questions: Does God exist? Is there anything out there? Do you believe in the God of the Bible? Do you worship a personal God?

Unfortunately these questions are more in tune with the media dominated, journalistic "black and white" age that we find ourselves in today. What an irony that at a time when philosophy acknowledges no single, fixed canon of Truth because all judgments are made on the shifting ground of our own socially constructed worldviews, religious leaders insist on hard and fast answers! There seems to be no place for shades of grey or careful theological exploration. Moreover, this recent turn to theological monism ("Thou shalt have no other theology than mine") betrays a lack of knowledge of the Christian tradition, which is far more diverse and exotically varied than its contemporary proponents are willing to recognize. Consider but one recent example: the publication of the Gospel of Judas reveals that early Christianity included many *differing* ideas of Jesus. For nearly two thousand years, most people assumed that the only sources of tradition about Jesus and his disciples were to be found in the New Testament. But the unexpected discovery at Nag Hammadi in 1945 of more than fifty ancient Christian texts proved what the earliest church leaders knew and wrote long ago: that Matthew, Mark, Luke, and John are only a small selection of gospels from among the dozens that circulated among the first Christian groups. The Gospel of Judas—along with the Gospel of Thomas, the Gospel of Mary, and many others—opens up new perspectives on familiar gospel stories. Many of the first scholarly commentators on these gospels had been taught that they were "gnostic" and therefore "heretical." But this glib dismissal was way off the mark. As Elaine Pagels explains in the *New York Times*, the publication of these early Gospels "exploded the myth of a monolithic Christianity and showed how diverse and fascinating the early Christian movement really was."

What applies to the diversity of opinions about Jesus similarly applies to people's understandings of God. Throughout church history some Christian theologians have insisted that God was not an objective entity whose existence could be proved. The apophatic tradition of defining God by negation found in such writers as Meister Eckhart (c. 1260–1328) and St. John of the Cross (c. 1542–1591) so blurred the distinctions between theism and atheism as to make the two indistinguishable. In using such images as Nothing, a Void, a Desert, or a Cloud to evoke God, these Christian mystical theologians embrace a journey into the unknown and unknowing. In their view it is impossible to speak of a "personal God" because that would be to make God in our own image, and that would both constitute the height of human hubris and place limitations on our understanding of deity. As a radical Anglican I stand within that branch of the mystical tradition. Bishop Spong expresses it cogently:

> God is the Source of Life who is worshipped when we live fully,
> God is the Source of Love who is worshipped when we love wastefully,
> God is the Ground of Being who is worshipped when we have the courage to be.

The Ecological Imperative

And yet I also want more from my God than my own philosophical/theological introspection. As a planetary being in relationship with other planetary beings, humans and animals alike, I am disturbed by the disorder and dis-ease that we have created in relation to the natural world. I want my God to respond to the crisis of global warming, the reliance on nuclear power, and proliferation of the arms race. I must therefore embrace the notion of God so eloquently expressed by Gordon Kaufman;

> To believe in God is to commit oneself to a particular way of ordering one's life and action. It is to devote oneself to working towards a fully humane world within the ecological restraints here on planet Earth, while standing in piety and awe before the profound mysteries of existence.[5]

Rather than self-appointed rulers of the universe and the pinnacle of creation, we must recognize ourselves to be part of an interconnected web of existence. The responsibility for the future of the planet rests with us. We cannot look to another world and another life beyond this one, but must commit ourselves to an ecological imperative that will benefit succeeding generations. If we destroy the world, we obliterate both ourselves and God! My understanding of God, then, is tied in with the ongoing universe, the pressing concerns of our planet, and the well-being of its inhabitants. This view has been championed by another Fellow of the Jesus Seminar, Lloyd Geering, and I would endorse his appeal to live by a voluntary human protocol of Ten Resolutions:

1. Let us take time to stand in awe of this self-evolving universe.
2. Let us marvel at the living eco-sphere of this planet.
3. Let us set a supreme value on all forms of life.
4. Let us develop a lifestyle that preserves the balance of the planetary eco-system.
5. Let us refrain from all activities that endanger the future of any species.
6. Let us devote ourselves to maximizing the future of all living creatures.
7. Let us set the needs of the coming global society before those of ourselves, our tribe, society, or nation.
8. Let us learn to value the human relationships that bind us together into social groups.
9. Let us learn to appreciate the total cultural legacy we have received from the past.
10. Let us accept in a self-sacrificing fashion the responsibility now laid upon us all for the future of our species and of all planetary life.[6]

The "greening" of Christianity thus outlined stands in marked contrast, and indeed in direct contradiction, to much of the historic teaching of the churches.

It will be obvious by now that I stand within the Christian community and faith, seeking to radically recast its ancient theology into a form that is appropriate for those who live in postmodernity or even beyond postmodernity in post-postmodernity![7] So, what then is the Christian gospel for today?

The Christian Gospel

I will highlight my understanding of the Christian gospel by four defining incidents in my life. These incidents will reveal what I regard as the radical and subversive nature of the Christian good news.

Papua New Guinea

While I was a young teacher in Papua New Guinea, the dynamic and often problematic nature of the interface between religious belief systems and the lives of human beings first became evident to me. Assigned to teach in a remote outpost, I soon became acutely aware of the animist beliefs of those in my care. Moreover I had to constantly ask myself what *exactly* was the content of the gospel that I was trying to preach, a message that was necessarily altered by being filtered through a Western lens. Was the Christian gospel going to add anything to their spiritual health when for millions of years they had survived without it? My situation was similar to that described by the Roman Catholic missionary Vincent Donovan in his encounter with the Masai tribe in Africa:

> I told them I believed that they knew about God long before we came, and that they were a devout and very pious people in the face of God. It was not our belief that God loved us Christians more than them, nor that God had abandoned them or forgotten them until we came along. From the beginning it was evident that we were going to have to learn from them as well as teach them . . . . [However] I did not know that there would be whole areas in their life and language that would be blank as far as the Christian concepts go—no word in their language for person or creation or grace or freedom or spirit or immortality. There were times . . . when I found myself bitterly resenting the church that had sent me among them, so ill-prepared to deal with them, times when I wondered about the sincerity of that church which styled itself essentially missionary.[8]

I returned from Papua New Guinea with a mild case of malaria and a serious case of theological indigestion. The former was easily cured with tablets; the latter still induces heartburn. To be confronted with an indigenous spirituality that had a closer affinity to the world of the New Testament than did my Western gospel had been an unnerving experience. My gospel was so overlaid with individualism and Western values that in the eyes of the local populace Christianity was equated with material prosperity and cargo cults. Unfortunately, many fundamentalist Christian churches had reinforced that perception by sending missionaries who came laden with all the modern paraphernalia of the West and who built themselves houses suitable for an affluent American suburb. Worse yet, far from working together with other churches, many Christian ministers took to what was commonly called "sheep-stealing"—luring away members of other Christian denominations with promises of material prosperity and salvation. I was appalled that the churches were so intent on "saving people's souls" as to effectively deny their value as human beings.

While there were exceptions to this rule—indeed, I met a few fine missionaries who attempted to conceptualize Christ as Melanesian—the majority saw themselves magnanimously bringing God and Jesus to a pagan land. Very few could accept that they were only "bringers and revealers ('witnesses' would be better) of what God had done in their own parts of the world."[9] The key theological concern that I brought back from Papua New Guinea was a deep uncertainty as to whether the Christian gospel can offer anything of real value to an indigenous person who is already part of a spiritual and religious order that has long maintained and preserved his or her well-being and that of the community. As I looked at the greed of international companies, the exploitation of the natural environment, and the accompanying urban drift and unfulfilled expectations, I wondered whether my Western world and its religion was not doing more harm than good.

Believer-in-exile: Faith in the City

My understanding of the Christian gospel has always been wide-ranging and inclusive. I was "a believer-in-exile" long before Spong coined the phrase. I had more friends outside the church than within it. With Paul Van Buren I searched for "the secular meaning of the gospel." With Paul Tillich I discovered God as "the beyond in the midst of life." With Dietrich Bonhoeffer I came to see discipleship as "holy worldliness." The church must not serve as a religious sanctuary or a sheltered enclave, but must stand in the centre of the world/city. These ideas constituted the new teaching that would overtake the church. It had the breadth of vision to eradicate racism, social injustice, sexism and homophobia. The kingdom would be established here on earth. The church would be a New Jerusalem in which, as Sydney Carter exclaimed in his popular hymn *When I Needed a Neighbor*, "the creed and the color and the name won't matter."

The nearest I came to disturbing anyone's comfortable world was when, as a priest assigned to a wealthy suburban parish, I initiated an exchange program with one of the inner-city London parishes of Brixton in response to the Church of England report, *Faith in the City*. That groundbreaking report of 1985, the first to take inner-city deprivation in the United Kingdom seriously, was "a call for action by church and nation." This latter reference greatly annoyed the conservative Prime Minister Margaret Thatcher, who was particularly dismissive of any political advice from church leaders, especially the Archbishop of Canterbury.

My cross-parochial initiative was prompted by a priestly colleague who had adopted Dietrich Bonhoeffer's "holy worldliness" far more seriously than I and was attempting to stand alongside the poor and marginalized of inner-city Britain. Living in a small flat on the twentieth floor of a dilapidated high-rise block in one of the most neglected and violent neighborhoods of South London, my friend incarnated liberation theology by championing the cause of the downtrodden and powerless. I persuaded a group of my parishioners first to study the report and then to experience life in the Brixton parish for a weekend with a return visit by the Brixton people to our parish later in the year. Crossing the cultural divide of the nation and healing some of the wounds of injustice and social equality was a minor triumph, and I was impressed by the courage of some of those parishioners who stepped outside their prosperous world to be confronted by another side of Britain.

Hong Kong

My commitment to the Anglican Church then took me to the Far East when, newly married, I was posted to Hong Kong shortly before that British territory was handed back to China. Remnants of colonial rule were still in evidence, and much of the populace was uneasy as to what might follow the formal handover on 30th June 1997. The Cathedral Church of Saint John was a quite extraordinary social and cultural mix, with attendees ranging from the Governor to migrant Filipino domestic workers. Since Hong Kong's wealth derived from its lucrative international trade, many of those involved in the life of the cathedral were directly caught up in the accumulation of personal fortunes. A significant number were expatriates on short-term contracts, people whose connection with the cathedral was largely cultural: they might be far from the land of their birth, but the sight of a traditional Neo-Gothic church building, its features redolent of the thirteenth century and all painted in white, triggered an emotional response.

Hong Kong presented a challenge to my understanding of the gospel as a proclamation that privileged the poor and marginalized. I was continually haunted by Jesus' saying about how difficult it is for a wealthy person to enter the kingdom of heaven (Mark 10:25=Matthew 19:24=Luke 18:25). Could the force of the saying be blunted by taking it to mean that those who had comfortable bank balances needed God just as much as everyone else? And as long as they devoutly believed in God wasn't it all right to pursue the mighty dollar? What did it mean to be a Christian in a country whose preoccupation was material and financial prosperity? How could one preach that God's domain was "populated with the poor, the destitute, the tearful, the hungry" (as Bob Funk puts it in *A Credible Jesus*) when most members of one's affluent congregation were dedicated to increasing the wealth of large corporations and financial institutions? This pursuit of prosperity was evident at every level of society. Even the Filipino workers who occupied the lower end of the socio-economic scale had left their families in search of economic success, and worked as domestic servants rather than taking more skilled but less remunerative jobs in the Philippines. In one way or another, it seemed, everyone was trying to get rich at the expense of someone else.

If you are expecting that I managed to begin a religious and social revolution, then you will be disappointed. But I did make a few courageous decisions. First, my wife and I were one of only two families in our block of apartments who did not employ a live-in amah (house-keeper or maid). It was a small token of our opposition to a social system that still endorsed something we considered tantamount to slavery. For us, the Jesus story repudiated such a way of life. Second, after visiting an island off Hong Kong where Vietnamese refugees had been dumped by authorities with inadequate sanitation and accommodation, I preached a sermon—at which the Governor of Hong Kong was present—in which I outlined this appalling state of affairs. Whether these words directly affected the governor's decision I cannot tell, but mercifully the camp was closed a few months later. Third, in my pastoral work I attempted to emphasize the radical inclusiveness of the gospel and the corollary requirement of an equitable distribution of the world's resources.

For the most part, however, like most in full-time ministry I had to compromise and allow myself to be compromised. My wife and I wined and dined at the best restaurants and hotels, we frequented the social round of cocktail parties, never refused an invitation to go on a junk trip or ride in a Rolls Royce, enjoyed the endless shopping emporiums, and in effect were members of an exclusive private club. We were caught up in a tempting and tempestuous whirl—a world of few friends but many acquaintances, fed by insincerity and what all too easily became an habitual concern for how to turn others to profitable use. It was a milieu of high contradiction: enticing yet ultimately unsatisfying, magical yet unreal. When the church hall was being refurbished and the Sunday school needed accommodation, the cathedral rented the ninth floor of the Hilton Hotel next door. At the time, well conditioned to the life and expectations of my parishioners, I made no objection to this decision. Today, I wonder what it says about those who claim to be followers of one who cautioned that God and the preoccupation with wealth are incompatible.

Secular Australia

Australia, to which we came at the beginning of the 1990s, proved to be another culture shock. Far from being "England with lots of sun," Australia has an ancient and rich history that thrums to the sound of the didgeridoo (a large musical pipe) and a feeling of oneness with its dusty red earth. My ministry was not focused on the indigenous inhabitants of this country, however, but with the "late-comers"—descendants of the early pioneers who, depending on one's reading of history, had either cultivated or despoiled the land. What immediately struck home was the lack of religious observance of Australians. In Hong Kong I had been used to a church packed with hundreds of people; my first Sunday in Perth found just *ten* faithful in the pews. Here was a glaring theological issue: the lack of relevance of the Christian church, the arrival of the post-Christian era. I was informed that only a minority attended church services on a Sunday and that the traditional rites of passage—baptism, marriage, and funerals—were now performed by civil celebrants. The church building was ignored in favor of ceremonies in the open air: gardens, beaches, and riverbanks had become "holy ground."

Just as I had swapped the concrete jungle of Hong Kong for the cry of the indigenous kookaburra bird and the venomous sting of the red-back spider, so I had exchanged ecclesiastical community for apathy and indifference. With nineteen per cent of the population openly declaring themselves to have "no religion," and a corresponding decline in Christian belief and increase in popular spirituality, my role as a clergyperson was in serious jeopardy. Nor had a number of notorious sexual scandals involving clergy in Australia enhanced public respect for my role. Christian communities were deemed irrelevant and unnecessary. People in large numbers had voted with their feet and found other strategies for coping with what life threw their way. The "church alumni association" was alive, well, and indeed thriving in Australia.

Jesus

As my life journey clearly attests, the Jesus story has been deeply influential. Being the product of a Christian family and Anglican Church education, it is hardly surprising that I have lived, as Gerd Theissen famously put it, in "the shadow of the Galilean." I am a Fellow of the Jesus Seminar and have a passionate interest in Bob Funk's renewed quest for the historical Jesus. Moreover, my definition of the New Testament has broadened to include such very early writings as the Sayings Source (Q) and the Gospel of Thomas, and I concur in the Seminar's attempt to distinguish the historical Jesus from the Christ(s) proclaimed by the early Christian churches. The historical person known as Jesus of Nazareth that has emerged from the Seminar's scholarly research is at variance with the figure preached by many in the church. The "official" mythical matrix put forward by the church has given way to the Seminar's portrait of an itinerant wisdom teacher who proclaimed the reign of unconditional love.

And yet, I find myself strangely at odds with the notion of Jesus as exclusively a wandering wisdom teacher. I'm not convinced that an itinerant Jewish sophist would have been put to death by the Roman authorities. I would contend that to have been crucified for political reasons he must have been more of a firebrand preacher. And I remain unconvinced that Albert Schweitzer's portrait of Jesus as a failed apocalyptic prophet was entirely wrong. To dismiss *all* the apocalyptic references in the gospels as literary creations of the early church seems rather contrived. The New Testament period was well supplied with apocalyptic expectations and it is evident that the apostle Paul believed that he would live to see Jesus' return in glory. Schweitzer's portrayal of Jesus as a failed Jewish prophet, who by being crucified thought he would return after three days as the Lord of a world transformed into total peace and perfection (the Kingdom of God) scares Christians because that would show Jesus was mistaken. The kingdom of God never occurred, and later Christian theologians recast Jesus' message to mean that he will appear at the "second coming." Where perhaps the Jesus Seminar and Schweitzer's Jesus overlap is in their insistence that Jesus called for an ethical reverence for life reflected in humanistic activity (Schweitzer) and an end to "tribalism," "ethnic privilege," and "nationalism" (Funk). What matters is the *good news* of a transformed humanity; the apocalyptic shell can be discarded and Jesus' message of universal love is still relevant. So while *my* Jesus (can there be any other?) may have been wrong about the imminent reign of God, he was correct in pointing towards a more inclusive vision of the world, humanity, and religion.

The Future Faith

But immediate problems remain: human sexuality; the challenge of "the new atheists" that "religion poisons everything"; evangelism and the relationship of Christianity to other faiths and cultures; Jesus' vision of a kingdom transcending human diversity; the harmful effects of fundamentalist teaching; the decline of Christianity; and the emergence of a post-Christian era. These are the pressing issues I now face on a journey that began with a young boy listening to the bells of my home church four decades ago. What do I make of it all? What do I see as the future of faith?

It will have been apparent that I am still wedded to the cause of radical Anglicanism. During my lifetime this radical vision has had some notable successes. A decrease in racist attitudes has resulted from the courage of those like Desmond Tutu; the awareness of multiculturalism has matched the growth of inter-faith dialogue; the enhancement of the role of women has followed their ordination to the priesthood and in some parts of the Anglican Communion as bishops (and is of particular interest to someone like myself who is married to a woman priest); efforts to ease the plight of refugees have expanded as has the fight against HIV/AIDS, most notably led by the unsung heroism of African Archbishop Njongonkulu Ndungane. Yet despite all this, resistance to radical change has been fierce. We have seen the victimization and even dismissal of clergy who openly probe the deepest issues of faith; the coalition of conservative theological forces against the appointment of Bishop Gene Robinson and Canon Jeffrey John because of their sexuality; and the demonizing of those who are considered "unsound." All these conservative initiatives smack of pulling up the drawbridge lest any but true believers be allowed to enter.

Moreover, many of the controversies in which we church folk are caught up were decided decades ago by those outside the church. I am now at a stage where ecclesiastical discussions very often bore me stiff. I am embarrassed by the irrelevancy of church councils and edicts. Among other issues, I no longer care to debate the suitability of women as bishops, the theological diversity within scripture, and the recognition of sexually active gays and lesbians. *These should be accepted as arguments that have been won: there can be no turning-back.* I have moved beyond these disputations and wish to explore new ways of being religious that have meaning for those who have seen the former certainties fade away. We need to be forging a new ethical commitment to life in the here and now. Yet, while the looming crisis of global warming should be galvanizing us to formulate a religious response, some in my church are decades behind the latest scientific and ecological thinking. The recent debate about "intelligent design" (creationism repackaged!) shows that many church folk still do not have a theology that coheres with Darwinism. It is no wonder that Richard Dawkins and "the new atheists" have been able to so easily make an assault on an intellectually bankrupt church. Where is an understanding of "God" that takes evolution by means of natural selection seriously? How many churches have responded in an intellectually satisfying way to the claim that the "God-hypothesis" is unnecessary? As I write this essay I have just spent three hours discussing the "mutual recognition of ministries" with representatives of another denomination, and am flabbergasted by the report we are expected to read. Some four hundred or so years after the Reformation we are still debating whether to accept each other's ministers. What disgraceful irrelevancy! No wonder people have abandoned the churches.

Indeed, Christianity and the world's other major religious traditions are content to immunize themselves from the world with myths of their special rabbi, prophet, or guru—myths that have been continually embellished and rewritten to fit the prevailing cultural norms and practices. As a cultural product, faith is continually refined and redefined. To be sure, I have come to recognize my own particular faith (radical Anglicanism) as a resource that has helped me shape my life: its emphasis on a human community that is "all embracing" and "radically inclusive" has both inspired and challenged me. In contrast to the insistence on "difference" found in most religions (and interestingly in canonical postmodernity), radical Anglicanism has championed the vision of a common future—a reign of justice, love, and equality.

Conclusion

Thus I face a most painful question: Is the church an institution that I wish to save? Don Cupitt has advocated taking leave of God; is it now time to take leave of the church? Will it remain forever locked in theological contradiction and social irrelevance? Should I leave the dead to bury the dead or remain and fight my corner of the battle? Even if at some future date (and it could be decades hence) my church should, for example, allow gay priests to openly express their sexuality and permit radical theology to thrive again, is it worth the effort? Is it reasonable to give one's life to an organization that is always at least a generation behind the rest of the world's best and latest thinking?

It is an interesting dilemma. I oscillate between depression and hope. I am filled with despair by those who use religion as a force for evil, constantly manipulating it to ostracize or terrorize those who are different. I weep over those who use sacred texts as a battering ram to justify hatred and fear. I am continually perplexed by the hate-filled "lovers of Christ" who divide humanity into "us" and "them." More and more I identify with those on the margins of the church, with those who have left its embrace, and with those in centers, networks, and forums that combine doubt and uncertainty with reverence for life. I find more spiritual wonder in watching the sun set over the West Australian Ocean than in many liturgical services. And yet I have also met many fine fellow Christian travelers who love the Lord even as they share my frustration with a conservative and often narrow-minded institution.

And so I choose to stay the course and pursue the radical Anglican vision that first inspired me all those years ago and nourished me through university studies and along the path to ordination. I look to the time when the church becomes a beacon leading to a fully inclusive and transformed humanity in which "the creed and the color and the name won't matter." I am happy to play in my writing the role of theological gadfly, to be one who challenges the church to make the necessary changes in its thinking to the disputations thrown up by the latest scientific and intellectual discourse. *Indeed, my own Anglican theological training was one that urged us to relentlessly plumb the depths of not only ourselves but also our scriptures and traditions.* **I am in so in many ways a true product of the Anglican system and its theological methodology**. Theological investigation *is* expected to be a life-long passion. Faith *is* an ever-evolving process that shall never end for, as T. S. Eliot put it in his poem "Little Gidding," "we shall not cease from exploration." It is only by so doing that the church will become the fully inclusive kingdom that Jesus proclaimed.

In short, I journey on in faith and life "looking in the distance" for a more compassionate Anglican church that has the vision to change the world for good.

Notes

1. Vasilii Rozanov, quoted by Richard Holloway in *Looking in the Distance*, 3.

2. In 2006, in an interview with the Dutch newspaper, *Nederlands Dagblad*, Rowan Williams said that homosexual practice was incompatible with the Bible and that homosexuals must change their behaviour if they are to be welcomed in the Anglican Church. This statement contradicted an earlier paper he had written in 1989 while a Professor at Oxford University, when he argued that the Anglican Church must revise its outdated attitude towards homosexuality.

3. Spong, *Rescuing the Bible from Fundamentalism*, 116–18; *Living in Sin*, 151–54; *Here I Stand*, 373–75. Nock's book, *St. Paul*, was written in 1938. His suggestion is all the more remarkable in an era that considered homosexuality "unnatural" or an illness.

4. Armstrong, *Spiral Staircase*, 328.

5. Lloyd Geering, quoting Gordon Kaufman in Jones, *God, Galileo and Geering*, 163.

6. Geering, *Greening of Christianity*, 53–54.

7. One current view is that we now have passed through postmodernity and are in post-postmodernity. Post-postmodernism is the inelegant and tentative name for whatever comes after postmodernism. The relationship between post-modernism and post-postmodernism is analogous to that between postmodern-ism and modernism: it builds on, reacts to, and is critical of what it deems to be deficiencies in what preceded it.

8. Donovan, *Christianity Rediscovered*, 25.

9. Gaquare, "Indigenization as Incarnation," 147.

Works Consulted

Archbishop of Canterbury Commission on Urban Priority Areas. *Faith in the City: A Call for Action by Church and Nation*. London: Church House Publishing, 1985.

Armstrong, Karen. *The Spiral Staircase*. London: HarperCollins, 2004.

Blakney, Raymond B. *Meister Eckhart: A Modern Translation*. New York: Harper Torchbooks, 1957.

Bonhoeffer, Dietrich. *The Cost of Discipleship*. London: SCM Press, 1959.

Boulton, David. *The Trouble with God: Religious Humanism and the Republic of Heaven*. Arlesford, UK: O Books, 2002.

Cupitt, Don. *Life, Life*. Santa Rosa, CA: Polebridge Press, 2003.

Dawkins, Richard. *The God Delusion*. New York: Houghton Mufflin, 2006.

Donovan, Vincent. *Christianity Rediscovered: An Epistle from the Masai*. London: SCM Press, 1982.

Funk, Robert W. *A Credible Jesus: Fragments of a Vision*. Santa Rosa, CA: Polebridge Press, 2002.

Gaquare, Joe. "Indigenization as Incarnation—the Concept of a Melanesian Christ." Pp. 146–49 in *Christ in Melanesia: Exploring Theological Issues*. Goroka, Papua New Guinea: POINT, 1977.

Geering, Lloyd. *The Greening of Christianity*. New Zealand: St Andrew's Trust, 2005.

Hart, David A. *Faith in Doubt: Non-Realism and the Christian Faith*. Oxford: Mowbray, 1994.

Hitchens, Christopher. *God is Not Great: How Religion Poisons Everything*. New York: Twelve Books, 2007.

Holloway, Richard. *Looking in the Distance: The Human Search for Meaning*. Edinburgh: Canongate, 2005.

Jones, Robert. *God, Galileo, and Geering: A Faith for the 21st Century*. Santa Rosa, CA: Polebridge Press, 2005.

Leaves, Nigel. *The God Problem: Alternatives to Fundamentalism*. Santa Rosa, CA: Polebridge Press, 2006.

Miller, Robert J. *The Apocalyptic Jesus: A Debate*. Santa Rosa, CA: Polebridge Press, 2001.

Nock, Arthur Darby. *St. Paul*. New York: Harper & Brothers, 1938.

Pagels, Elaine. "The Gospel Truth." *New York Times*, 8 April 2006.

Schweitzer, Albert. *The Quest of the Historical Jesus*. New York: Macmillan, 1986 (first published in 1906).

Spong, John Shelby. *Here I Stand: My Struggle for a Christianity of Integrity, Love and Equality*. New York: HarperCollins, 2000.

——. *Jesus for the Non-Religious: Rediscovering the Divine at the Heart of the Human*. New York: HarperCollins, 2007.

——. *Living in Sin: A Bishop Rethinks Sexuality*. San Francisco: Harper and Row, 1988.

——. *Rescuing the Bible from Fundamentalism: A Bishop Rethinks the Meaning of Scripture*. San Francisco: HarperSanFrancisco, 1991.

——. *The Sins of Scripture: Exposing the Bible's Texts of Hate to Reveal the God of Love*. SanFrancisco: HarperCollins, 2005.

Theissen, Gerd. *The Shadow of the Galilean: The Quest of the Historical Jesus in Narrative Form*. Philadelphia: Fortress Press, 1987.

Tillich, Paul. *The Courage to Be*. London: Collins Fontana, 1962.

Van Buren, Paul. *The Secular Meaning of the Gospel*. London: SCM Press, 1963.

Footsteps in the Quicksand

Robert M. Price

Remember the tongue-twisting slogan from biology: "Ontogony Recapitulates Phyogeny"? The point of it was that every embryo, as it develops in the womb, passes through the major stages of evolution, initially possessing a tail and gills, etc., and eventually losing these pre-human traits before birth. I believe that every biblical scholar goes through something equivalent upon departing from the fundamentalism in which we were raised or to which we converted as adolescents. We raise new (to us) biblical questions for which church instruction never prepared us, and we find ourselves forced to leave the once-comfortable nest in order to find answers in a wider intellectual world. We may begin by nuancing the doctrine of biblical inerrancy, and before long we begin to see the inevitability of the whole apparatus of historical and literary criticism. Along the way we find we have repeated in miniature the long historical process by which biblical scholarship escaped the cloying tutelage of Medieval orthodoxy. But then we find ourselves forced to rehearse in our own case the theological revolution occasioned by Modernity, too. What are we to believe, once we drop traditional religious authority? How are we to decide?

I have found that Paul Tillich makes sense of many things for me. I've loved Tillich and Rudolf Bultmann most of all, with a special fondness also for the 1960s "Death of God" theologians: Thomas J. J. Altizer, William Hamilton, and Paul van Buren. Some of these thinkers have since moved on to other positions themselves, but back then they were describing the place where I found myself: holding a (perhaps vestigial) fixation on Jesus as the religious ultimate, but standing in the air with no real beliefs or expectations. I see in Altizer's theology the heroic prospect of Christians as bastard children of an uncaring and impersonal universe, facing it down like pioneers at the edge of a primeval forest, and ready to impose their own habitat of values upon it, using the saw and ax of Christian discipleship. It might not succeed, but then the image of the cross already implies that.

But what a way to live! What a bid for authentic existence! One would have lived for something. And that's what Tillich said faith was: not a set of beliefs in unseen verities, but an "ultimate concern," a gut-commitment to a larger-than-life cause. I remember one night hearing then-Christian Bob Dylan on *Saturday Night Live* singing, "You Gotta

Serve Somebody." And I thought, here I am, bereft of beliefs, with no way ever to know any better about Jesus and God, but I can still read the gospels and see sketched out there the way of discipleship—a way to live that is characterized by showing compassion, cherishing integrity, discarding pretension and self-righteousness, going beyond the minimum requirements of duty. Discipleship remains an option, even without doctrines, even without any hope of heaven. The door is open, and it hangs ajar like a lingering question: will you go through it? Malcolm Boyd's writings have always appealed to me, too: no doctrines, just experience, and experience close to the ground, with people in a universe of ambiguity. The cameos displayed in his *Are You Running with Me, Jesus?* seem to flesh out what Altizer describes so abstractly but powerfully: the pouring out of the sacred into the profane.

Campus ministry and teaching and hosting religious discussion groups have all taught me that the quest for answers is itself a spiritual exercise, one more bracing and more productive than thinking one has all the answers. In *The Great Divorce*, C. S. Lewis finds endless seeking without discovering answers akin to masturbation. But I disagree. Dogmatic beliefs seem to be sleeping pills for the spirit. And who could possibly imagine he or she had grasped all the answers, even to the major questions? Even Paul, the opinionated apostle, admitted that he, like everyone else, saw only the vaguest image of the truth (1 Cor 13: 12). Seeking without finding answers is not some kind of clever reversal of traditional spirituality designed to make a skeptic feel less guilty. Doesn't the most ardent traditional devotion gauge spiritual growth precisely by the depth of yearning and emptiness the seeker feels? It is the one who hungers and thirsts, not the one who is filled, who receives the gospel beatitude. That, I think, is what poverty of spirit is all about. Tillich and Bultmann hold that we must apply the old Lutheran principle "simultaneously righteous and a sinner" to the cognitive realm of belief and opinion, that is, a thinking Christian must be able to be "at the same time righteous and a doubter." And it's the doubt that makes one's faith commitment more than a comfortably pat certitude. Doubt makes faith a wrestling match with the angel on the riverbank. It makes faith no mere possession, but a living thing.

To me the universe appears neutral and empty of any personal God pulling the strings. Claims to answered prayers, even the claims I used to make, seem like striking coincidences or else self-fulfilling prophecies. Nor do I believe in historical miracles. The ones in the Bible look too much like miracle stories found outside the canon, legends and myths that no one takes very seriously. I cannot demand special treatment for one group of miracle stories just because they appear in the Bible and cross off the rest as legends. Hume was right: every time I hear of a supposed miracle, I recall the constantly reiterated human tendency to jump the gun and accept rumors or misinterpretations as fact, and I think, "What are the chances?" The legends of the Bible I take as powerful symbols that (at least sometimes) convey the Holy to us. The way I look at it, the stories, even if factual, can be of value only if they possess a catalytic power to spark spiritual experience in us. I mean, suppose you had a videotape of Adlai Stevenson rising from his tomb. It would be astonishing, yes, but would it have any more religious significance than flying saucers or the abominable snowman? Such an event would be more than a mere freak phenomenon only insofar as it participated in the Holy, as Tillich says, and allowed us to participate in it, too. So, if the stories do in fact have this symbolic, transformative character, what difference does it make whether there is any factual basis to them or not? They "work" either way.

For a long time, I conceived of God as abstract Being-Itself, a fullness of Reality and Holiness revealed to us in moments of mystical contemplation and of occasional surprising "encounters." As I imagined it, the Trinity and all the heavenly realities of Christian belief were abstract truths far past the mortal mind's ability to conceive, but the mythical symbols we must perforce use to talk about them were true as far as they went. I was content not to try to crack the Divine Mystery as a code, but rather to bask in the Mystery *as a Mystery*, to be led to the Rock that is infinitely higher than I. I still believed in Idealist metaphysics, the notion of a "more real" invisible dimension of the spirit. A few years later, I would see this approach as a strategic retreat into vagueness, what Don Cupitt calls "Objective Symbolism." What changed me?

I became intrigued by Deconstructive philosophy and literary theory. This led me into Cupitt's "Non-Realist" theology, and marked the end of Idealism, of believing in unseen Transcendence. As I read Cupitt's *Taking Leave of God*, which deftly skewered my theology, I felt as if the author were whispering to me, "You don't really believe that stuff, do you, Bob?" And in my imagination I replied, "No, Don, I guess I don't."

I soon accepted the fully atheistic implications of the Religious Humanism I espoused. And I came to view liberal religion as what Cupitt calls "a theology of nostalgia." Every step of religious progress Liberal Christianity heralded was in reality a step toward Secular Humanism— though it never quite arrived, always clinging to some shred of religious sentiment tortuously redefined. I soon found myself working for the Council for Secular Humanism.

But I began to irritate some atheist colleagues because I could not be as virulently anti-religious as they were. You see, I had seen it from both sides, and as a scholar I knew one could not simply write off the whole cultural creation of religion as a baneful delusion, not even if one were an atheist. If one considered oneself a humanist, one was obliged to understand human religion as empathetically as possible. So I was a religion-loving atheist, trying to promote keen criticism and respectful coexistence.

One November afternoon in 2000, as I sat waiting for a friend in Newark International Airport, I passed the time with some light reading: *Ressentiment* by the Protestant sociologist-philosopher Max Scheler. One particular passage brought me up as short as if I had run into a brick wall. Scheler drew a distinction between a genuine convert to a new viewpoint and a mere "apostate." The apostate was a person bitterly disillusioned with his first-loved cause who joined up with another but used it only as a platform to attack his old allegiance. Immediately I felt pinned down by his words like a bug in an entomology lab! In that moment, as the marginal notes I scribbled in the book still attest, I knew that religion was too much a part of me for me to imagine I could simply reject it. I should have to make my peace with it and re-assimilate it in some way that would not require forgetting all the lessons I had learned. I could not just go back on my critical analyses and pretend they didn't matter.

For some time I had been thinking and writing about the essentially dramatic and theatrical character of religion. I had pretty much come to think that the power of religion stemmed from what Coleridge called "poetic faith" or the "temporary, willing suspension of disbelief." Maybe going to church was like going to a play or a movie. It was a transformative experience: esthetic, emotive, ethically challenging. For the duration of the service you allow yourself to forget about the mundane world of electricity and radios and the laws of physics, where no God seems to be in evidence. You let yourself be imaginatively swept away to a never-never land like Middle Earth or Oz or Camelot, where you can experience wonders of the imagination and the elevation of the spirit.

Unlike his mentor Sigmund Freud, Carl Jung did not dismiss religion as a complete neurosis. Jung thought the deep unconscious was hard-wired with symbols ("archetypes") that (to use a more recent analogy) work like computer screen icons. They hint at the hidden presence of built-in programs one must access in order to become computer-proficient. But to activate these programs, one must click on the icons. What if the religious symbols on parade in church and scripture are like those icons, and rituals are the way we click on them? Maybe it is precisely by means of its mythic symbolism, none of it literally true, that religion works as well. Church is a kind of psychodrama, and we participate in it, our imagination on "high," as part of a process of integration, individuation (as Jung called it), and maturity. Maybe one need not "believe in" an historical Jesus any more than one would have to believe in an historical Oedipus for the plays of Sophocles to make their impact.

I came to realize that I could participate in religion again on such a basis if I so desired. And I realized I *did* so desire. Secularism was becoming just too arid for me. Before long, I returned to the Episcopal Church. I rejoice to sing the great hymns, to repeat the litany, to receive the Eucharist, to be a Christian. Like wise old Judaism, Episcopalianism finds its center of gravity not in unanimous beliefs (about which the less said the better) but in a common worship. For me, this means that I can do the Christian thing without having to subscribe to a set of historical and theological opinions. Even the creeds are, after all, part of the poetic liturgy denoting historical continuity and not, as in many denominations, a litmus test.

With Jung, I regard God as a dweller in the depths, a powerful image in the deep unconscious rather than some kind of being (or Being!) external to me. God, as Psalm 22 says, dwells enthroned upon the praises of his people, or *inside* the ark of the covenant, not outside, as if sitting at some control panel programming tsunamis and earthquakes. I love the way Cupitt puts it in *Taking Leave of God.* He simply points out how little we really imagine God has to do with the physical universe. When a plane goes down, does anyone pause to ponder why God swatted it? The very idea is ludicrous, even to religious believers. Even one who says, "Thank God I cancelled my flight at the last minute!" doesn't mean to imply God actually decided to spare him while killing the rest of the passengers. The lucky survivor would recoil in disgust if anyone suggested it! He is merely using expressive language about his feelings. "God" has come to mean what it meant when Origen said, "But who wrote the epistle [to the Hebrews], in truth, God knows" (Eusebius, *Ecclesiastical History*, 6.25). No man or woman knows. Nobody knows. I have no one to thank for my good fortune, and that makes the good fortune all the more remarkable. And that is what one is remarking on when one says, "Thank God!"

Cupitt says that God makes sense only in religion, just as numbers make sense only in math. I admit it is a mind game. When we ask God to scrutinize our unfaithful hearts and to point out hidden sins, we are, I realize, assuming an imaginary vantage point from which *we* will scrutinize what we usually miss about ourselves. We are setting up a receptive mood that may enable something to pop up from our subconscious. You may well ask how I can go on with it when I am fully cognizant of the "gimmick" involved. The play's the thing to catch the conscience. Just as Freud said that behaving like a crazy person *makes* you a crazy person, I should say that behaving like a worshiper *makes* you a worshiper.

Old Testament theologian Gerhard von Rad argued that the faith of Israel was not so much in history as in a saga, an epic of their origins and of God's mighty acts to deliver them—even if those acts didn't exactly happen! It was *Heilsgeschichte*, a narrative of religious meaning, not necessarily

of historical facts. He called it "a theology of recital." I find myself participating in just such a recital theology in church. Only, probably unlike the
ancient Israelites, I know good and well it is fiction. And as a member of
the living extension of that tradition, that is, as part of the worshipping
community, I know I am an actor in the same drama. I am playing a fictive role, and that role has great power. Ask those who act on stage if they
remain unaffected by the roles they play.

I even suspect that church has some similarity of function to William
Sargant's "abreactive therapy," a technique he developed for helping trau-
matized war veterans get past their flashbacks. He found that they could be
cured by voluntarily reliving battlefield horrors in their imagination. Then,
to his surprise, he found that other patients who could not trace their neu-
roses to wartime crises were helped in the same way by "reliving" *imaginary*
"pasts." That's psychodrama—literally, "the drama of the soul"—and that's
what I think is happening in church when it is effective.

I think back to what a Pentecostal pastor named Alan Babcock told
me many years ago: if you think you might want to worship God, but
you say, "Lord, first let me resolve all my doubts and questions," you are
never going to worship God. So why not just decide now to worship and
enjoy religion, even if you leave all the intellectual questions wide open,
and even if the twin railroad tracks are veering farther and farther apart?
If you are going to stay honest, you have to call historical judgments as
you see them, as objectively as you can, without being influenced by what
you'd like to believe happened. And it works the other way, too. You can't
restrict faith to the piddling amount of factuality you can scrape together.
I think it is pathetic to see New Testament scholars trying to scale faith
back so that it ventures no farther than the facts: a religion of the historical
Jesus, for example. Can't they see they are still fundamentalists—chastened
fundamentalists, maybe, but fundamentalists nonetheless. They're like
tight-lipped Detective Sergeant Joe Friday on the old *Dragnet* TV series:
"The facts, ma'am, just the facts." No wonder such "religion" inevitably
devolves into liberal politics and utilitarianism. I think religion, via myth
and ritual, makes the soul take flight to higher realms, kingdoms not of
fact but of Mystery.

I celebrate Easter, even though I know Jesus did not rise from the dead
any more than Osiris or Jimmy Hoffa did. In fact, I am no longer convinced
that there was an historical Jesus to begin with. As a scholar and historian
I can be frank about that. I do not need to engage in mental gymnastics to
find some vague, redefined way in which I can still say that Jesus "really
lives" or "actually did" rise. No, I just go with the flow of the gospel passages and the liturgy for the occasion. But that is worship, not scholarship.
They are two different "language games." Look, what would it even *mean*

to say you took the traditional creed "literally"? How, in "literal" terms, could Jesus or anybody else be the Son of God? How could there be a penis involved in the matter? Or what about the gospel miracles? As David Friedrich Strauss asked, what are we supposed to picture when we read of Jesus multiplying the loaves and sardines? Did he stretch them like sponges and then rip them in half? Did a star, a ball of blazing hydrogen millions of times the size of the earth, hover only a few yards above the Judean countryside to guide the Wise Men? If the Risen One still had his wounds, that is, if he still bore the same physical damage that killed him—why wasn't he still dead? If he was trying to demonstrate his corporeal reality, why did he walk through a locked door like Jacob Marley's ghost in Dickens's *A Christmas Carol*? When Jesus ascended, did he—as the Flying Saucer cults teach—keep going till he arrived on another planet? Philosopher D.Z. Phillips asks just how magnificent a dining hall would have to be to convince an awakening Viking that he had died and gone to Valhalla. In the same way, even supposing you're a fundamentalist, if you saw (probably on CBN) Jesus Christ descending through the air to the Mount of Olives with angelic trumpets blaring, wouldn't you have to suspect it was some kind of special effects show? It would make you wonder what kind of observable phenomenon you had ever expected—if any. I suspect the so-called literalists have never thought it out very far. Like mine, deep down, their religious faith is a different sort of language, one that expresses feelings, not facts. As Paul says, "I will sing with the spirit, and I will sing with the mind also" (1 Cor 14:15). Maybe not at the same time. Maybe not the same tune. I agree with Bishop Pike: I sing the creed; I don't say it.

Let me tell you just how far I go with this. With my mind I work with Atheist Alliance International and the Secular Humanists. With my spirit I am a happy Episcopalian and teach for Johnnie Colemon Theological Seminary. I have no "beliefs" any more and don't miss them. The question for me is whether religious experience is wholesome and edifying. And if so, how do I go about getting it? I can't tell you what I expect after death besides a cold grave. But I figure that is beside the point anyway. If there is no postmortem hope, then, as the writer of Psalm 90 knew, this life seems all the more precious. I also recall what Pascal said: if you choose the religious life, and there turns out to be no postmortem payoff, what have you lost? It will have been a great ride.

Works Consulted

Altizer, Thomas J. J. *The Descent into Hell.* New York: Lippincott, 1970.

———. *The Gospel of Christian Atheism.* Philadelphia: Westminster Press, 1966.

Altizer, Thomas J. J., and William Hamilton. *Radical Theology and the Death of God.* New York: Bobbs Merrill, 1966.

Berger, Peter L., and Thomas Luckmann. *The Social Construction of Reality: A Treatise in the Sociology of Knowledge.* Garden City: Doubleday Anchor, 1967.

Boyd, Malcolm. *Are You Running with Me, Jesus?* New York: Avon, 1967.

Bultmann, Rudolf. *Jesus Christ and Mythology.* New York: Scribners, 1958.

Coleridge, Samuel Taylor. *Biographia Literaria.* Eds. James Engell and W. Jackson Tate. Bollingen Series 75. Princeton: Princeton University Press, 1983.

Cox, Harvey. *The Feast of Fools: A Theological Essay on Festivity and Fantasy.* New York: Harper & Row, 1969.

Cupitt, Don. *Life Lines.* London: SCM Press, 1986.

———. *Taking Leave of God.* New York: Crossroad, 1981.

Dickens, Charles. *A Christmas Carol.* Pp. 89–151 in *The Complete Ghost Stories of Charles Dickens.* Ed. Peter Haining. New York: Franklin Watts, 1983.

Freud, Sigmund. *The Future of an Illusion.* Trans. W. D. Robson-Scott. Rev. and ed. James Strachey. Garden City, NY: Doubleday Anchor, 1964.

Hamilton, William. *The New Essence of Christianity.* New York: Association Press, 1966.

Hoeller, Stephan. *The Gnostic Jung and the Seven Sermons to the Dead.* Wheaton, IL: Quest, 1982.

Hume, David. *"An Enquiry Concerning Human Understanding."* Section X: "On Miracles." Pp. 205–29 in *David Hume on Religion.* Ed. Richard Wollheim. New York: World Publishing Company/Meridian Books, 1964.

Jung, Carl. *The Archetypes of the Collective Unconscious.* Trans. R. F. C. Hull. Bollingen Series XX. 2nd ed. Princeton: Princeton University Press, 1968.

Kaufmann, Walter. *The Faith of a Heretic.* Garden City, NY: Doubleday Anchor, 1963.

Lewis, C. S. *The Great Divorce.* New York: Macmillan Company, 1963.

Pascal, Blaise. *Pensees.* Trans. A. J. Krailsheimer. Baltimore: Penguin Books, 1995.

Phillips, D. Z. *Faith and Philosophical Enquiry.* London: Routledge & Kegan Paul, 1970.

Pike, James A. *A Time for Christian Candor.* New York: Harper & Row, 1964.

Sargant, William. *The Mind Possessed: A Physiology of Possession, Mysticism and Faith Healing.* Baltimore: Penguin, 1975.

Scheler, Max. *Ressentiment.* Trans. Lewis B. Coser and William W. Holdheim. Milwaukee: Marquette University Press, 1994.

Sophocles. *The Oedipus Cycle: Oedipus Rex, Oedipus at Colonus, Antigone.* Trans. Dudley Fitts and Robert Fitzgerald. New York: Harvest Books, 2002.

Strauss, David Friedrich. *The Life of Jesus Critically Examined.* Trans. George Eliot. Lives of Jesus Series. Philadelphia: Fortress Press, 1972.

Tillich, Paul. *Biblical Religion and the Search for Ultimate Reality.* The James W. Richard Lectures in the Christian Religion. University of Virginia, 1951–52. Chicago: University of Chicago Press, 1955.

———. *Dynamics of Faith.* New York: Harper & Row, 1958.

van Buren, Paul M. *The Secular Meaning of the Gospel.* New York: Macmillan, 1966.

von Rad, Gerhardt. *Old Testament Theology.* 2 vols. Trans. D. M. G. Stalker. New York: Harper & Row, 1962.

A Mystical Christian Credo

Paul Alan Laughlin

Like most Americans, I was born into and reared within a rather traditional sort of Christianity. Mine was of the Southern-evangelical Methodist variety, which suited me well in the naiveté of my childhood. But it utterly failed me in my early adolescence on two grounds: its strong strain of Wesleyan pietism was too emotion-based for my disposition, and its biblical literalism and strict monotheism made little or no sense to a bright kid interested in science and analytical thinking. My pubescent alienation obtained some relief *and* reinforcement when I was eighteen and a new minister arrived at our little church. He was an unknown factor appointed to our congregation out of the blue (that is, from another Conference), and he decidedly broke the previous pattern of pastors by being intellectual, highly educated, and well-read in theology and comparative religions. Due largely to his influence, I became fascinated with the academic study of religion, and eventually entered and graduated from seminary, was ordained into the (by then) *United* Methodist ministry, and studied for and earned a doctorate in religious studies.

After a mercifully brief but surprisingly rewarding stint in the pastoral ministry in my native Kentucky, I became a full-time professor of religion and philosophy at a small liberal arts college in central Ohio, a position that I hold to this day, nearly three decades later. In that post, my research interests and teaching responsibilities gradually shifted from the Christian historical theology I had focused on in graduate school to comparative religions, with a special emphasis on Eastern faiths and philosophies. In retrospect, I can see that this career adjustment, which at the time seemed rather circumstantial and pragmatic (largely a result of shifting curriculum, faculty, and student needs) really did have a personal motivation and rationale—a rhyme *and* a reason, as it were. I had slowly realized, albeit subliminally, that along with my obvious intellectual interest in things religious and spiritual I also had a strong mystical bent, one that would eventually lead me to abandon the decidedly non-mystical United Methodist Church and its ministry.

I now attribute my mystical inclination in large part to my having been since childhood an improvisational and later jazz musician, a

pursuit that had the effect of re-orienting (or re-Orienting) me spiritually. Artists, I have come to believe, or at least the more spontaneous and
creative among them, are mystics by inclination, evidencing as they do
an introverted spirituality; for whatever creativity they experience feels as
though it emanates from within themselves, rather than being bestowed
by some outside entity.

The following affirmation sets forth my current and still tentative thinking about the Christian faith from my mystical vantage point at age 62.
I present it under the banner of "a mystical Christianity" because from
beginning to end, my credo reflects a spiritual orientation toward introspection, inwardness, and deep-self understanding and affirmation that at
least since middle age has become a kind of equilibrium for me. The original working title of this faith-statement was "An Enlightened Christianity
Credo," because it keyed on the last chapter of my *Getting Oriented*, where
that phrase meant simply a Christianity viewed *in light of* Eastern mystical spirituality and philosophy. But *Fourth R* editor Robert J. Miller rightly
pointed out to me that at face value "enlightened" sounded presumptuous
or even smug, suggesting (unintentionally) that other forms of Christianity
were *de facto* unenlightened and therefore inferior. The word "mystical" is
therefore better, because it implies no such thing *and* is more accurate and
descriptive, especially as I define it throughout this article.

What follows, therefore, is a very personal and no doubt idiosyncratic affirmation of faith, though it is not without its antecedents in the
Christian tradition. (Prominent and very accessible examples of Christian
mystics would include Meister Eckhart, Pierre Teilhard de Chardin, Thomas
Merton, and Anthony de Mello.) This credo comprises nine articles, starting
with conceptual or doctrinal considerations (1 through 4) and proceeding
to more pragmatic matters—spiritual practice, ethics, community, interfaith
relations, and faith development (5 through 9). It is not offered as a (much
less *the*) final word on faith in general or the Christian faith in particular;
much less is it intended to serve as a norm for anyone else, including other
mystics. Its main purpose is to stimulate reflection, self-searching, and
self-clarification in the reader, even if (as is likely) it does so by generating
dissonance, discomfort, or—worst case scenario—disdain.

Article 1: An Immanent, Emanating God

*I believe in God the Mystery Eternal, Source and Essence of all that is; and in God
the Manifest Expression, the Identity in diffusion, the Unity in Diversity, the One
and All that is in one and all.*

My credo begins with the central theological issue: the basic nature of
God. It reflects a fundamentally mystical spirituality, which in its highest

expressions (mostly found in Eastern religions) is typically characterized by a profound intuitive experience of the unity of all things. In Hinduism, Buddhism, and Daoism—where mysticism is more honored and highly developed than in the West—this experience has usually been expressed philosophically as a particular sort of *monism*, which is the belief in a single ultimate principle, being, force, etc., in contrast to dualism, which posits two constituent elements (usually matter and mind or God and the universe), or *pluralism*, which postulates three or more such components. The specific type of monism found in the philosophies generated by these religions is best termed *neutral monism* because the Ultimate that they attest is neither physical nor psychical, these latter qualities being but manifestations of the One Something. (Neutral monism is a term coined by William James in the first decade of the twentieth century to reflect a viewpoint dating back to Baruch Spinoza in the seventeenth century.) This position very closely resembles pantheism, which is the belief that everything is God (and vice versa) or essentially God—or, as the *Oxford English Dictionary* puts it, "that God is immanent in or identical with the universe." Eastern religions are not really pantheistic, however, since their respective Ultimate Realities—*Brahman, Shunyata,* and *Dao*—are not conceived of as God (though Hindus occasionally call *Brahman* God as a concession to Christian and Muslim sensibilities). Christians who embrace neutral monism, however, may rightly be called *pantheists* if they continue to use the traditional name "God" for their untraditional view of the Ultimate Reality.

The most important characteristic of the *monistic-pantheistic* God of our first article is Its immanence. I use "Its" intentionally because the God described here is non-personal or, more accurately, is beyond any such distinction as personal versus impersonal. All of the synonyms for God contained in this article are therefore non-personal, as imagistic representations (e.g., metaphors) should be as well. "Immanence" literally means "within-ness," and in monism-pantheism, the Ultimate-God profoundly indwells nature and human nature—innately, inherently, and indelibly. This God is *transcendent* as well, but only in the relatively weak sense of being *beyond* our abilities to perceive, comprehend, or express It verbally—transcendent, in other words, not by virtue of the Divine nature *per se*, but due to our limited human capacities to grasp It.[1]

The God of Article 1, then, stands in stark contrast to the monotheistic God of traditional Christianity, Who is personal and profoundly transcends nature and human nature as an Other Being "above and beyond" even the cosmos itself. This divine transcendence in its most intense sense is an *essential*—or in fancy philosophical terms, *ontological*—otherness, a quality that renders this God not natural, but supernatural. Our newly-conceived God, by contrast, is a Principle, Power, or Force that is thoroughly within the universe rather than in a supernatural realm that is empirically inaccessible and thus impervious to analytic and experimental investigation.

Article 2: Nature and Humanity as Divine Manifestations

I believe in Nature and Humanity as manifestations and expressions of the profoundly immanent and incarnate God, whose pervasive Presence and Power are active and unfailing, though often subtle and elusive.

A mystical Christianity typically treats nature and human nature as being a part of God, rather than apart from God, as monotheistic traditionalists would have it. In keeping with the preceding article, therefore, nature and human nature are understood here not as creations of an ontologically transcendent God, but as emanations of an ontologically immanent God, comparable to photons of light that are simply given off by the sun as part and parcel of its inherent thermonuclear process. Creation-language suggests a discontinuity between Creator and the created order (including its creatures), and thus implies a relationship between two separate entities. It further opens up the possibility—if not the inevitability—of an alienation, which traditional Christianity has framed theologically in terms of *sin*. That in turn becomes the premise for a soteriology (that is, a doctrine of salvation) and Christology (the so-called Person and Work of Christ, which is to say the doctrines of Incarnation and Atonement). Emanation, by contrast, entails continuity and thus connotes not a dichotomous relationship between God and the believer, but an essential *identity*. That identity is not obvious, of course, for it lies at a spiritual level much deeper than the ego-self and its perceptions, hence the "subtle and elusive" phrase that closes Article 2. Hinduism's *Upanishads* say that the Ultimate *Brahman* is hidden in the world the way cream is hidden in milk or salt in salt water. These images work just as well for the mystically-conceived Christian God with regard to nature and human nature.

This second article, in effect, universalizes the traditional Christian doctrine of the Incarnation, which says that God was "enfleshed" in the man Jesus, who therefore and uniquely had in his one integral person two complete natures, one human and one divine, seamlessly fused. A *mystical* Christianity, however, sees God as Incarnate—suffused or interfused—throughout the cosmos and all its constituents as their Inner Spirit, or in the words of Ralph Waldo Emerson (in "The Over Soul"), "the Soul of the whole." Properly understood, such references to Spirit and Soul do not reintroduce a dualism to the picture, for they are merely terms for the depth aspect or dimension of a single unified Reality. (The reconception of matter and energy as matter-energy posited in modern physics is analogous.) Again, the acknowledgement that this pervasive Presence is "subtle and elusive" is a simple recognition that detection and awareness of this Divine

Within are not automatic—hence the need for specific spiritual practices designed to access and actualize It.

Article 3: The Multifaceted "Messiah"

I believe in Jesus Christ, historical and mythical, metaphysical and archetypal, the perfect image of a fully realized person, complete humanity wholly and seamlessly interfused with pure divinity.

Article 3 expresses my belief that the common distinction between the historical Jesus and the Christ of faith, methodologically useful as it is for New Testament studies, is in a broader theological context a false dichotomy and too simplistic to fill the needs of the wide variety of dispositions and spiritualities found among Christians. In a recent *Fourth R* article, "The Once and Future Christ of Faith," I argued the virtues of the historical Jesus, the fictional-narrative Jesus, the celestial Christ, and the archetypal Christ. In this credo, however, I exclude the third of these images because as an essential element of faith in and love of an external Other, the celestial Christ is of little use in a mystically-based (and therefore introverted) faith. In place of "celestial," therefore, I insert the word "metaphysical" to indicate that it is entirely proper for a mystic to understand the word "Christ" as referring to every person's inner-spiritual aspect that is waiting to be touched and tapped—what Buddhists call our "Buddha-nature" and Daoists dub our "Inner-Nature." This article, then, reinforces the universalization of the traditional Christian doctrine of the Incarnation implied in Article 2.

Decidedly absent here is the sin-redemption model upon which the traditional doctrine of the Atonement is based. Like Incarnation, Atonement (At-one-ment) is universalized in this credo as the truth about all of us and the universe that we inhabit: we are literally "at one"—a Unity. In a fundamentally monistic system, all is One by definition. Any sense of multiplicity and duality—to say nothing of alienation—is illusory at best. The human predicament is framed in terms of ignorance of one's truly divine nature rather than sin; and with sin no longer the problem, the notion of assuaging it through a blood sacrifice of any kind is stripped of meaning, with self-knowledge replacing propitiation as the appropriate amelioration for our existential plight. If ignorance is the root problem, the remedy will necessarily be something on the order of *enlightenment*.

Article 4: Scriptures as Word-Windows

I believe in the Bible and all inspired scripture as fallible, finite words imperfectly conveying the Infinite Word that brings both the peace of our unity with the Absolute and the passion to spread joy, love, and peace.

The fact that my version of Christianity is mystically based means that the locus of authority is shifted from outside the believer or practitioner to within. Put another way, we move from a situation of *heteronomy*, in which we are ruled by external authorities (e.g., scriptures, creeds, and clergy), to one of *autonomy*, in which we become our own authorities based on our own experiences and reason. The issue with the Bible then becomes not a matter of its authority, but of its *authenticity*—by which I mean not its historical accuracy or factuality, but rather the extent to which it resonates with the world, existence, and life as we experience and understand them. The related issue of inspiration also takes on new meaning: a scripture is "inspired" only to the extent that its reader finds it inspiring. Our newly found autonomy also allows us to look for authenticity in the scriptures of other world religions, especially those that have proven inspiring to many readers over time and across cultures. Our motto at this point might be: "The more you like scripture, the more scriptures you'll like."

The use of "Word" in Article 4 simply introduces another synonym for the monistic-pantheistic God I described in Article 1. It also picks up on the Greek term *logos* (Word) in John 1:1: "In the beginning was the Word, and the Word was with God, and the Word was God." *Logos* is a complex concept derived from the Greek philosophical tradition and connotes, among many other things, a cosmic organizing Principle not unlike the monistic-pantheistic God of my Article 1. While this brief discussion cannot do the term justice, let me simply note that when the American Bible Society translated this passage from John into Chinese, the word they used for *Logos* was *Dao*, the ultimate Way of Daoism. A mystical Christianity allows for the possibility of a variety of scriptures—as well as other literature not generally considered as scripture—to be, in effect, windows to this Word-Way.

Article 5: Practice as Prerequisite

I believe in the importance of intentional spiritual practices that may lead to the direct experience of the Spirit that sustains us, the Light that illumines us, and the Love that connects us to all persons and things.

Article 5 turns from the theoretical (theological-philosophical) to the practical issue of spiritual discipline, which is the very heart of mystical Christianity: the ongoing quest for the direct, unmediated experience of the immanent God sketched in the first four articles. The God of a mystical Christianity is not simply a concept to be considered, weighed, and accepted because of its plausibility or aesthetic or emotional appeal. On the contrary, It is the innermost aspect of the whole of reality and of every individual constituent; and It is both accessed and verified empirically, not so much with the five senses and intellect (though they are by no means excluded in the search) as with intuition—the right hemisphere of the brain, as it were. The search for the immanent Ultimate Within defines mysticism, at least in those highly developed expressions found in Eastern religions and a few notable Christian examples (especially the medieval German Dominican mystic Meister Eckhart). Mystical spirituality is by nature introverted and introspective: it entails a journey within oneself in search of radical At-one-ment.

The terms "Spirit," "Light," and "Love" are not mutually exclusive, but merely evocative. They add to the pool of non-personal images already used for God in this credo. Such images of the Ultimate suggest an essential continuity between the human and the Divine, and therefore imply that the purest experience of It would be direct. One would be wrong, however, to exaggerate the unmediated nature of mysticism. Indeed, the desire for such experiences can be triggered by many things. A mentor, a book, or even a credo like this one, for example, may be instrumental in this regard—not because they are authoritative in any heteronomous sense, but simply because they ring true as authentic. Even common experiences may provide mystical moments spontaneously, and often without being recognized as such. I believe that such episodes are much more commonplace than most people realize. They occur in moments of extraordinary profundity: while making a special connection with nature or another person, or being absorbed in a piece of music, or a painting, or a dance, or even a sport—and whether as performer-artist-player or as observer-audience-spectator. In short, the only thoroughgoing non-mystics, if such people exist, would be people who live purely superficial lives in a vapid flatland of everydayness and ordinariness, blithely unaware of any depth dimension to human existence. In our model, we might figuratively call such a life "Hell."

Article 6: World Affirmation and Amelioration

I believe that our inward spirituality must be demonstrated in a radical acceptance and affirmation of the planet and all of its inhabitants, and in a burning passion to work for their wellbeing, justice, and peace.

One of the gross misperceptions and misrepresentations of Eastern mysticism is that it is escapist and world-denying. Nothing could be further from the truth. Such a misunderstanding is grounded in the spiritual trajectory of mysticism, which is away from the ego-self and its physical environs—what Hinduism and Buddhism call the realm of *samsara*—and into the inner *sanctum sanctorum* of the true or deep Self, which turns out to be none other than the Ultimate One. Mystics do not abide there, however. In fact, quite the opposite: they return to the plane of worldly existence better able to see it for what it is, to cope with its vicissitudes, and to engage it with compassion for other people and creatures and the planet itself. Meditation, then, is best thought of as a temporary tactical withdrawal or retreat.

Article 6 does two very timely things relative to modern life and its peculiar challenges. First, it consciously distances us from the charge of the God
of Genesis 1 to the man and woman just created in the divine image and
likeness: "Have dominion over the earth and subdue it" (Gen 1:28). With
or without this injunction in mind, we human beings have accomplished
this task with such a vengeance that we have not only estranged ourselves
from nature, of which we are obviously a part, but made ourselves its worst
enemies—and thus, ironically, our own. I affirm here something very different and ecologically promising: our continuity with nature, which, by
virtue of a theology of immanence, is itself inherently divine, rather than
purely secular (i.e., unsacred) "stuff" to be used (and abused), manipulated,
and depleted at our whim. The other (but not unrelated) side of this article
is the ideal of justice, which may be the point at which Christianity could
inform and benefit Eastern thought; for Christianity has a much more
deliberate, self-conscious impetus toward social justice by virtue of its
grounding in the Hebrew prophetic tradition, which counsels believers to
"Let justice flow down like waters, and righteousness like a mighty stream"
(Amos 5:4). This theme was also taken up in the teachings of the historical Jesus, which repeatedly express concern for the poor, the hungry, the
widowed, and other socially oppressed and outcast people. Admittedly, this
pro-justice dynamic is often ignored by those who most vociferously claim
Jesus as their source of inspiration, but it is clear and unavoidable for those
who truly "have ears to hear," and no Christian affirmation—mystical or
otherwise—should be without it.

Article 7: Communal Considerations

I believe in the universal spiritual community of open-minded seekers and compas-
sionate servants, whether it be manifested in formal symbols, rituals, and institu-
tions or in more informal, impromptu ways.

Article 7 raises (without really settling) the classic Christian doctrine of
the Church. Its first line suggests that people who are on this particular
spiritual and conceptual wavelength already belong to a universal community, one perhaps analogous to "The Body of Christ" of St. Paul, "the
holy catholic Church" of the Apostles' Creed, and the "mystic sweet communion" posited in the hymn "The Church's One Foundation," where
it includes even the like-minded dead. Testimony to the reality of such a
seemingly abstract entity has been communicated to me from all over the
world by fans of the kind of spirituality sketched out in my *Getting Oriented*;
they indicate a widespread recognition that we not only are but probably
long have been in the same spiritual-conceptual circle or set, whether we
knew it or not.

The credo leaves completely open the issue of whether people who embrace this or a similar affirmation need to associate with one another either physically or at a distance (e.g., via telephone or correspondence). It is entirely conceivable that some mystically oriented individuals might, by virtue of having reached a satisfactory spiritual plateau, feel no need for an actual spiritual community—being content, perhaps, with the virtual Universal One intuitively realized in spiritual practice. But human beings seem to be social creatures, so I suspect that most would want ongoing personal relationships and interactions, if only informally as regular lunch mates, Internet friends, book clubs, or study groups. In my experience, the ongoing sharing of experiences and discussion of their meaning promotes spiritual growth. But some people also seem to require a more formal social structure, as well as set ritual expressions of their shared spiritual orientation and experiences. They may want to build institutions around their mystical Christianity.

If so, they will probably find it necessary to devise new sets of symbols and rituals as well as communal spiritual practices, or at least to reconfigure old ones. The traditional cross and crucifix, for example, will have to be dispensed with or radically redesigned and reinterpreted to eliminate the connection with blood-sacrifice atonement. Something suggesting Light might be appropriate, perhaps within a circle, since circles suggest centers and a mystical Christianity is all about spiritual centering. Rituals involving circles, would also seem fitting—circumambulation or circle-dancing, perhaps. Prayer as communication with an Other would have to go, replaced by a Quaker-style silent introspection, Zen-like meditation, Father Thomas Keating's centering prayer, or some such affirmative *mantra* as "I AM the One and the All."

Article 8: Pluralism in Practice

I believe in the necessity of appreciating, honoring, and learning from other humane and life-affirming religious, spiritual, philosophical, and scientific traditions, and of recognizing that none of us has a special claim to the truth.

Article 8 is an appreciative nod to the fact that we live in a world of globalization and pluralism. A fair definition of globalization might be this: *the already profound and ever-increasing interconnection and interdependency of the world's peoples, nations, cultures, politics, economies, and technologies.* Two of the prime causes of globalization are the increasing ease of international travel and transportation and the instantaneous worldwide communication of thoughts, data, and feelings via the Internet. The upshot of globalization is the sense that the world is getting smaller. Pluralism is the handmaiden of globalization in two senses. First, pluralism as a condition of modern life is the coexistence of different ethnic, cultural, and/or religious groups (and their competing beliefs and practices) within a society. Second, as an attitude toward that situation, pluralism means the appreciation of and perhaps even a drawing upon existing ethnic, cultural, and/or religious groups and their competing beliefs and practices within a society.

A Christianity that appropriates mystical strains in Eastern religious traditions is inherently pluralistic. Its choice of autonomy over heteronomy and its preference for authenticity over authority (see Article 4) free its adherents to search for spiritual truth wherever it might be found. A mystical Christianity values rational inquiry and critical thinking as well as the more intuitive and imaginative mental processes that are typically less appreciated in intellectually based Western philosophies as opposed to those more spiritually grounded ones of the East. But the wording of the article suggests that mystical Christians should not be indiscriminate, gullible, or so open-minded as to be swayed by every spiritual system or claim that clamors for acceptance. On the contrary, a mystical Christianity rejects out of hand any faith system that is intellectually unsustainable or, for that matter, that is inhumane or physically or psychologically harmful in thought or practice, or that promotes itself via fear, guilt, or shame.

Article 9: Spiritual Stages and Dynamic Development

I believe in continuous personal growth, psychological development, intellectual edification, and spiritual transformation; and in the right to change my mind at any point along the way.

Excellent work has been done in the area of faith development over the past quarter century or so, thanks largely to James W. Fowler of Emory University. His highly regarded and widely used Faith Development Theory is based on the developmental psychology of Jean Piaget and Erik Erikson, but also draws heavily on the work of Harvard's Lawrence Kohlberg, whose model of moral development was the subject of an excellent paper presented at the Fall 2005 Westar meeting. It is impossible to do justice to Fowler's schema for faith development in an article like this, and a simple Google search of his name and the phrase "faith development" will provide many excellent summaries. For the present, let it suffice to say that I see myself as having come through messy fluidity of thought in early childhood (Stage 1), the tidy, literal certainty of late childhood (Stage 2), the conformist and largely unexamined peer-consensus faith of adolescence (Stage 3), the critical and often skeptical reflection and radical doubt of early-to-mid-adulthood (Stage 4), and having reached a fairly comfortable equilibrium in a deliberate re-embracing of items discarded in Stage 4, but now interpreted much more freely and in a larger context, which includes science and the world's other great religious traditions (Stage 5).

The final article of my credo, therefore, while not specifying Fowler's system, does affirm both that various types of faith are appropriate to particular levels of maturity and that faith is not a static constant in life, but a dynamic force impelling an exciting, ongoing, and ever-changing existential journey. As already indicated, the final affirmation of the durable right to change one's mind[2] is part and parcel of this dynamic view of the spiritual life, and is a hedge against becoming doctrinaire or absolutist about any particular religion or religious tenet.

Conclusion

Taken as a whole, the credo certainly looks rather formal and final; but the very last line indicates the contrary: every article in it is negotiable, open to tinkering or torpedoing. Nor is this credo an invitation to a new orthodoxy, for it does not pretend to present the definitive version of Christianity. Rather it offers a single very personal and plausible interpretation of that faith, suitable for modern or even post-modern times, especially for other Christians who may be inclined toward a mystical spirituality and a monistic-pantheistic *God*. But even such diverse folks as the traditionalist right and the humanist left of the faith spectrum might find value in this formulation to the extent that it helps them clarify, if only via contrast, their own understanding of the faith and the spirituality that it reflects or implies. That is my intention and modest hope.

Notes

1. A mystical Christianity is also compatible with the relatively new theology of panentheism, which posits two aspects for God, one transcendent and the other immanent, both adhering to the Divine Nature. My only real problem with this model is that however aesthetically pleasing it may be, it appears to be *purely* an intellectually-based construct (and indeed compromise) rather than an articulation of a specific spirituality or spiritual experience

2. I am echoing here a favorite saying of the co-founder (with his wife, Myrtle) of the Unity School of Christianity, Charles Fillmore: "I reserve the right to change my mind."

Works Consulted

de Mello, Anthony. *Awareness*. Ed. J. Francis Stroud. New York: Image Books (Doubleday), 1990.

Eckhart, Meister. *Selected Writings*. Trans. Oliver Davies. New York: Penguin Classics, 1995.

Emerson, Ralph Waldo. *Essays: 1st and 2nd Series, by Ralph Waldo Emerson*. E. P. Dutton & Company, 1909 [1st ed. 1906]. "The Over-Soul" is in the 1st Series.

Fowler, James W. *Stages of Faith: The Psychology of Human Development and the Quest for Meaning*. San Francisco: Harper & Row, 1981.

————. "Faith Development at 30: Naming the Challenges of Faith in a New Millennium," *Religious Education* 99.4 (2004) 405–421.

Hanh, Thich Nhat. *Interbeing: Fourteen Guidelines for Engaged Buddhism.* 3rd ed. Berkeley, CA: Parallax Press, 2005.

Keating, Thomas. *The Divine Indwelling: Centering Prayer and Its Development.* New York: Lantern Books, 2001.

Laughlin, Paul Alan. "A Mystical Christian Credo." *The Fourth R* 20.5 (2007) 3–9, 18. This is an earlier, longer version of the present article.

————. *Getting Oriented: What Every Christian Should Know about Eastern Religions, but Probably Doesn't.* Santa Rosa, CA: Polebridge Press, 2005.

————. "The Once and Future Christ of Faith: Beyond the History-Faith Dichotomy." *The Fourth R* 18.2 (2005) 2–7, 18.

———— with Glenna S. Jackson. *Remedial Christianity: What Every Believer Should Know about the Faith, but Probably Doesn't.* Santa Rosa, CA: Polebridge Press, 2000.

Merton, Thomas. *The Asian Journal of Thomas Merton.* New York: New Directions, 1975.

————. *Thomas Merton's Rewritings: The Five Versions of Seeds/New Seeds of Contemplation as a Key to the Development of His Thought.* Ed. Donald Grayston. Lewiston, NY: E. Mellen Press, 1989.

Teasdale, Wayne. *The Mystic Heart: Discovering a Universal Spirituality in the World's Religions.* Novato, CA: New World Library, 1999.

Teilhard de Chardin, Pierre. *The Divine Milieu.* New York: Harper Perennial, 2001.

————. *The Phenomenon of Man.* New York: Harper Perennial, 1976.

The Upanishads. Trans. with an introduction by Juan Mascaró. London: Penguin Classics: 1965.

What I Believe

Trust in God = Selflessness

James M. Robinson

This presentation is not intended to be a theological autobiography, much less my bibliography, both of which I have already published. As to my relevant biography, I grew up in a strict Calvinist home in faculty housing at a Presbyterian Seminary in Decatur, Georgia, I did my doctoral work under Karl Barth in Basel, Switzerland, and moved from there to study with Rudolf Bultmann at Marburg, Germany, where I became involved in the post-Bultmannian "new quest of the historical Jesus." Some years later I digressed into the real world to organize a team to break the European monopoly on the Nag Hammadi Codices. After the publication of the those codices, I returned to New Testament studies to organize a team to reconstruct the Sayings Gospel Q, and most recently summarized that effort for a popular audience in *The Gospel of Jesus*. What I present here is what has worked its way through these various avenues to emerge as my present religious position.

Rather than cherry-picking those elements I prefer, I could say I believe all the theology I was taught, and I could say I believe none of the theology I was taught. Both alternatives would be both true and false, which of course calls for some explaining. So let me work my way through these apparent contradictions to a somewhat clearer statement of what I believe. Simply stated, I equate trust in God with selflessness.

What I Do Not Believe: Antiquity's Belief-Structure

My problem with antiquity's belief-structure does not have to do with the individual items, but with the world of thought, the cultural language, and the concept of reality in which these beliefs were formulated. The three-story universe of the heavens above, the earth beneath, and the waters under the earth is not unbelievable considering each element in its own right (what is wrong with believing at least in "the earth beneath"?). The problem is the culture that presupposed in its thinking such a three-story universe.

That culture had astrology as its frame of reference; we, on the other hand, have astronomy. In the ancient view the planets move because they are alive; they are gods or angels or spirits that move among the

61

fixed stars ("planets" means moving stars). The heavenly animals have highlights, the stars of the zodiac. Astrology was something figured out by nomads sleeping out in the open all night, with nothing better to do than look at the heavens and figure out what was going on in the starry night sky. Such astrology is not something that I as a modern human being can believe.

Nor am I to believe that God slowed down the sunset long enough for the Israelites to continue slaughtering their opponents they had on the run (Josh 10:12–14), not because I do not believe God would do such a thing (or believe that God would because it is in the Bible), but because I do not live in a culture that thinks the sun revolves around the earth.

I do not believe that Yahweh rather than Baal is God, because on Mount Carmel Yahweh lit the fire on his altar and Baal did not light the fire on his altar (1 Kgs 18:20–40). My reason for not believing this narrative is not that I am an unbeliever, but rather that my culture does not explain lightning as fire hurled by God. My culture does not put me in a position either to believe or disbelieve that story. I would try to understand lightning by understanding climatology.

God ordered the chosen people to kill off the Canaanite tribes inhabiting the Promised Land so as to make room for the Israelites to whom Yahweh had given it (Deut 20:16–18). My reason for not believing this is not Jesus' injunction that we should love our enemies; rather I am confused by the very structure of the argument: Each tribe has its God, and each God fights for its tribe. Hence tribal warfare is theologically necessary. But I, thank goodness, do not live in a culture where that is the case. Our culture rejects genocide, however it is packaged.

Natural disasters used to be ascribed to God, and in archaic legal terminology are still classified as "acts of God." Yet today we have scientific meteorologists who explain what makes hurricanes happen in one season and region, but not in another. Even Evangelicals believe the meteorologists when they tell us that a hurricane is moving across the Gulf of Mexico and will reach land in a day or so, and they evacuate as fast as possible along with the rest of us. For we all live in the modern world and react accordingly, even those who should not want to because to do so is not consistent with the pre-modern worldview in which the Bible was written.

The culture of the ancient world in which the Bible was conceived has continued largely unbroken down to the present in places (such as in the Third World and among the functionally illiterate) where the Renaissance and the Enlightenment have not produced the new culture that conditions our thinking. Elements of this pre-modern culture still persist among Evangelicals to the extent that they do not know how to translate their beliefs from one culture into another, and hence cling to the thought patterns of the ancient world when their beliefs seem to demand it.

The ancient world was thought to be infested by demons, especially in the monotheistic culture of Judaism, where the existence of superhuman forces who were not Gods was still presupposed as an explanation for abnormal conduct such as epilepsy. An evil spirit or demon would take possession of a person so forcefully that the demon would think for the person, speak through his mouth, and torture his body by making him writhe in pain. Only a superhuman opposing force could fight such a superhuman demon, and Jesus, himself possessed since his baptism with the superhuman force of the Spirit, did just that, and won: the demon was cast out!

Much of the public ministry of Jesus seems to have been characterized by this cultural presupposition, though even in antiquity it was largely confined to the less-educated classes. It may be no coincidence that in the New Testament the casting out of demons is limited to the Synoptic Gospels, and does not occur in the Gospel of John or the Epistles of Paul or the rest of the New Testament. Yet the positive side is retained: the Paraclete in the Gospel of John and the gifts of the Spirit in Paul. Demons are not part of the thought world of the well-educated today, though it does continue in more traditional parts of society. Most of us know that the medical profession and therapists do a better job of handling what we prefer to call mental illnesses.

It is not a matter of believers versus unbelievers, but rather one of persons who have, for better or worse, been born and bred in the modern world and hence quite appropriately think that way, versus those who try to separate their modern worldview from such biblical "truths," and thus seek to have it both ways.

Jesus and his initial disciples came from small, largely illiterate, Aramaic-speaking villages in Galilee, where the higher education of their day was completely unknown. "How is it that this man knows his letters, when he has never studied?" (John 7:15). "I praise you, Father, Lord of heaven and earth, for you hid these things from sages and the learned, and disclosed them to children" (Q 10:21). "Peter and John . . . were uneducated, common men" (Acts 4:13). The Jesus people would no more have been able to wrap their minds around the dogmas of subsequent Christianity than, in retrospect, are we.

Yet from the second century on some Christians did have higher education, and felt obliged to make sense of Christianity as the ultimate truth in terms of what "truth" meant in that day. In Alexandria, Egypt, the leading cultural center back then, this "learning" tended to boil down to Middle Platonism, the intellectualism that spilled over into Judaism in the case of Philo, and then into emerging orthodox Christianity in the case of Clement and Origen.

But even before these proto-orthodox theologians came on the scene, precocious philosophical theologians of the early second century tried to figure things out, each in his own way. They took Plato's knowledge of ultimate reality, both the higher realms of pure ideas and the lower levels of material imitation, and plugged Jesus into the system as best they could. These first Christian intellectuals ("gnostics") came to be rejected by what emerged as main-line Christianity as much too speculative, and survived only in the snide quotations of heresy-hunting orthodox Christians such as Irenaeus and Epiphanius—that is, until the gnostic texts themselves were discovered in our own times and published as the Nag Hammadi Codices, plus the Gospels of Mary (Magdalene) and Judas (Iscariot).

But these earliest Christian "egg-heads" left their mark even on ortho-dox Christianity in that the orthodox felt obliged to produce as a foil their own intellectual constructs ("creeds," "dogmas") so as to be able both to retain the monotheism of their Jewish point of departure and to absorb the pluralism of Hellenistic religion: angels, saints, and, of course, the Trinity—according to which Jesus somehow has two "natures" in one (of the three) "person(s)." Jesus himself would not have been able to think his way through all of that any better than we can today.

Christians today should no more be expected to "believe" the creeds for-mulated in terms of the Neo-Platonic intellectual climate of Late Antiquity than they are expected to "believe" the rest of the culture of that day. But it is not simply a matter of "believing" or "not believing" those dogmas. It is a matter of not being able to penetrate into the cultural world of Late Antiquity and embrace it as our own. It is not that we do not "believe" the dogmas—rather, we do not think in the thought world that produced those dogmas. Considering them to be perhaps the best solution for their day and age (surely better than the gnostic "heresies"!) is about as near as we can come to "believing" them in our day and age.

We live in a different philosophical age, one created by Immanuel Kant, a leading figure in the Enlightenment, and updated by Ludwig Wittgenstein, a major twentieth-century philosopher. We can't do anything about that either. The door to the "beyond" has simply become closed to us, and so for all practical purposes, and perhaps even "metaphysically," the "beyond" is non-existent for us. In our thinking we are limited to time and space. Does this make of us "non-believers"? Philosophically, yes, but not necessarily "unbelievers" in the religious sense.

It is in this sense that I neither believe nor disbelieve the traditional doctrines of Christianity. I simply do not live in that world of thought, and should not be blamed for living in the modern world. I did not choose the age when I was born or the culture in which I live! No doubt if I had lived in an earlier century or been raised in a third world context today, I would more nearly "believe" those doctrines, since I would live more nearly in their thought world. Therefore it is not for me to stand in judgment on persons in that situation, and I would hope that they could reciprocate. My problem is not "disbelief," but simply living in a different culture. Just as missionaries had to translate the Bible and their evangelizing message into the language and thought patterns of those whom they were seeking to convert to Christianity, just so I have to translate the Bible and the Christian message into the cultural context in which I live, for only then do I have something that I can actually "believe."

The Positive Side of What I Do Not Believe

I have tried in the first section of this paper to make it clear that my problem is not really disbelief in those doctrines of yesteryear. Rather, mine is the problem of the culture, the world of thought, in which they were believed. If I were in that culture, I might well have believed them. Why not? (I might even have believed what the orthodox regarded as "heresy"!) But we will never know, since in fact I am not there, but here, and I have to make do with what I have.

In any case, I would like to begin my discussion of what I do believe by emphasizing the positive side of what I do not believe. Nearly 175 years ago David Friedrich Strauss refuted the rationalists of his day when he wrote the first (super-radical) Life of Christ. They explained away the miraculousness of Jesus' public career so as to rescue the historicity of his walking on water, feeding the five thousand, healing the sick, casting out demons, and the like. Strauss pointed out that far from *rescuing* the gospels as they claimed, these rationalists were *repudiating* them, since the miraculousness of such stories was precisely the point the evangelists were scoring by telling them. Thus Strauss came out on the side of the orthodox supernaturalists, for whom, as in traditional Christian belief, the miracle was precisely the point of the story. Of course as a modern person Strauss himself did not believe in miracles. Hence his own position was that the stories did not happen, but were created out of such currently available myths as the Elijah and Elisha stories in the Old Testament—for example 1 Kgs 17–19 and 2 Kgs 2–8.

Much the same position was renewed by Rudolf Bultmann in his famous/notorious proposal that we "demythologize" the Christian message, that is, state its point in existential language. Actually, he began the famous essay in which he made that proposal by scoring the same point as did Strauss: biblical criticism was throwing the baby out with the bath in simply eliminating the miraculous from the stories of Jesus, since that is precisely their point. Rather than "myth" having the negative overtone of falsehood, he pointed out that myth was the way ancient authors conveyed ultimate meaning. Thus the meaning of Christianity for the first Christians lurks hidden (for us) in the mythology of their stories. If we simply eliminate what we know did not happen, the meaning of Christianity itself is eliminated. Over against such "higher criticism" of Protestant Liberalism, Bultmann proposed that the task of New Testament scholarship is not to eliminate, but rather to interpret. What is the existential meaning of the mythological stories of the New Testament?

Bultmann's focus was on the biggest miracle of all, the resurrection of Christ. Being the good Lutheran he was, his focus was on Paul. Jesus was hopelessly apocalyptic (Albert Schweitzer), and his ethical teaching was on the wrong side of the "Law versus Grace" dichotomy (Karl Barth); in any case he is inaccessible to modern historical scholarship (Bultmann's own Form Criticism). Furthermore, according to Bultmann, the quest of the historical Jesus has misled us into thinking that focusing on the historical Jesus is focusing on the center of Christianity. Rather, the message of Christianity has its center in Christ crucified: he died for our sins on the cross, on the third day he rose from the dead, and he appeared to the apostles. Bultmann used for this message the Greek loan-word "Kerygma" (proclamation of the message), a synonym for the all-too-common and hence worn-out term "gospel." Bultmann's "kerygmatic theology" was then what had to be "demythologized," so as to get to the central message of Christianity that one should believe today—that is, if one would maintain a continuity with the early Christian tradition.

This new focus revived the old-fashioned discipline of hermeneutics, which is the art of interpretation. Bultmann and his followers updated "hermeneutics" to mean the art of translating the message from the thought patterns and language of one culture into those of another. His own effort in this direction made use of the language of Existentialism. The "New Hermeneutic" of Bultmann's followers preferred the concept of the "Word Event" as the saving event (Gerhard Ebeling). In America, the concept of "performative language" was used, where attention was not focused on the kerygma, but rather on Jesus' parables (Robert W. Funk). Of course parables by definition do not "mean what they say"; but this is true not only in the sense that a metaphor says one thing in the language of another thing, but, in the case of Jesus, in the sense that the parables were not primarily teaching that "one thing," but were themselves the upsetting of the apple cart; they were "God happening," and not just the coded teaching of some higher truth.

Jesus' Trust in God

It is in this "Post-Bultmannian" direction that my own theological development has moved. But I had to digress from theology for a number of years, to break the monopoly on the Nag Hammadi Codices by assembling the fragments and reconstructing the ancient books in the Coptic Museum in

Cairo and eventually publishing *The Facsimile Edition of the Nag Hammadi Codices.* This led me to focus on the Nag Hammadi text most important for the study of Jesus, the Gospel of Thomas, where it was Jesus' sayings that were the whole point. This experience suggested to me that as I returned to New Testament scholarship, I might try to reassemble the fragments of the Sayings Gospel Q imbedded in Matthew and Luke and lurking just below the evangelists' "improvements."

Q, like the Gospel of Thomas, is a collection of Jesus' sayings rather than a narrative gospel like those in the New Testament. Q does not even go to the trouble of identifying any disciple as hearing them or repeating them or handing them on. No disciple is named or even referred to, for the sayings have their own say. This speaking in the present stands over against the canonical gospels with their nostalgic reminiscence of the past, stories about Jesus' wonderful public career that unfortunately is ended—in other words, looking back is the stance and scope of the canonical narrative gospels.

Once the crucifixion put an end to it all, the only sensible thing for the disciples to do (and which they therefore promptly did) was to run for their lives, return to fishing for fish in Galilee (Matthew and Mark, versus Luke and John), and remember sadly those wonderful things that Jesus had said, but which they had to admit had not come true. But in Q it is as if Jesus himself has resumed saying his sayings in their ears, and soon on their lips, as if (incredible as it must have seemed, given the crucifixion) it was all somehow still true, as if Jesus somehow were still speaking. This experiencing of Jesus' voice is probably the earliest form of "Easter faith" that one can postulate. (Bultmann said that Jesus rose into the Kerygma, but it is more accurate to say he rose into the re-proclaiming of his own Word.) The Sayings Gospel Q does not tell the Easter story (no empty tomb, no appearances), but is, so to speak, its own kind of "Easter story." Jesus is still speaking, only now through disciples' lips.

Jesus was not a trained theologian. He seems to have launched only one theological concept, which hardly existed before or after his use of it. We know it as "the kingdom of God," but that is a mistranslation, not only because it suggests real estate, but because that mistranslation has been used to justify the territorial expansion of "Christian" nations. But Jesus was talking about the reign of God, about God reigning in the human realm where we find ourselves. One is to pray to God to provide a day's ration of food, and, like the ravens and lilies, trust him to do just that. One is to heed his call for us to share what we have with others, to turn the other cheek, to give the shirt off our back, to go the extra mile, to give, expecting nothing in return, to love even our enemies.

What help others get from us is not due to our being so virtuous, but rather to what God does through us when we listen to him. In fact, God's action cuts both ways: God does for us through others, and for others through us. The most "authentic" sayings of Jesus about the kingdom of God make this clear: "If I by the finger of God cast out demons, then God's reign has come upon you" (Q 11:20). When you are admitted to the house of the "son of peace" for bed and breakfast and there you heal the sick, tell them that "God's reign has reached unto you" (Q 10:9). God acts both through the "son of peace" providing you with lodging and food, and through your providing for them the healing of the sick. The emphasis that this is God's action denies the idea of the action being our own. (Even Jesus does not point to himself as the one doing what he says God is doing—and this in spite of the Gospel of John often putting that on his lips.)

Such conduct is "selfless," for it bypasses "self-interest." We are not to help the other so that the other will help us (the patron-client relationship of *do ut des*; I give [to you] so that you give [to me]). We help someone, and that person helps some other person (as the "Parable of the Unforgiving Servant," Matt 18:23–35, exemplifies). If everyone thought this way, the chain reaction would move through society and replace self-interest—the driving power ruining society—with selflessness as God's action in building society.

Thus the naming of this action as "God's" stands over against naming it as my own. We are familiar with the idea that Jesus' constant talk about "the kingdom of God" had a political overtone that the Romans could not fail to detect. Indeed, it was apparently abrasive enough to produce the sign on the cross to the effect that this imposter claimed to be "the king of the Jews" (Mark 15:26; John 19:19). But naming this saving action "God's" also has a clear implication at the individual level: it stands over against designating the good deed my own (or the Church's), even though it is through me that God acts for others and through others that God acts for me. The world is not to be saved by Manna falling from heaven. Thus "God's" means not only "not Rome's," but also "not mine." My not looking out for number one, in other words my selflessness, is not my own virtuous achievement far surpassing the less-worthy conduct of those around me and therefore something to be proud of. No, one is to be selfless even about one's selflessness!

The theological name for this selflessness is trust in God. The Greek word for "belief" can also be translated "faith" or "trust." And that very ambivalence is in large part to blame for the plight in which we find ourselves as a church that does not practice what it preaches. You may have to pause when you read in the Bible stories of miracles that according to the modern mind-set did not happen, or swallow hard when you recite in the creed things that cannot possibly have happened. But for most Christians it is much easier to accept as factual these intellectual bitter pills than it is to trust God for your daily bread! This attitude is one major reason that Paul had more success with the Gentile mission than Peter did with the Jewish mission.

Thus the point of departure, "What I Believe" becomes, when better understood, "Do I Trust God to Care for Me?" or, in a more secular idiom: can I risk giving up looking out for number one and replace it with selflessness as my life-style? We are always haunted by the rich young man who was simply too well off to give all he had to feed the poor and follow Jesus in a mendicant itinerancy (Mark 10:17–22). Francis of Assisi was also well off, but he did give away all he had, and many followed him on his path. On his death he was "domesticated" by being made a Saint, and his followers were domesticated by being made into a religious Order with the marching orders to get rid of the "spiritualists" among them, those who were the most committed to what Francis (and Jesus) had practiced and preached.

Thus "what I believe" boils down to "trust in God," which in turn boils down to selflessness. Jesus did not intend to found a movement with an improved *belief*, but rather to show the way with improved conduct. He launched a movement based on *trust*ing God with a lifestyle of selflessness. When we thus translate from belief into trust, into selflessness, and thus into practice, none of us is a true believer. We talk about "walking in his footsteps," but walking in his footsteps means far more than "talking the talk."

Trust in God = What I Do = Selflessness

Let me conclude by summarizing what I have tried to say thus far. Being a Christian today should not mean *believing* what Christians have traditionally believed. It should mean *trusting* God as Jesus did, and in this way being his disciple to whatever extent we can figure that out in terms of our situation today.

Jesus himself was not a Christian, but a Jew. His trust in God was not Christian "belief." So "following in his footsteps" cannot mean "believing" Christian doctrine. It can only mean committing oneself to the same trust in God that he exemplified and advocated, and that means not looking out for number one! I can only trust that God is looking out for me! This trust means selflessness toward those one encounters in everyday living. This openness to hearing God when he sends one to help the neighbor (or enemy!) in need—and conversely, this humility to receive what one needs from others as a gift from God—is the kind of trust Jesus exemplified.

This "doing" is harder than "believing." I do not mean to suggest that I myself have replaced traditional "believing" with an unselfishness that is at once "trusting" and selfless "doing." The hardest saying of Jesus is: "Why do you call me: Master, Master, but do not do what I say?" (Q 6:46). For me, the bottom line on "what I believe" can be no better than "I believe, help my unbelief!" (Mark 9:24)—or, better, "I trust, help my selfishness!"

Works Consulted

Asgeirsson, Jon Ma., Kristin de Troyer, and Marvin W. Meyer, eds. *From Quest to Q: Festschrift James M. Robinson*. Bibliotheca ephemeridum theologicarum lovaniensium 146. Leuven: University Press and Uitgeverij Peeters, 2000. The Bibliography of James M. Robinson is found on pages xxv-xliv.

Bultmann, Rudolf. *Jesus Christ and Mythology*. London: SCM Press, 1958.

———. "New Testament and Mythology: The Problem of Demythologizing and New Testament Proclamation." Pp. 1–43 in *New Testament and Mythology and Other Basic Writings*. Ed. and trans. Schubert M. Ogdon. Philadelphia: Fortress Press, 1984.

Funk, Robert W. *Language, Hermeneutic and Word of God. The Problem of Language in the New Testament and Contemporary Theology*. New York: Harper & Row Publishers, 1966.

Robinson, James M. *A New Quest of the Historical Jesus*. Studies in Biblical Theology 25. London: SCM and Naperville, IL: Alec R. Allenson, 1959. Many other reprints.

———. *Das Problem des Heiligen Geistes bei Wilhelm Herrmann*. Marburg: Karl Gleiser, 1952.

———. General Editor, *The Nag Hammadi Library in English*. Leiden: E. J. Brill and San Francisco: HarperSanFrancisco, 1977. Several revisions and reprints.

———. "Introduction." Pp. xi-xxxiii in Albert Schweitzer, *The Quest of the Historical Jesus*. Trans. W. Montgomery. New York: Macmillan Publishing Company, 1968.

———. "Jesus' Parables as God Happening." Pp. 45–52 in *A Meeting of Poets and Theologians to Discuss Parable, Myth, and Language*. Ed. Tony Stoneburner. Cambridge, MA: Church Society for College Work, 1968.

———. *Language, Hermeneutic, and History: Theology after Barth and Bultmann* Eugene, Oregon: Cascade Books, 2007. "The German Discussion of the Later Heidegger," 1–68; "Hermeneutic since Barth," 69–146, "Revelation as Word and as History," 147–240.

———. Permanent Secretary of the International Committee for the Nag Hammadi Codices. *The Facsimile Edition of the Nag Hammadi Codices*. 12 vols. Leiden: E. J. Brill, 1972–84.

———. *The Gospel of Jesus: In Search of the Original Good News*. San Francisco: HarperSanFrancisco, 2005. Paperback edition 2006.

———. "Theological Autobiography." Pp. 203–34 in *Jesus According to the Earliest Witness*. Minneapolis: Fortress Press, 2007.

———. "Theological Autobiography." Pp. 3–34 in *The Sayings Gospel Q: Collected Essays*. Eds. Christoph Heil and Joseph Verheyden. Bibliotheca ephemeridum theologicarum lovaniensium 189. Leuven: University Press and Uitgeverij Peeters, 2005.

Robinson, James M., and John B. Cobb, Jr. *The New Hermeneutic*. New Frontiers in Theology: Discussions among Continental and American Theologians, 2. New York: Harper and Row, 1964.

Robinson, James M., Paul Hoffmann, and John S. Kloppenborg, eds. *The Critical Edition of Q: Synopsis Including the Gospels of Matthew and Luke, Mark and Thomas with English, German and French Translations of Q and Thomas*. Leuven: Peeters and Minneapolis: Fortress, 2000.

Strauss, David Friedrich. *The Life of Jesus Critically Examined*. Ed. Peter C. Hodgson. Trans. George Eliot. Philadelphia: Fortress, 1972.

Ears to Hear
Learning to Listen to Jesus

Mahlon H. Smith

Like other voices in this volume, I am a creature of the twentieth century, who has had the good fortune of surviving, with most of my marbles, into the next millennium. Who I am and what I think have been shaped by the myriads of persons and events I happened to encounter during the more than 25,000 days of my existence to date. Yet not all have had an equal influence. Some—family, friends, teachers, great books, and current crises—have made a greater impact on my mind and life than others in forming and transforming how I view the world and existence in general. In retrospect, however, I would have to say that none has played a more persistent role in the evolution of my life than a person from a culture and era far from my own: a first-century Galilean Jew, known to his contemporaries as Yeshu bar Yosef of Nazareth (John 1:45) but more commonly referred to in my culture simply as Jesus.

The Presence of Jesus

I have no memory of my first encounter with this Jesus. As the son of a Methodist preacher, I heard this name and was encouraged to probe the implications for my life of his purported words, deeds, and fate as far back as I can recall. My father had a gift for making biblical stories relevant to contemporary life—not just for me, but for thousands whose lives he touched in a ministry that spanned forty some years. Thus, I could never identify with reported experiences of Christians who claimed to have "found Jesus" or to have been "born again," for Jesus has always been a persistent presence in my world—at least the world as I came to imagine and experience it.

Presence, as I understand it, is not necessarily visible. Even though the operations of my brain and my other internal organs are not visible to me as I write this, I am confident that they are present and functioning in the world as I now experience it. Although I cannot see with a naked eye the molecules and atoms that constitute me and the world around me, I am sure that they are actually present. Without their presence I would not exist.

Likewise, other persons can be present to me even when they are not immediately perceptible to my physical senses—present insofar as they still impact my memory and current patterns of thinking and acting. As a child, I was never bothered by the fact that the presence of the person named Jesus was not immediately perceptible. For although during much of my early life my own father was physically absent while serving as a naval chaplain during World War II, I was confident that he was alive and really *with* me—in spirit, at least, if not in the flesh. His pictures on our mantle and end tables kept his face fresh in the minds of our family; and his periodic letters kept us in touch with what he was currently—or at least recently—thinking and doing. By analogy, Jesus was and *is* present to me insofar as his words and graphic stories about him continue to shape my fundamental values and how I relate to the world. In this sense, persons cease to be present to us only when they cease to influence our daily lives *or* when we discover that the images and echoes in our minds do not accurately represent them.

My concern for an accurate image of Jesus and clear understanding of his words and deeds antedates by more than a decade my formal introduction half a century ago to the modern scholarly "quest of the historical Jesus." I trace this concern to the weekly Sunday dinner table debates over the morning sermon between my father, a socially liberal preacher, and his own more conservative, pietistic sire. The fact that these intense father-son debates involved rigorous questioning of the sources and logic assumed by each party taught me that *any* person's claims or statements concerning factual matters need to be subjected to close critical cross-examination before they are accepted as true. The added fact that my father and grandfather conducted their ongoing debates with due respect and clear affection for each other also taught me to show proper regard to those whose views are at odds with mine and to avoid *ad hominem* attacks in a mutual quest for truth.

Such experiences as these have helped me see the pragmatic sense in Jesus' paradoxical teaching to love one's opponents (Matt 5:43//Luke 6:27, 35). Without an opponent's challenge I probably would not bother to examine my current opinions and beliefs or bring them into closer conformity with the actual evidence. It is in this sense of a dialectical opponent—a dialogue partner, that is, who persistently provokes me to reexamine my facile presuppositions—that Jesus has been a presence throughout my life.

The Bible

My lifelong training in dialectics—the art and science of interaction between those with conflicting perceptions and convictions—has convinced me that absolute truth cannot be the property of *any* statement, argument, or text composed by a human mind. While any formulation using a human language may *seem* true to the person who composed it and those who accept it at face value, every such statement is in fact the product of a particular mind or group of minds and, therefore, inevitably only an expression of one person or group's view of reality at a particular point in time. Moreover, since the experience of all humans is limited by the conditions of their historical existence, any assertion of truth by any human can never be anything more than a declaration of what that particular person *believes* to be true at that particular moment. The adequacy of such affirmations of faith is always open to question by any whose outlook and experience differ, or whenever new discoveries challenge the adequacy of the evidence presupposed by those formulations.

For me, these insights not only confirm the wisdom of the American forefathers' principle of religious tolerance, they also underlie my lifelong support for ecumenical and interfaith dialogue. For one can recognize the limitations of one's own current view of reality only when one takes seriously the views of those whose experience makes them think otherwise.

As far back as I can remember, therefore, I never considered the Bible to be literally, simply "*the* Word of God." Insofar as the biblical books were demonstrably written long ago in archaic human languages, by *various* authors who did *not* claim to be divine, and for audiences that lived in historical circumstances quite different from my own, I could never pretend that the text of the Bible was the "Word of God" addressed personally to me. From my point of view, anyone who makes such a claim is bound to confuse the different voices and mindsets that actually formed the biblical texts and therefore to mistake what each passage in scripture was originally formulated to say.

Whenever anyone not of the original intended audience reads a particular scriptural text, he or she is, as it were, reading someone else's mail. Failure to take this into account has led to countless distortions and conflicts, holy wars and holocausts, pogroms and crusades throughout Jewish and Christian history, since those who view the Bible as the Word of God are prone to mistake their own very human and selective reading of the text for absolute truth.

But if recognized for what it really is—a collection of faith declarations by humans who, like the contributors to this volume, do *not* share a single belief system—and is read with historical perspective, the Bible can be a salutary means of promoting mutual understanding and common cause between persons with quite diverse backgrounds and individual agendas. Over the years I have found that scholars who have been trained to study the Bible as an historical artifact show an even greater openness to honest dialogue and exchange of insights across religious divides than exists among confessional peers who take it upon themselves to defend what they—individually or collectively—hold to be the truth of "holy" scripture.

That said, I do believe that passages from the text of any scripture, canonical or otherwise, can have a formative or transformative influence on the lives of persons who lived long after those who formulated those words were dead and gone. Witness for example Augustine, Francis of Assisi, Martin Luther, John Wesley, and others whose lives were changed by reading passages from the Bible. Whenever and wherever recorded human speech has a seminal influence in shaping or altering any human life, then I am prepared to grant that it has *become* the living "word of god" (metaphorically speaking) for that particular person. It is only in this sense that I would acknowledge words credited to Jesus (and taken as a foundational formula or pivotal principle in a particular person's life) to have the power to *become* a creative "word of god." Whether that "god"—that is, the driving force in such pivotal experiences—is, in fact, the same that inspired the author of the influential words depends entirely on whether the consequences of those words in the life of the reader remain consistent with the logic of their author.

Whether in the Christian church's collection of canonical texts or in any scripture or great book held sacred by any human anywhere, whether identified as "Christian" or not, any passage can become a source of God's revelation. I come to this conclusion not from agnostic or secular presuppositions, but from a close reading of the canonical biblical texts themselves. For the "God" depicted in both Old and New Testaments is not limited to revelation through a particular book or set of books canonized by any earthly authority.

On the contrary, the Bible itself begins by portraying *ha Adam*—"the earthling": that is, the human species *per se*, female as well as male—as *in essence* a reflection of the primal Force that generated the stars and the rest of the universe (Gen 1:27). The Hebrew prophets Isaiah, Jeremiah, Ezekiel, and Malachi assumed that this creative Power addressed its revelation to all nations; and even that first-century Christianized Pharisee who identified himself simply as Paul protested that the "power and nature" of this "God" was available for *all* humans to find—and *not* through studying sacred scripture, but through exploring the fabric of the cosmos itself (Rom 1:19–20).

Thus, from the perspective presupposed by the scriptural canon itself, any alleged conflict between faith and reason, revelation and science, reflects a false dichotomy. Instead, biblical texts regularly present rational arguments to counter false beliefs (for example, Job 34:16–20, Hos 8:5–6, Jonah 4:9–11, Mark 3:22–27, Acts 17:22–29) and encourage clear-eyed study of the real world (for example, Prov 6:6, Matt 6:26–30) in order to challenge superstitious traditions and hypocritical piety. Therefore, I never thought that to take something "in faith" meant to swallow it without question. Rather, my Wesleyan heritage prepared me to view the story of Jacob's wrestling match (Gen 32:22–32) as paradigmatic of the human condition. One often has to grapple with the presence of the Unknown to come to a clearer view of whom or what one encounters on life's journey. When such experiences involve ultimate questions of existence, one's prior convictions are not likely to emerge unscathed. Rather, like Jacob, one may gain a more realistic image of oneself and the forces one faces only by risking permanent dislocation of one's prior self-understanding.

Wrestling with the
Images of God

To borrow a metaphor from the mystics, my own night-long wrestling match with God—more precisely, with the images of God in biblical texts—began with passages presenting Jesus material. The New Testament's emphasis on Jesus' crucifixion and death convinced me that whatever else he may have been, he was fundamentally a mortal human like me. I neither doubted my own inevitable mortality nor naïvely thought of death as divine punishment for sin, since observation of the real world told me that all species of living creatures were also mortal. For me, the eventual death of any organism, myself or Jesus included, is nothing more than evidence that *no* single creature or species can rival or avoid the ultimate undying Power that generated and remains operative within this ever-changing universe. If Jesus was really born and really died, then he was a mortal human like you and me, plain and simple.

The authors of Jewish scripture were unanimous on one point: the Creator tolerates no rivals. There is no place for a plurality of persons in Israel's view of the Godhead. Hebrew prophets, who presumed to speak for this God, both predicted and celebrated the demise of all earthly entities that dared to claim or tried to exercise totalitarian power—a fate that offered dramatic evidence that their God was in fact active and supreme. Therefore, *if* Jesus and his first followers were in fact Jews, as New Testament authors assert, neither he nor they would have claimed that he was God. For had they done so, their Jewish contemporaries would rightly have regarded them as blasphemous pagans and their movement would have effectively ended with Jesus' death. Since Jesus was *not* stoned—the scripturally mandated penalty for blasphemy—and the movement around him not only survived but spread, I long ago concluded that much in the development of gentile Christian images of Jesus as a divine being has been misguided. Not only could the historical Jesus *not* have uttered many of the claims ascribed to him in the gospel of John (such as John 10:30, and most of the "I am" sayings), it is highly unlikely that *he* would have approved of the general tendency of Christians to elevate him to the status of sole mediator of divine authority.

But my personal struggle with the images of God I inherited from orthodox Christian tradition was far more existential than the intellectual challenge of trying to reconcile the logical paradoxes of post-biblical Trinitarian creeds with the claims of scripture. My faith was tested and shaken to the core precisely *because* I firmly believed the biblical claims that the Force ultimately directing human history supports social justice rather than ritual worship.

Justice and the Problem
of Human Suffering

Accounts that I have heard since childhood depicting Jesus' crucifixion at the hands of other humans have shaped my understanding of the fate of any martyr for a just cause, such as the assassination of Abraham Lincoln or Martin Luther King. For study of history has assured me that injustices *can* have the paradoxical effect of galvanizing other advocates of the martyr's cause and attracting enough support to alter the eventual course of history. I remain confident that even the horrific brutalities of Hitler's Holocaust *can* have humane consequences, providing their recollection leads enough people of all religious persuasions to dedicate themselves to opposing any policy of genocide or ethnic cleansing. But the paradigmatic power of such senseless events depends entirely upon whether those who recall them will eliminate ethnic prejudice from their own worldview.

While I have had little trouble reconciling the fact of human injustice towards fellow humans with an understanding of a just God, my worldview was severely challenged by events in my young adult years that occurred closer to home. Since like my Pilgrim ancestors I truly believed in a divine Providence that tends to support social underdogs and topple tyrants, I was ill-prepared to come to terms with my own mother's twenty-two year painful deterioration into complete paralysis and eventual death due to Parkinson's disease. Here was a brilliant, articulate woman who had devoted her whole life to helping others, but who through no fault of her own was slowly being reduced to total silent impotence. I was troubled not so much by contemplating the inevitable death of a parent as by the helplessness I felt in having to watch her prolonged suffering without being able to do anything to relieve it. While my mother bore her deteriorating condition with grace and even self-effacing humor, her family was crushed. Despite our deep-seated faith in a just and loving God, there was no miraculous healing. Gospel stories of Jesus' cures became for me mocking myths. For in this case, at least, the lack of positive results could not be blamed on either the perversity of the patient or the weakness of her family's faith in Jesus' vision of God.

The concrete facts of this inescapable situation made post-modern analyses of the absurdity of the human condition seem to me more realistic than any optimistic scriptural promise of eternal life. For a time, the only biblical texts that made any sense were the poetic core of Job and Ecclesiastes. But neither gave much spiritual solace. Since no one in our family could rightly be charged with hubris, we did not need such a prolonged encounter with the existentially devastating effects of the cosmic storm to teach us that the ways of the Almighty are inscrutable. While I could heartily second Qoheleth's conclusion that the unpredictable vicissitudes of life revealed human existence to be a mere vapor in the cosmic Void, the realities of my mother's condition precluded me from heeding his advice to content myself with my work (Eccl 2:24).

The only immediate benefit I found in such a situation was that it motivated me to devour the works of a wider range of philosophers and theologians than I might otherwise have done. It was only after my mother died and almost a thousand people attended the service of thanksgiving that she had requested instead of a funeral, that I began to put this experience into a more positive perspective. For most—including many who had known my mother only as an invalid—made a point of telling us that the way in which she faced her condition had helped them deal with troubles of their own.

While benign consequences of human suffering and tragedy are never assured, I have come to think that Paul's eudemonistic pronouncement that "*all* things work together for good" (Rom 8:28) is not so much of an exaggeration after all. So long as one sees that forces inherent in the on-going evolution of this ever-changing cosmos really tend to generate and support the development and triumph of life—if not the life of any individual creature, at least the lives of others—then no situation or experience can ultimately destroy faith or hope. As an intellectual historian who has spent almost half a century tracking trajectories in the development of Christian theology, I have found that the most persistent pious distortion of biblical texts can be traced to a widespread "gnostic" mindset that views "the world and the flesh" *per se* as the handiwork of "the devil" instead of the field for the cultivation of a triumphant faith. I myself could easily have succumbed to some such view that *this* world is inherently evil—or at least absurd—if historical circumstances had not kept me grappling with the logic inherent in the words of Jesus.

Distinguishing Jesus from
the Tradition

Close reading can convince any unbiased reader that sayings ascribed to Jesus in the gospels cannot be taken as *verbatim* utterances of this Galilean. The wide range of divergent wordings of the same saying in different gospels makes it clear that at best these are translated paraphrases of something that the author heard that Jesus allegedly said. The historical question of whether such recollection was accurate cannot be satisfactorily answered by either a leap of faith in the basic honesty and reliability of the gospel writers or a blanket skepticism that *a priori* takes all elements of their narrative portraits to be figments of their vivid individual or collective imaginations. While either thesis remains theoretically possible in the abstract, the credibility of such conclusions depends entirely on whether they are supported by the details of the texts themselves.

New creations are extremely rare—rarer, in fact, than any creationist would care to admit. Since most things in this cosmos are the product of the impact of one thing upon another, the probable source of anything can be accurately identified only by careful analysis of trace elements in its composition. Thus, it is important to sift and compare the actual data in the gospels, before accepting *or* rejecting the accuracy of anyone's ascription of the logic of any statement to Jesus.

The gospels themselves authorize and encourage the task of distinguishing the voice and worldview of Jesus from those of others. While the story of Jesus' transfiguration (Mark 9:2–8//Matt 17:1–8//Luke 9:28–36) may owe more to the mythic imagination of some early Christian than to recollection of any particular historical event, it clearly illustrates the tendency of Jesus' would-be disciples to confuse his voice with those of others whom they regarded as agents and revealers of God. Though the synoptic portrayal of Jesus' disciples as persistently misunderstanding his message may be an exaggerated caricature, almost forty years of teaching have convinced me that *most* students are more apt to misinterpret their teachers than not. Selective hearing and misinterpretation are the rule rather than the exception, particularly in oral communication. We all tend to hear what we are prepared to hear; and when we listen to someone else we are naturally prone to be more concerned with reconciling what we thought we heard with our own *a priori* worldview than with trying to understand the presuppositions of the speaker. Thus, the voice near the end of the transfiguration account (Mark 9:7//Matt 17:5//Luke 9:35) that urges disciples and readers alike to listen to the voice of Jesus *on his own*—without confusing him with other revered figures—justifies an historical hermeneutic distinguishing the logic of Jesus from that of other voices in either the Jewish or Christian traditions.

Despite recent scholarly studies trying to discredit the attempt to isolate the real Jesus by focusing on distinctive elements in his words and behavior, differentiating the characteristics of one phenomenon from those of another remains *the* fundamental human tool for developing an accurate understanding of anything in this universe. It is *only* by focusing on the differences in the characteristics of elements, persons, or things that we can tell one from another. Concentrating on such distinguishing characteristics is a necessary prerequisite to "separating the wheat from the chaff" or "finding a needle in a haystack." Thus, *if* one is concerned to develop an accurate description and understanding of Jesus as an historical individual, one *must* concentrate on elements in the gospel record whose inherent logic is distinct from and in tension with that of other voices in the biblical tradition.

My Essential Jesus

There is neither time nor space here for me to lay out a complete inventory of items in the gospel accounts that I think, after critical examination, can be reasonably accepted as accurate representations of Jesus' thinking. Nor is this the proper occasion to attempt a detailed portrait of Jesus himself by drawing lines between these dots. These are tasks that all who have any honest interest in understanding Jesus will have to wrestle with for themselves. Any description that I develop of Jesus would at best offer an impression of how I as an individual see him at this particular moment in time.

By way of summary, however, let me list several of the traits I find in Jesus' sayings that have left a lasting impression on my understanding of my own existence.

First and most important, Jesus illustrated the realm and activity of God by focusing his hearers' attention on the observable behavior of phenomena in the physical world around them rather than by reporting his own personal mystical visions of an other-worldly paradise. Moreover, in comparing God's rule to the natural behavior of leaven or mustard seed, for example, Jesus called his hearers' attention to phenomena they might otherwise overlook or disparage as unworthy of theological reflection. By so doing, he pointed them to an organic, evolving understanding of divine activity within the universe. These observations convince me that, were he a child of our current era, Jesus would side with experimental scientists rather than biblical literalists or apocalypticists.

Second, Jesus' parables and aphorisms challenged conventional family, social, and economic values. And since this practice of his is not something that makes me comfortable, I can hardly be accused of reinventing Jesus in my own image. As an obedient son who feels fortunate in having been blessed with understanding and supportive parents, I am constitutionally inclined to empathize more with the dutiful older son in the parable (Luke 15:11–32) than with the spendthrift who wasted his inheritance in excess and debauchery. As a father who feels proud of his children, I find Jesus' sayings involving parent-child relations deeply disturbing (for example, Matt 8:21–22//Luke 9:59–60, Matt 10:34–36//Luke 12:51–53, Luke 14:26). And as a child of the Great Depression whose family often had to struggle to survive from one day to the next, I never saw any sense in "selling all" and depending on God to provide me with my daily bread (Matt 6:10//Luke 11:3). While I have long viewed such sayings as rhetorical exaggerations, I have never been able to dismiss them as fictions invented by either Jesus' Jewish followers or gentile evangelists. To me they remain dramatic warnings against confusing Jesus' perspective with the agendas of nominally Christian champions of the so-called moral majority or traditional family values.

Finally, genuine Jesus tradition proves that he did not think of himself as better than other people. On the contrary, he identified himself with those of least influence and power. He fraternized with and defended those whom law-abiding religious contemporaries criticized and avoided. Instead of posing as sole "son of God," he encouraged others to see *themselves* as offspring of the Creator and Sustainer of the universe and therefore worthy to appeal to their cosmic parent directly rather than through him or any other religious mediator. And he warned them not to imitate those who flaunted their righteousness or authority (Mark 12:38–40//Luke 20:46–47).

Such observations make much in the Christian religious tradition problematic for me. If Jesus were a child of our own era, I am sure that he would be a secular social gadfly rather than the founder of any religion. While I firmly believe that on balance the historical triumph of Christianity over its ancient alternatives has been for the good, in the process Christian triumphalism has too often left self-proclaimed Christians deaf to the voice of Jesus himself.

Conclusion

Given the evidence, Jesus will always be a disturbing presence in history. All must decide for themselves whether to listen closely to the logic inherent in the most likely authentic of his sayings or to give priority to the promptings of other voices in shaping their personal values and views of the real world. While others are free to come to other conclusions, I for one have found that Jesus' view of God as the often paradoxical Parent of all humans who provides the basic necessities of life—food, sun, and rain—for all without regard for their moral merit (Matt 5:45) to be a far more realistic understanding of the transcendent Force that actually propels this universe than the image of God as an other-worldly Judge who rewards the righteous and punishes the wicked. And I am attracted by Jesus' view of the ironic nature of this God who sometimes motivates even those like the despised Samaritan in the parable (Luke 10:30–37) to do good while those who are concerned for religious purity pass by on the other side. This is, in my eyes, a far more accurate paradigm for human history than that of preachers who promise paradise for the faithful and consign all others to hell. Learning to distinguish the logic of Jesus from that of other biblical authors has finally helped me believe in God.

Works Consulted

Buber, Martin. *I and Thou*. Trans. Walter Kaufmann. New York: Charles Scribner's Sons, 1971.

Crossan, John Dominic. *The Historical Jesus: The Life of a Mediterranean Jewish Peasant*. San Francisco: HarperSanFrancisco, 1991.

———. *In Fragments: The Aphorisms of Jesus*. San Francisco: Harper and Row, 1983.

Davis, Stephen T., ed. *Encountering Jesus: A Debate on Christology*. Atlanta: John Knox Press, 1988.

Dawes, Gregory W., ed. *The Historical Jesus Quest: Landmarks in the Search for the Jesus of History*. Louisville, KY: Westminster John Knox Press, 2000.

Funk, Robert W. *Honest to Jesus: Jesus for a New Millennium*. San Francisco: HarperSanFrancisco, 1996.

———. *Language, Hermeneutic, and Word of God*. New York: Harper and Row Publishers, 1966.

———. *Parables and Presence: Forms of the New Testament Tradition*. Philadelphia: Fortress Press, 1982.

Funk, Robert W., Roy W. Hoover, and The Jesus Seminar. *The Five Gospels: The Search for the Authentic Words of Jesus*. New York: Macmillan Publishing Company, 1993.

Hedrick, Charles W. *When History and Faith Collide: Studying Jesus*. Peabody, MA: Hendrickson Publishers, 1999.

Michalson, Carl. *Worldly Theology: The Hermeneutical Focus of an Historical Faith*. New York: Charles Scribner's Sons, 1967.

Patterson, Stephen J. *The God of Jesus: the Historical Jesus and the Search for Meaning*. Harrisburg, PA: Trinity Press International, 1998.

Tatum, W. Barnes. *In Quest of Jesus*. Revised and Enlarged edition. Nashville: Abingdon Press, 1999.

Teilhard de Chardin, Pierre. *The Phenomenon of Man*. Trans. Bernard Wall. New York: Harper and Row Publishers, 1959.

Theissen, Gerd, and Annette Merz. *The Historical Jesus: A Comprehensive Study Guide*. Minneapolis: Fortress Press, 1998.

Theissen, Gerd, and Dagmar Winter. *The Quest for the Plausible Jesus: The Question of Criteria*. Louisville, KY: Westminster John Knox Press, 2002.

A Faith Odyssey
The Journey of My Mind and My Soul

Theodore J. Weeden, Sr.

Professional Background

I am an ordained minister of the United Methodist Church. I received
a B.A. in 1953 from Emory University, a B.D. in 1956 from Emory
University's Candler School of Theology, and in 1964, a Ph.D. in New
Testament from the Claremont Graduate University. I sought the Ph.D.
to be a more effective pastor, and have served churches in Georgia,
California, New York, and Wisconsin for thirty-six years—including
small rural churches, medium-sized city churches, and the two-
thousand member, "flagship" church, Asbury First United Methodist
Church, Rochester, New York, which I served as Senior Pastor from
1977 until retirement in 1995.[1] I have taught in colleges, universities,
and seminaries for eighteen years. I have been a participating Fellow of
the Jesus Seminar since 1996.

Jesus

For sixty years Jesus has been singularly significant in my life and indispensable to my faith. But my present understanding of Jesus is radically
different from the faith of my childhood and adolescence. Back then
my faith in Jesus was defined by Christian Orthodoxy as celebrated
in the liturgical seasons of Advent, Christmas, Lent, and Easter, and
as articulated in the Apostles' Creed, which I recited in worship and
believed literally—heart, soul, and mind—as historical truth.

After a fifty-year journey of my mind (left brain, if you will) in inves-
tigative historical scholarship, my mind, contrary to the desire of my
heart and soul, can no longer assent to my childhood and adolescent
beliefs taught to me by Christian Orthodoxy. Consequently, in all intellectual honesty, I can no longer hold as historical truth Jesus' virgin
birth, resurrection from death, ascension into heaven, and exaltation
to God's right hand, where he remains until he will "come again to
judge the quick and the dead," as the Apostles Creed puts it. Nor do I
hold any longer that Jesus was pre-existent with God. With respect to
his passion and death, I no longer hold as factual Jesus' "Palm Sunday"
entry into Jerusalem, his betrayal by Judas and denial by Peter, his
"Last Supper" commemoration of his anticipated martyrdom, followed

by his departure to Gethsemane, where he was arrested. I do not hold as historical truth Jesus' trials before the Jewish high priest Caiaphas and the Roman governor Pilate. With the exception of the Last Supper, which was conceived by Hellenistic Jewish Christians, all the following are inventions of the Gospel of Mark: Jesus' "Palm Sunday" entry into Jerusalem, his prayer and arrest in Gethsemane, his betrayal by Judas (himself a Markan invention), Peter's denial, the Jewish and Roman trials, as well as the crucifixion, burial and empty-tomb stories. The only historical kernels behind the Gospel events from Palm Sunday to Easter morn are Jesus' provocative act against the temple money-changers and Jesus' crucifixion.[2]

I can no longer hold in good conscience that God delivered Jesus up to death for our sake as a sacrifice for our sins, or that his death in itself has any saving significance. I do not hold that Jesus historically ever viewed himself as the Messiah or Son of God, nor held any other exalted understanding of himself, nor perceived God to have bestowed on him any elevated status. Nor do I hold that Jesus chose an inner circle of twelve disciples to accompany him on his ministry, to serve as his apostles, and to represent symbolically the restoration of the twelve tribes of Israel (Luke 22:28–30).

Jesus was born in Nazareth, not Bethlehem. His birth was not heralded by wise men, angels, or shepherds. Nor was his birth noted by Herod the Great, in whose final year of reign (4 BCE) Jesus was born. Jesus was one of five sons of Mary and Joseph—the other four being James, Joses, Judas, and Simon (Mark 6:3).

All the above delineates the results of the scholarship of my mind (left brain). But what about my heart and soul (right brain)? While I no longer hold Jesus' virgin birth, his "Palm Sunday" entry into Jerusalem, Last Supper, Gethsemane prayer, Jewish and Roman trials, crucifixion as narratively described, and the reported Easter experiences as historically true, I do believe they point to another form of truth: metaphorical truth. Fabricated as these events are, they were created to interpret metaphorically the greater existential and transcendent meaning of Jesus' life and death among the earliest Christians. As metaphorical truth, they are indispensable to my faith.

To cite just one example: the most moving experience I have had as pastor is participating in Christmas Eve services: the reading of the nativity texts, hearing the beautiful traditional Christmas music that tells their stories, the congregational lighting of Christmas candles while "Silent Night" is sung with violin obbligato, within the transcendent ambience of a candle-lit Gothic cathedral, with illuminated Rose window over the seasonally decorated high altar. What I mystically intuit in that experience is the transformative presence of God who in those moments inspires human spirits to believe that Jesus is the light for our darkened world, the Prince of Peace and Son of Love, whose way offers peace, goodness, love and well-being for all. I could speak similarly to the metaphorical truth acclaimed in the Easter stories: God is never defeated in actualizing God's vision for humanity as intuited by Jesus, but always transforming death's end into life's new hopeful beginnings.

How does the metaphorical truth of Christmas and Easter alert me to the existential and transcendent meaning of Jesus in my life? Three things about the historical Jesus have enduring, existentially compelling importance for my life, and constitute the meaning for my being: (1) his intuitive experience of God's presence and character; (2) his vision of the kingdom of God and its inclusiveness; and (3) his opposition to the Judean establishment's rejection of its non-conformists as sinners. In what is the earliest gospel, the Sayings Gospel Q ("Q"=abbreviation for *Quelle*, a German word meaning "source"), a gospel which Matthew and Luke incorporated in *their* Gospels, I find Jesus' articulation of (1) and (2) most authentically preserved.

Specifically, in unique departure from Judaism and other ancient Near East cultural traditions, Jesus intuited God's self-disclosure in the natural world. Observing the intricate processes of nature, he noted that lilies of the field achieve effortlessly a beauty that exceeds the glory of Solomon, and that ravens do not have to labor to produce something to eat. Even grass, as short-lived as it is, is cared for. The shining sun and the falling rain exhibit a dependable process that benefits all life. The tiny mustard seed becomes a great tree, offering birds a nesting place in its branches. Yeast plays its part in the natural process of making bread, and salt helps sustain life by its indispensable preservative role.

From his observation of the natural world Jesus arrived at two profound insights. First, the world of nature is God's realm, where God reigns as a benevolent creator, providentially sustaining all life. Nature is not abandoned to chance, but God compassionately supplies all its needs. While this represents an idealistic view of the natural world on the part of Jesus, he is not unaware that nature can be "red in tooth and claw," as Tennyson put it. Jesus alludes to this savagery when he sends his missioners out "like sheep in the midst of wolves."

Second, from his observation of God's benevolent provision for all natural life, Jesus inferred a corresponding relationship that God desires for and offers to human beings. In this regard, Jesus made a conceptual transition from his intuition of God as compassionate creator to seeing God's relationship with humans as symbolically represented by the role of "father."

Jesus apparently reasoned that if God benevolently sustains the natural world, then as an ideal parent who gives "good things to those who ask him," God must provide for human needs as well. Thus, if in trust we petition God for daily bread, the bread will be ours. Nor need we be anxious about finding clothes to wear: God sees that our needs are supplied.

And having inferred God's presence in the natural world as evincing God's involvement in the human realm, Jesus espoused a unique ethic. Its radically idealistic program transcends the moral protocols of both Jesus' own Judaism and other Near Eastern cultures and religious ideologies of his day. Based upon beneficent, unconditional love, it follows the divine model that Jesus intuited from God's providential care of the natural world. It is so utopian that it calls upon us to love not only friends and neighbors, but enemies as well, just as God shows no partiality in equally blessing the just and unjust with sunshine and rain.

By invoking that universal care and love, Jesus was able to envision human relationships taking on a reconfigured disposition and dynamic. Not only will we love our enemies and pray for them when they persecute us, but when slapped on one cheek, we will turn the other to the slapper. When someone tries to take our coats, we will offer our shirts as well. When conscripted to walk one mile, we volunteer to go a second mile. When approached to borrow, we give expecting nothing in return. Our compassion for others is to match God's compassion for us. Rather than pass judgment on others, we will forgive others no matter how much they offend us. For the way we must treat people is the way we want them to treat us. When such an ethic is practiced, according to Jesus, there will no longer be any poor, or hungry, or sick, or exploiters, or enemies.[3]

Jesus' vision of God's kingdom and its idealistic ethic arose largely in response to the Judean establishment's hegemonic oppression of Galilean peasants. The Judean establishment's authorities robbed poor Galileans of their personal dignity and self-worth by insisting that they were sinners unless they faithfully observed the rules and regulations of Torah (particularly its Holiness Code: Lev 17–26), kept the precepts of the oral law, and supported the temple system with tithes and offerings. But these were impossible demands for those who suffered the poverty and vicissitudes of peasant life.

This brings me to the third reason why Jesus has such importance for my life. He aligned himself with the downtrodden Galilean peasants against their Judean establishment oppressors. In his parable of the "Good Samaritan" Jesus attacked the insensitivity of priests and Levites toward the plight of the helpless by contrasting to it the innate compassion of a despised Samaritan, an ethnic hybrid vilified by the Judean establishment's "holiness" ideology as a contemptible idolator.

Jesus lambasted Pharisees (Q [Luke 11:43]) and scribes (Mark 12:38–39) for flaunting their prestigious status. He utilized a self-effacing tax collector to denounce the self-righteousness of Pharisaic authorities (Luke 18:10–14a). He rejected the strictures of the purity laws that rendered defiled any who failed to wash their hands before eating, rebutting that what defiles a person is not outer uncleanness but inner uncleanness (Mark 7:15). He dismissed kosher dietary laws by declaring that since what one eats is immaterial to God, his followers could eat and drink whatever was provided (Q [Luke 10:7–8]). Contrary to the Ten Commandments, he declared that strict observance of the Sabbath (Exod 20:8) could be set aside for human need (Mark 2:27) and that discipleship took precedence over honoring one's father (Exod 20:12) in proper burial (Matt 8:21–22).

Further rejecting holiness as the sole criterion of Godliness, Jesus employed unclean and disreputable things as symbols of God's kingdom: in addition to the aforementioned Samaritan and tax collector, we find the mustard seed (a weed) and leaven representing the presence of God's kingdom (Q [Luke 13:18–21]). The "fallen" prodigal son is affirmed before his righteous older brother, and those who finally sit down at a feast (symbolic of banqueting in the kingdom) are a random gathering swept up in a search of roads and byways (Q [Luke 14:16–23])—a procedure that inevitably resulted in a mixture of "saints and sinners" at table together.

Jesus' vision of the kingdom of God was liberating to his followers. His assurance that, though scorned outcasts, they were loved by God and included in God's kingdom ("Blessed are you poor, for God's kingdom is for you!" Q [Luke 6:20]) restored their lost dignity and self-worth. His practice of table fellowship demonstrated God's acceptance of all—even those scorned and rejected by religious authorities claiming to speak for God.

In my judgment, it was Jesus' opposition to the Judean establishment and his championing of the cause of its outcasts that finally led to his martyrdom. During a visit to the temple, he became so enraged at the fleecing of the poor by the money-changers that he lashed out in protest, overturning the tables of coinage and scattering coins all over—thereby enabling the poor to pocket the dispersed coins. Perceived to be a thief, Jesus was arrested by the temple guard and turned over to the high priest Caiaphas, who immediately delivered him to Pilate, who summarily crucified him— the customary Roman punishment for thievery.

But Jesus' vision lived on in the hearts and minds of those who had found new life as members of God's family, and that vision was preserved in the Sayings Gospel Q. For these earliest followers neither Jesus' death nor his resurrection was important, but rather his life and his restorative message of God's unconditional love and nurture.

My Faith Response

I am an idealist and incurable romantic. One of my favorite songs is "Over the Rainbow," a song I, as a child, heard Judy Garland sing in "The Wizard of Oz." The song's last verse captures my idealism and romanticism:

"Somewhere over the rainbow, skies are blue, and the dreams that you dare to dream really do come true." As an idealist and incurable romantic, I am inescapably drawn to Jesus' utopian vision of the kingdom of God. While I am not as sanguine as Jesus that such a vision can be actualized, I *want* his dream to come true. I dare to dream that it can, and am committed, however inconsistent and faltering my efforts, to working for its realization.

Jesus' championing of the oppressed against the injustices of his society has transformed my attitude and behavior toward the devalued people of my own time. Growing up in a White Anglo-Saxon Protestant society, I was indoctrinated with its religious, racial, ethnic, sexist, and sexual prejudices. In both my early childhood in Asbury Park, New Jersey, and later childhood and adolescence in Atlanta, Georgia, I was taught that boys and men are superior to girls and women; African Americans are an inferior and incompetent race; Jews are intrusive, money-grubbing opportunists, who put Jesus to death; Catholics are papists, conspiring to turn our Protestant nation into a papal state; and homosexuals are abhorrent sexual deviates. I was also taught that unless you are Christian and believe that Jesus died for your sins, providing, thereby, the only path to God, you will not have eternal life. Those of other religious traditions "need not apply."

The lyrics of Oscar Hammerstein's "You've Got to Be Carefully Taught" (*South Pacific*) epitomizes my indoctrination: "You've got to be taught before it's too late, before you are six or seven or eight, to hate all the people your relatives hate."

But discovering Jesus' radical inclusiveness and his opposition to the dehumanizing oppression of his day changed me. Jesus' compelling vision enabled me to overcome the White Anglo-Saxon Protestant prejudices of my upbringing and transform my attitudes and behavior toward the vilified and oppressed of my own day. His resolute call for universal justice and compassion was the catalyst that empowered me to exorcise my inherited prejudices and strive to redress the injustice and bigotry endemic in my social and religious environments, and in the following ways.

Racism. Disillusioned with the Methodist Church's failure to support the civil rights movement, I left the pastorate in 1966 and joined the faculty of Shaw University, an historic Black institution in Raleigh, North Carolina. During the summer of 1967, a Shaw student and I successfully organized the Raleigh Black community against "urban renewal" (a euphemism for Black removal). In the fall of 1967, I organized some White Raleigh citizens in an endeavor called HOME (Housing Opportunities Made Equal), with the purpose of ending housing segregation in Raleigh. In 1968 we succeeded in enabling an African American family to purchase a home in an all White Raleigh neighborhood. Some years later, in a move from a White suburb in Wilmington, Delaware, I sold my home to a Black couple. Years after that, I brought an African American onto Asbury First United Methodist Church's pastoral staff. He was the first Black pastor in the church's history.

Sexism. In 1973, as a faculty member of Colgate Rochester Divinity School, I was appointed chairperson of a faculty committee to address the lack of women on the faculty. I was successful in persuading the all-male faculty and administration to adopt a protocol that assured equitable hiring of female applicants. Furthermore, when my bishop appointed me in 1977 to Asbury First United Methodist Church, I became the senior pastor of a church with a one-hundred-fifty-seven year tradition of male pastors. In 1981, I persuaded the bishop to appoint a woman to the four-pastor staff, and soon after succeeded in having another woman fill a pastoral vacancy, and later a third.

Anti-Semitism. My sister, raised as a Methodist, married a Jewish physician, converted to Judaism, and raised her two daughters as Jews. The warmly embracing, inclusive spirit of her husband and my sister's passionate dedication, driven by her Jewish faith, to helping under-privileged children in Florida cured me of my inherited anti-Semitism.

Anti-Catholicism. Being raised anti-Catholic (even forbidden by my parents to play with a Catholic neighbor boy) was another prejudice to overcome. From 1974–1981, I had the great privilege of being the first Protestant to teach New Testament at the Roman Catholic St. Bernard's Seminary, Rochester, New York. My warm reception by its Catholic students, faculty, and administration, as well as close friendships with its priests, made me feel I had found a new spiritual home. I am indebted to them for introducing me both to Catholic spirituality, particularly the modern writings of Thomas Merton and Henri Nouwen, and to the monastic community at the Abbey of the Genesee, where I met Nouwen, and where I often experienced its deeply moving contemplative worship.

Christian bigotry. While living in Appleton, Wisconsin, from 1995–2004, I was invited by the Fox Valley Muslim community's Imam to be a panel member on his public access TV program devoted to Islamic and Christian approaches to critical issues of the day. The Imam soon became a good friend. He often invited me to the Muslim community's festival celebrations, on one occasion as guest speaker. Warm, self-effacing, compassionate, and serene, he is both devout in his faith and respectful of others' faith. Indeed, he is "Christ-like." Yet, he is a Muslim! I deplore and reject Christian bigotry that thinks it knows who is loved and accepted by God.

Homophobia. Throughout childhood and adolescence, the family member I felt closest to was my father's brother. Affable, gregarious, and caring, my uncle was both deeply serious about life's vital issues—himself a pastor—and delightfully playful. He introduced me to classical music, a life-long love, for which I am eternally grateful. After two failed marriages, he apparently came to terms with his homosexuality. Recognizing that my beloved uncle was inherently gay cured me of my own homophobia. The transformation was further facilitated by my sister's daughter, a wonderful lesbian niece. Accordingly, I reject any religious dogma, ecclesiastically or biblically grounded, that considers homosexuality deviant or sinful.

To epitomize my faith response to Jesus' exemplification of God's inclusive love for all, I often quote from the fourth verse of the hymn, "When I Survey the Wondrous Cross," *not* with the focus on Jesus' death, but *on his life*—a life that calls us to make the same resolute, self-giving commitment to the realization of God's kingdom in *this* life:

Were the whole realm of nature mine,
that were an offering far too small;
love so amazing, so divine
demands my soul, my life, my all.

God

As a child and adolescent I was taught the traditional Christian doctrine: God is wholly other, all-powerful, all-knowing, all-seeing, all-loving, and immutable, who manifests as the trinity: Father, Son, and Holy Spirit. I was indoctrinated to believe in a three-storied reality—heaven above, hell below, and earth in between. In this view, God—imaged as a man, referred to as "He" and "our Father"—resides in heaven and intervenes on earth in behalf of the faithful, and against the wicked. God is depicted as wrathful judge, but also as merciful and compassionate, blessing those who faithfully respond to God (see Deut 27–28). Those who do not repent of their sins are condemned to hell. The righteous, of course, are destined for heaven.

I heard stories from the Bible and Christian tradition of God's self-revelation to others. I was taught and believed that God was ultimately and fully revealed in God's *only* Son, Jesus, whom God sacrificed for our sins. I was taught that *only* through the sacrifice of Jesus on the cross are we saved and by God's mercy granted eternal life. I was taught that I should pray to God and that "prayer changes things." A cherished memory of my childhood is of my mother praying with me at night as I lay in bed, reciting: "Now I lay me down to sleep. I pray the Lord my soul to keep. If I should die before I wake, I pray the Lord my soul to take. God bless mama and daddy. God bless. . . ."

Here is what I now believe about God and the universe God has created.[4] I submit that God created the universe as a dynamic, vibrant, organic web of interdependent relationships. Everything in the universe is interrelated with everything else. I heard a physicist once speak to this point when he said: "A physicist knows that the cry of the smallest baby effects the movement of the most distant star." In our world all of life is intricately interrelated. That reality has been made tragically clear in global warming, the human sin against all planetary life.

I take it as axiomatic that community precedes individuality. Each of us is born into community. We do not exist in isolation, however much we may at times think or wish we did. John Donne was right: "No man is an island, entire of itself, every man is a piece of the continent, a part of the main. . . . Any man's death diminishes me, because I am involved in mankind; and therefore never send to know for whom the bell tolls; it tolls for thee."

I believe that God created this interdependent web of relationships—human and natural—to grow in harmony, unity, goodness, and beauty through the wonder of complexity and intensity. I believe that God is all-loving, all-giving and all-forgiving, the source of all goodness, harmony and beauty, the source of the impetus toward empathy, compassion, altruism, and love in human relationships, as well as empathy and altruism when manifested in the animal world.

As pure spirit and dynamic energy, God both transcends and fully encompasses all creation. Moreover, God empathically experiences everything and everyone, and therefore empathically experiences us exactly as we experience ourselves.

Envisioning all possibilities for the creative order and always promoting the most positive outcomes, God both enables and inclines every aspect of creation to enrich life in accordance with ideal harmony, goodness, and beauty. Although God inherently possesses absolute power, God chooses not to wield it to achieve God's will. Out of love, God chooses to employ persuasion to lure creation toward self-fulfillment. However, the effectiveness of God's persuasive influence is often impeded by forces that keep creation from attaining the ideals God envisions. So then, in the natural world, its creatures' God-given power of self-fulfillment can work adversely to God's intention, just as in the human sphere our God-given free will can work adversely to God's intention when we make self-serving choices.

Since God does not dictate creation's choices, God cannot know the future in advance of its realization, though God does know the possibilities and the probabilities of the future. Therefore, when we choose to act to our detriment and that of others, God can only accept the future consequences of our sinfulness. Yet, even then what God envisions for us is not cancelled: its realization, even if modified by the consequences of our ill-fated choices, awaits only our transformative response to God's passionate love and persuasive lure.

While God's active presence in the natural world cannot be empirically verified, it can be inferred from those moments when harmony and goodness in the natural world is manifested through creaturely empathy and altruism. Examples of such behavior in nature are well documented: from mother/infant bonding, to social insects caring for their brood, to dolphins rescuing a dolphin in peril, to dogs offering comfort to distressed humans, to buffalo risking their lives to free a calf from devouring lions—all of which suggest to me God's direct, compassionate influence.

Similarly, when humans rally to the support of one another in the face of disaster, divinely infused compassion is the catalyst. To be sure, such outpouring of human compassion cannot be empirically verified as divinely instilled. Awareness of God's presence can never be empirically verified. I know that to be the case because when I have tried to verify God's presence through some empirical test generated by my left brain (my rational intellect), the test always fails. But when I shift to right brain and become open to its mystical and transcendent receptivity, I experience the presence of God. I experience God's presence in the uplifting bliss of those moments when I am transfixed by the mystical ambience of Christmas Eve services, as I described, the awesome sight of a mountain vista, the soaring beauty of a Handel oratorio, a Gounod mass, a Brahms requiem, the redemptive inspiration of Wagner's opera "Parsifal," or in the soul-felt singing of my favorite hymn, "Be Thou My Vision"—particularly these words: "Be Thou my vision, O Lord of my heart; naught be all else to me, save that thou art. Thou my best thought, by day or by night, waking or sleeping, thy presence my light. Be thou my wisdom, and thou my true word; I ever with thee, and thou with me, Lord; . . . Heart of my own heart, whatever befall, still be my vision, O Ruler of all."

The Church and Its Bible

I have a lover's quarrel with the institutional church. Although I am deeply indebted to the Christian community for its early nurture, its support during times of crisis, and its appreciative responsiveness to my ministry, I have a lover's quarrel with the institutional church's historic failure to be faithful to Jesus' vision. More often than not the institutional church accommodates itself to the prevailing culture. This is already clear in New Testament writings that impose subservient status and guilt-filled roles upon women: wifely subservience (Col 3:18; Eph 5:22–23), silence and submissiveness before men, and responsibility for the origin of sin, with childbearing their only hope for salvation (1 Tim 2:11–15).

Similarly, Paul denounces the homosexual lifestyle (Rom 1:26–27), a position never attributed to Jesus and inconsistent with his inclusive practice. The church has also subscribed to Western culture's anti-Semitism despite the obvious fact that Jesus himself was a Jew. Worse yet, churches of the American South historically sanctioned slavery and segregation on the ludicrous grounds of Noah's curse upon Ham (Gen 9:18–27). Other examples of the institutional church's violation of Jesus' ethic of unbounded love are its persecution of dissident Christians, medieval crusades against Islam, and warfare between Catholics and Protestants.

Furthermore, in my judgment, from its earliest days Christian Orthodoxy's establishing of the New Testament canon and its creedal formulations has almost completely misrepresented Jesus and the intent of his life and mission. Why do I say that?

For 2000 years the indispensable tenet of traditional Christian faith has been the salvific atonement wrought by Jesus' death. This doctrine has been the underpinning of its christology, promise of salvation, and Eucharistic observance; as well as the force behind its evangelistic mission and confidence in eternal life. For all that, Christian Orthodoxy is almost solely indebted to Paul, the first expositor of the cult of the dying and rising savior from which the church has never deviated.

From Paul's perspective, virtually the only important elements of the story of Jesus are his death by crucifixion and his resurrection by God. Jesus' death mattered for Paul because he interpreted it as the sole means by which fallen humanity is saved from the wrath of God, redeemed and reconciled to God. Paul even declared that God sacrificed Jesus, God's only son, for our atonement—a doctrine that Orthodoxy has promulgated ever since.[5]

The notion that God would sacrifice anyone, let alone Jesus, contradicts my perception of God's character. Such an interpretation totally misrepresents the historical Jesus. That misrepresentation stems from Pauline ideology, as well as Christian Orthodoxy's canonization of its belief structure—a process that was not finalized until almost four hundred years after Jesus. In actuality the pluralism of the early Jesus movement produced not only the four gospels finally chosen for the New Testament canon, but, also, some twenty others. One of these, the Sayings Gospel Q, originated as early as the late 30's or 40's CE, long before our Matthew, Mark, Luke, and John.

Like Q, the Gospel of Thomas, the Gospel of Mary, and the Didache, a first-century church manual, present radically different views of the life and significance of Jesus. Contrary to the Pauline tradition and the canonical gospels, they show no interest in Jesus' death and resurrection per se, but focus instead on applying Jesus' life and teaching to the purpose of realizing God's kingdom in this life. For that reason they represent what New Testament scholar John Dominic Crossan calls the "Life Tradition" as opposed to the "Death Tradition" reflected in the New Testament and Orthodox creeds and doctrines.

I suspect that the ideological foundation of the Death Tradition is a Christian fiction based on Greek and Hellenistic Jewish traditions of the revered martyr. I submit that the scenario of Jesus' passion and death was the creation of Hellenistic Jewish Christians—an ideological construct which Paul adopted—to explain why Jesus was crucified and, with the help of Isa 53:1–12, to attest that "Christ died for our sins, according to the scriptures, . . . was raised, . . . and appeared . . ." (1 Cor 15:3–5). With the same apologetic purpose in mind, these Christians created the Last Supper account, in which Jesus casts himself in the role of a sacrificial martyr.

Contrary to the Death Tradition, I do not hold that, prior to the temple incident in which Jesus overturned the money-changers' tables and was arrested as a thief, Jesus anticipated his death, that he ever viewed his death as sacrificial, much less as a means of atonement for human sinfulness, or that he imagined he would be raised from the dead. Moreover, Jesus did not institute the remembrance of his death in a last supper, as the Death Tradition would have us believe. For since he was arrested immediately after his provocative act against the temple, he could not have shared such a memorable occasion with his disciples.

I am persuaded that the Life Tradition, particularly as represented by the Q Gospel, comes closest to being an authentic depiction of Jesus' vision, mission, and purpose. Unfortunately, it was suppressed by early Christian churches and overshadowed by their advocacy of the Orthodox Death Tradition. Since then, in my judgment, Christianity has misrepresented the historical Jesus.

I am convinced that Jesus' focus was on life and that he considered each individual life a sacred gift of God. All but certainly reflecting an oral tradition that antedates the Orthodox account, the Eucharistic prayer found in Didache 10:3 acclaims, as Didache scholar Aaron Milavec phrases it: "You, almighty Master, created all things for the sake of your name, both food and drink you have given to people for enjoyment in order that they might give thanks; to us, on the other hand, you have graciously bestowed Spirit-sent food and drink for life forever through your servant Jesus." Instead of the salvific death of Jesus, this Eucharistic prayer celebrates *life*, and God's bountiful gift of physical and spiritual nourishment. This prayer is far more congruent with Jesus' vision of life in God's kingdom than is traditional Christianity's focus on Jesus' death as a passport to life eternal.

As I see it—and as I believe Jesus saw it—the greatest gift we have is *this* life *now*. As a teenager I pondered the staggering thought, "What if I had never been born?" That persistent thought has redirected my life to a deep appreciation and thankfulness for life itself and made me deeply grateful that I *am*.

As I write I am recuperating from fracturing my neck in a near-fatal fall, in which I fell twelve feet, landing on the back of my head. Fortunately, my next-door neighbors, alerted by their dog, rushed to see what had happened, and called 911. Prior to my neighbors' intervention, as I lay helpless on the ground without feeling from the head down, and plaintively crying for help, I thought to myself: "If I die here, I am fortunate to have had a wonderful life. Whether or not there is life after death does not matter. I have been blest with the gift of life. That is treasured gift enough. Thanks be to God!"

Notes

1. In 1981, I was offered a faculty position at the University of Chicago's Divinity School. In 1984, I was nominated as a candidate for the Episcopacy of the United Methodist Church. I declined Chicago's offer and withdrew as a candidate for the episcopacy because, were either honor actualized, I would no longer enjoy the professional gratification of being pastor of one of United Methodism's great progressive churches.

2. See, also, the Jesus Seminar Fellows' judgment on the non-historicity of these various events, Funk et al., *Acts of Jesus*, pp. 119–20, 138–61, 449–95.

3. The relevant Q citations, which serve as the basis for formulating Jesus' intuition of God's providential care of natural life and for profiling Jesus' ethic, can be found in the following Lukan texts: 6:20–21, 27–31, 34–37, 43–44; 10:3,7–8; 11:2–3, 9–13; 12:22b-30; 13:18–21; 17:3–4. See, also, the Matthean citation of the text of Q in Matt. 5:41. In subsequent Q references, I indicate I am citing Lukan or Matthean textual versions of Q by specifying the respective texts within brackets. For much of my understanding of Jesus' vision of God's kingdom and ethic, I am indebted to James M. Robinson, my New Testament mentor: see his *Gospel of Jesus*.

4. In what follows, I am heavily indebted to John B. Cobb, Jr., my theological mentor: see his *Process Theology*.

5. For the relevant Pauline texts, see Rom 3:23–25; 5:9–11; 8:31–32; 1 Cor 1:30; 2:2; 2 Cor 5:18–19; Gal 3:13; 1 Thess 1:10; 5:9.

Works Consulted

Allott, Robin. "Evolutionary Aspects of Love and Empathy." *Journal of Social and Evolutionary Systems* 15.4 (1992), 353–70. [Online Journal]. Uniform Resource Locater: http://www.percepp.com/lovempat.htm.

Byrne, Mary E., trans. "Be Thou My Vision." *The United Methodist Hymnal.* Nashville, TN: United Methodist Publishing House, 1989.

Cobb, John B. Jr., and David R. Griffin. *Process Theology: An Introductory Exposition.* Philadelphia: Westminster, 1976.

Crossan, John Dominic. *The Birth of Christianity: Discovering What Happened in the Years Immediately after the Execution of Jesus.* San Francisco: HarperSanFrancisco, 1998.

Donne, John. "Meditation XVII." *Devotions upon Emergent Occasions.* Ed. Antony Raspa. London: Oxford University Press, 1987.

Funk, Robert W., and The Jesus Seminar. *The Acts of Jesus: The Search for the Authentic Deeds of Jesus.* Polebridge Press Book. San Francisco: HarperSanFrancisco, 1998.

Funk, Robert W., Roy W. Hoover, and the Jesus Seminar. *The Five Gospels: The Search for the Authentic Words of Jesus.* Polebridge Press Book. New York: MacMillan, 1993.

Harburg, E. Y. (Lyrics), and Harold Arlen (Music). *The Wizard of Oz: Vocal Selections*. Arranger David Nelson. Design Susan Marzio. Miami, FL: Warner Brothers, 1995.

Kloppenborg Verbin, John S. *Excavating Q: The History and Setting of the Sayings Gospel*. Minneapolis: Fortress, 2000.

Merton. Thomas. *New Seeds of Contemplation*. New York: New Directions Publishing Corporation, 1961.

Milavec, Aaron. *The Didache: Faith, Hope, and Life of the Earliest Christian Communities, 50–70 C.E.* New York: Newman Press, 2003.

Nouwen, Henri. *Reaching Out: The Three Movements of the Spiritual Life*. New York: Doubleday, 1966.

Popular Science Blog. "When Lions, Buffaloes, and Crocodiles Attack—At the Same Time." [PopSciBlog, November 2, 2007]. Uniform Resource Locater: http://popsci.typepad.com/popsci/2007/06/when_lions_buff.html.

Robinson, James M. *The Gospel of Jesus: A Historical Search for the Original Good News*. San Francisco: HarperSanFrancisco, 2005.

Rodgers, Richard, and Oscar Hammerstein. *South Pacific: Vocal Selections. Music by Richard Rodgers; Lyrics by Oscar Hammerstein*. New York: Williamson Music, 1981.

Tennyson, Alfred Lord. *In Memoriam: An Authoritative Text, Backgrounds and Sources, Criticism*. Ed. Robert H. Ross. New York: Norton, 1973.

Watts, Issac. "When I Survey the Wondrous Cross." *The United Methodist Hymnal*. Nashville, TN: United Methodist Publishing House, 1989.

The Myth of the Human Jesus[*]

Walter Wink

This essay shares in a growing effort to cast the original truths of Christianity in new molds that have a more lively appeal for people in our day. For my part, I have been searching among the records of Judaism and Christianity to see if there are perhaps other ways to interpret and live out the original impulse of Jesus. In this essay I want to reflect both exegetically and theologically on how that impulse can open to us the present possibilities of the past. I do so as one who is deeply committed to what Jesus revealed, yet who believes that Christian churches have to a tragic extent abandoned elements of that revelation. I do not wish to throw the whole enterprise overboard, however. The gospels continue to feed me, as does all of Scripture, even the worst parts of it, and some churches are impressively faithful. But if Scripture is to speak to those who find its words dust, we will have to radically reconstitute our reading of these seminal texts.

My suspicion is that something terrible has gone wrong in Christian history. The churches have too often failed to continue Jesus' mission. I grant that the church fathers sometimes understood the implications of the gospel better than the earliest Christians, who lacked the perspective of hindsight. But there is a disappointing side as well: anti-Semitism, collaboration with oppressive political regimes, the establishment of hierarchical power arrangements in the churches, the squeezing of women from leadership positions, the abandonment of radical egalitarianism, and the rule of patriarchy in church affairs. Those of us who are to varying degrees disillusioned by the churches feel that it is not only our right but our sacred obligation to delve deeply into the church's records to find answers to these legitimate and urgent questions:

Before he was worshiped as God incarnate, how did Jesus struggle to incarnate God?

Before he became identified as the source of all healing, how did he relate to, and how did he teach his disciples to relate to, the healing Source?

Before forgiveness became a function solely of his cross, how did he understand people to have been forgiven?

Before the kingdom of God became a compensatory afterlife or a future utopia adorned with all the political trappings that Jesus resolutely rejected, what did he mean by the kingdom?

97

Before he became identified as messiah, how did he relate to the profound meaning in the messianic image?

Before he himself was made the sole mediator between God and humanity, how did Jesus experience and communicate the presence of God?

It is, of course, conceivable that the surviving data do not permit us to distinguish the Jesus of the gospels from the gospel of Jesus. However, it is my considered judgment that there is sufficient evidence to develop an alternative mode of access to Jesus. Specifically, clues and traces in the canonical gospels provide flashes of authenticity that seem incontrovertibly to go back to Jesus or to clear and vivid memories of him. When we finish our quest, however, we will not have the historical Jesus "as he really was," for such a feat is impossible. If we are successful, we will have contributed, through historical reflection and interpretation, to a new myth, *the myth of the human Jesus.*

The Original Impulse of Jesus

In my struggle to become human, I find myself returning over and over again to those ancient texts that for me still contain the original impulse of Jesus. That impulse was the spirit that drove Jesus through the villages of Galilee and ultimately to death in Jerusalem. It was the inner fire that impelled him to preach the coming of God's reign, the spirit that caused him to cry out, "I came to cast fire upon the earth, and how I wish it were already kindled!" (Luke 12:49). Even though that impulse may lie buried under the detritus of routinized religion, I am convinced that we can recover priceless rubies from the rubble. Nothing else can provide those who are seekers with the interpretive clues that might enable them to revitalize that sclerotic tradition.

I do not seek to get behind the text (for that implies that some other, superior text lies behind the received text). Rather, I wish to penetrate deeply into the text so as to provide an alternative means of access to Jesus. I seek a fresh picture of what Christianity might more truly be in our time. So I invite the reader to join me in the prophetic task of listening for what God might be saying to us today, individually and collectively. I will attempt to carry out that task by means of an "extremely verbatim reading," requiring what the great scholar of Jewish mysticism, Gershom Scholem, called "mystical precision." To that end, I will employ historical critical tools wherever they seem appropriate, and any other approaches that can render valid insights. I will hew to the biblical tradition with unrelenting determination, on the promise, as another Jewish scholar, Daniel Matt, puts it, that we will find God in the details. And if that happens, if the words dissolve into the reality, and language into experience, we will understand what mystics have always known: that the exegete stands, with Israel, at the Sinai of the soul, where God still speaks.

The Human Being in the Quest
for the Historical Jesus

The End of Objectivism

What stands in the way of new/ancient readings of Scripture is the whole heritage of positivism and objectivism: the belief that we can handle these radioactive texts without ourselves being irradiated. Biblical scholars have been exceedingly slow to grasp the implications of the Heisenberg principle: that the observer is always a part of the field being observed, and disturbs that field by the very act of observation. In terms of the interpretive task, this means that there can be no question of an objective view of Jesus "as he really was." "Objective view" is itself an oxymoron; every view is subjective, from a particular angle of vision. We always encounter the biblical text with interests. We always have a stake in our reading of it. We always have angles of vision, which can be helpful or harmful in interpreting texts. The bankruptcy of objectivism has been redundantly pointed out. "Historical writing does not treat reality; it treats the interpreter's relation to it," according to Brian Stock. "All history," said the poet Wallace Stevens, "is modern history." All meaning, says Lynn Poland, is present meaning. "All truly creative scholarship in the humanities is autobiographical," says Wendy Doniger O'Flaherty. And "historical criticism is a form of criticism of the present," according to Walter Kasper (as cited by Hal Childs). Theodor Adorno writes "the detached observer is as much entangled as the active participant." Sheila Rowbotham (cited in Catherine MacKinnon) also says, "All revolutionary movements create their own way of seeing." All that is true, but only partially. For historical criticism still can help us discover an understanding of that past which holds out to us present meaning.

According to Hal Childs, the past is not an object we can observe. It is an idea we have in the present about the past. History is constantly being rewritten from within history. Thus, as O'Flaherty observes, there is no absolute perspective available outside of history that could provide a final truth of history. Childs contends that Jesus of Nazareth, as a real person who once lived but now no longer exists, is unapproachable by historical critical methods. Obviously it is possible to continue to reinterpret the documents that reveal his one-time presence in history. But this is a reinterpretation of meaning in the present and not a reconstruction of the past. Following Jung, Childs believes that the question of whether we can ever know what happened in the past is, in the final analysis, undecidable. All we can know is its effect on us today.

While I agree with much of Child's critique, I believe he goes too far when he declares that the past is unapproachable by historical methods. For historical criticism still can help us recover an understanding of a past that holds out to us the possibility of present meaning. The text is a brute fact, not a Rorschach inkblot onto which any conceivable interpretation can be read. The great if limited value of the historical critical approach is that it debunks arbitrary notions of what the text might mean. From every hypothesis and reconstruction it demands warrants, or reasonable evidence within the text. Arguments can sometimes be falsified by historical and literary data. Not just anything goes, but only positions that other scholars can examine and debate. In order to discern the past in its present meaning, it is absolutely essential that we have as accurate a picture of the past as possible. We do not need "a final truth of history," but only approximate truth backed up by evidence.

We can find meaning in the present, not *instead of* a reconstruction of the past, but *by means of* a reconstruction of the past. We have not just one horizon, the present, but two, past and present; and it is their interplay and dialogue, often tacit and even unconscious, that provide meaning. It is this built-in, self-critical aspect of historical method that prevents pure subjectivity or the attitude that anything goes. In short, I want two things at once: to overcome the objectivist illusion that disinterested exegesis is possible, and to affirm the present meaning of the past by means of the most rigorous possible exegesis.

The *present* meaning of the historical Jesus has been the unconscious agenda of the Jesus-quest these past two centuries. Driving that enormous undertaking was an inchoate desire among Christian scholars to recover something numinous and lost *within themselves*, and within contemporary religion. The means used, however, were not capable of rejuvenating the springs of faith. In fact, the historical approach became a kind of Midas touch. The very act of projecting that longing for the numinous back into the first century concealed its present motivation. Consequently, the Jesus found in the past, however much a projection of modern religious ideals, could not then be brought forward into the present. To do so would violate those very scientific principles that had been used to recover Jesus in his original setting. Having found him again in all his compelling modernity, they had to abandon him to the past. For no one was aware, until Albert Schweitzer exposed it, that the real driving force behind this scholarly exertion was in fact a modern longing to be encountered by the divine. It was that very longing that scholarship pretended to be able to dispense with by its objectivist methodology and detached attitude. Paradoxically, the Jesus they found by scholarly means was located on the far side of an unbridgable gulf—the past—that was created by the very method scholars had chosen to recover Jesus as their contemporary.

No legitimate quest for the historical Jesus is possible as long as the real motives behind the quest are denied. Once the false objectivity of historians has been renounced, however, we can acknowledge that most scholars study the past *in order to change its effect on the present.*

The Myth of God Incarnate versus the Myth of the Human Jesus

It is not, however, a choice between the human, non-mythological Jesus versus the divine, mythological Christ; for both are archetypal images that are models or patterns that act catalytically to transform. The human Jesus of the Quest has already entered into the archetype of what it means to be human, and seems to have affected people even during Jesus' active ministry. Indeed, the son of man was already numinously charged.

The quest of the historical Jesus, then, functions in the service of the myth of the human Jesus. It attempts to recover the humanity of Jesus in order to liberate it from the accretions of dogma that have made Jesus a God-Man. For two centuries scholars have believed that they were simply going behind the gospel traditions to their earliest forms. But the scandalous lack of historical consensus among scholars reveals the true situation: they were not recovering Jesus as he really was; rather, they were forging the myth of the human Jesus. And this is as true of "unbelievers" as "believers," as true of liberals as conservatives.

No wonder there was no scholarly consensus. For every picture of Jesus that scholars produced was inevitably invested with that scholar's projections onto Jesus, positive or negative. And since these projections were by definition unconscious, and disguised the scholar's own personal needs and interests, scholars often became dogmatic about their exegetical conclusions where only tentative answers were appropriate. We had to be dogmatic, it seemed; the myth of the human Jesus that we were unwittingly helping to fashion offered us a kind of salvation. Since the driving spirit behind the quest was the hope of discovering our own humanness in God, the very meaning of our lives hung in the balance. And because each scholar brought his or her own set of needs to the quest, there could never be unanimity as to what the historical-critical results would be. Our contributions to the quest, then, are not "the objective truth" about Jesus, but rather personal probes of varying value into the humanity of Jesus. Each such contribution, however unavoidably subjective, adds to the wild proliferation of flowers and weeds that make up the riotous garden of Jesus studies.

I in no way deplore these efforts to construct a new, liberating Jesus-myth. I believe it is the most important theological enterprise since the Protestant Reformation, urgently to be pursued. The only problem is that so many scholars believed they were producing objective historiography rather than creating a necessary new myth. That myth, to be sure, draws on historical methodologies. But it marshals them in the service of what I hope will become a powerful mythic alternative to the Christ-myth that we have known these past two thousand years. *Historical criticism is essential for Jesus research because the myth of the human Jesus is itself historically constructed.*

In short, the quest for the *historical* Jesus has all along been the quest for the *human* Jesus. There is no need for consensus or unanimity as to what constitutes authentic Jesus tradition. The myth of the human Jesus is a wide field with room for many divergent views. And it continues to provide the dynamic impetus that has driven that quest ever since. We are not the drivers, but the driven.

The Jesus-quest is faced with two major limitations, however: the paucity of the biblical data, and the poverty of ourselves. The myth of the human Jesus cannot simply be spun out of the air, because that myth insists on the historicity of the human Jesus. The myth itself demands that we provide warrants for all our assertions and a plausible synthesis of the data. Fallible persons such as we can nevertheless exercise those critical judgments in such a way as to provide information about the human Jesus. It is precisely that wager that leads exegetes to engross themselves in that "extremely verbatim reading" the mystics talked about. We cannot abandon the historical method because it provides us with one of the most powerful tools we have for constructing the myth of the human Jesus.

Scholars seek to rectify the limitation on our data by turning over every leaf in search of new information about the ancient world. Newly discovered texts, new ways of reading texts, new disciplines applied to the texts—all provide invaluable aid in understanding Jesus' world and his own relation to it. Such research participates in a perpetual feedback loop in which our interpretation of solitary sayings and deeds of Jesus continually modify our overall picture of him, while our overall picture in turn exercises a powerful influence on the way we read the solitary pieces.

It is by now a truism that we lack adequate information to write a biography of Jesus, or even to profile his personality. And it is no doubt true that the scholarly reconstructions of the teaching of Jesus (for which we have considerably more data) do not carry the religious impact that the mythologized gospels do. That is why we must attempt to recover the archetypal meaning of "the son of the man," as Jesus is called in the gospels. Only then can we hope to offer an alternative to the perfect, almost inhuman Christ of dogma that has dominated these two millennia of Christian Orthodoxy. What I and others in the Jesus Seminar are trying to do is literally to reconstitute Christianity in a more humane direction, to build a Christology from below. For that task we seek a Jesus who is not the omnipotent God in a man-suit, but someone like us who quested for God at the center of his life and called the world to join him. What we do not know how to do, or even whether it can be done, is to position ourselves in such a way as to experience the Human Being as numinously activating, religiously compelling, and spiritually transformative. If such a thing is possible, then new liturgies, music, meditative practices, disciplines, and commitments will spring up spontaneously. Nor does that position need to be Christian.

Even if we are able to recover something of the human Jesus, we would still be subject to the second limitation mentioned above: the poverty of ourselves. No matter how vast our knowledge of Jesus' period, unless we are also doing something about our spiritual inadequacies, we will be unable to proceed closer to the mystery of Human Being (the son of the man), but will simply continue to circle its perimeter, accumulating ever more information without ourselves being changed by the encounter.

No scholar can construct a picture of Jesus beyond the level of spiritual awareness that she or he has attained. No reconstruction outstrips its reconstructor. We cannot explain truths we have not yet understood. We cannot present insights that we have not yet grasped. Our picture of Jesus reflects not only Jesus, but the person portraying Jesus; and if we are spiritual infants or adolescents, there are whole realms of human reality that will simply escape us. As Gerald O'Collins remarked, writing about Jesus betrays what we have experienced and done as human beings. The Jesus-quest as it is manifested today entails a high but necessary cost, and that is self-exposure, self-mortification, and personal transformation. Once we step out from behind the screen of historical objectivism into Heisenberg's universe, we become as much the subject of study as Jesus.

After all, "Jesus," "quest," and "Scripture" are not merely artifacts for study or the name given an inquiry. They are great religious impulses and archetypal powers, and they are not just "out there" in the texts to be studied, but already "in here," in the self who is fascinated, repelled, driven, wounded, and possibly healed by these realities.

The Myth of History
The historical critical method cannot deliver Jesus as he really was. But we should never have demanded that it do so. Its real contribution has been to sift through the Jesus traditions in order to establish the elements of a reconstruction. We can create the myth of the human Jesus because, as W. Taylor Stevenson has noted, the historical approach is basically a *mythic* way of perceiving the world. The idea of history *is* our modern myth.

To be sure, the myth of history is falsified when we pass from claiming that reality is historical in nature, to insisting that reality can be discerned *only* by use of historical method. Historical investigation cannot, for example, establish whether some people truly love others, or are acting from the motives they give for their behavior. Historical study, while indispensable, is incapable of providing the kind of insights that can make the Bible come alive with the power to facilitate transformation—which is the manifest intention behind its writing and preservation in the first place. Every historical image of Jesus that is created serves the myth of the human Jesus because today we *are* constituted by the myth of history. As Hal Childs commented to me:

> A significant dimension of our ontology today, our core being, is the myth of history. This is why "history" is so important to us, why it is so important to perceive and portray Jesus historically. We conceive of ourselves as historical be-ings; history is our be-ing. History does not mean "true facts." It is a grand narrative with ontological status, which because of its ontological status feels absolutely real at a pre-reflective level within us, as our being. I am trying to make this myth more conscious, but because it is still mostly unconscious, or we are mostly unconscious to it, there is ongoing confusion as we try to think about it.

In a sense, then, the quest for the human Jesus is the hunger for one's own emergent consciousness.

However much scholars differ on details, and however much they quibble over interpretations, what most do agree on is that Jesus really was a human being, and that our historical findings can help us recover aspects of his humanity. Because traditional Christianity suppressed his humanness in favor of his divinity, the recovery of Jesus' full humanity is felt as a remedial and even, for some, a sacred task.

That Jesus really lived is, to be sure, required, not by some putative historical science, but by the Christian myth itself. And faith, though not dependent on historiography, can certainly be helped by it. Historical criticism can fashion possible alternative images of Jesus that can free us from oppressive pictures spawned by churches that are too often themselves oppressive. Critical scholarship can help us recover Jesus' critique of domination. It also permits us to appreciate Jesus without an overlay of dogma that claims absolute truth and negates the value of other approaches to understanding Jesus.

Bruce Chilton's recent *Rabbi Jesus* is an excellent example of the careful use of historiography to paint a plausible picture of Jesus. It is full of speculation, informed guesses, and novelistic narrative. Because Chilton has performed such exhaustive research, and because he has tethered his imagination to reliable facts from the period and its places, he is able to make a significant contribution to the quest for the human Jesus. In a society in which the great living myths have lost their cogency for many, what we once held as beliefs can now be held self-consciously as "true fiction," as "creative nonfiction," or as "myths" in quotation marks. We no longer have to defend our meaning-stories, notes mythologist Betty Sue Flowers.

We simply watch them evolve as we tell them and live in the present that is created by the future we tell.

Jesus' Original Impulse

My goal in studying the gospels is to recover what Jesus unleashed—the original impulse that prompted the spread of his message into new contexts that required new formulations—and to keep it true to his spirit. Using a critique of the Domination System as my selective grid enables me to recover emphases lost as the gospel was domesticated in the early church. Although occasionally Jesus' teachings were further radicalized (as in Stephen's speech in Acts 7 or the extension of the mission to include Gentiles found in the Book of Acts), the more pronounced tendency of the tradition was to accommodate the gospel in significant ways to structures of domination (for example, the treatment of women in later New Testament writings). This critique of domination does not replace the historical criteria worked out with such care by New Testament scholars. It does, however, provide the primary criterion for discerning what was revelatory in Jesus' life and message.

The presence of a particular critical perspective does not spell the end of objectivity; we are still required to provide warrants for our claims. Once one abandons the chimera of disinterestedness, however, objectivity is free to become what it should have been all along: just another name for simple honesty and the willingness, like Schweitzer, to be changed by what we discover.

I listen intently to the Book. But I do not acquiesce in it. I rail at it. I make accusations. I censure it for endorsing patriarchalism, violence, anti-Judaism, homophobia, and slavery. It rails back at me, accusing me of greed, presumption, narcissism, and cowardice. We wrestle. We roll on the ground, neither of us capitulating, until it wounds my thigh with "new-ancient" words. And the Holy Spirit is right there the whole time, strengthening us both.

Such wrestling insures that our pictures of Jesus are not mere repetitions of the prevailing fashion. They can be a groping for plenitude, an attempt to carry on the mission of Jesus, and an effort to transcend the conditioning of the Domination System. And in the end, we may not just be conforming Jesus to ourselves, but in some faint way perhaps conforming ourselves to the truth revealed by Jesus.

My deepest interest in encountering Jesus is not to confirm my own prejudices (though I certainly do that), but to be delivered from a stunted soul, a limited mind, and an unjust social order. No doubt a part of me wants to whittle Jesus down to my size so that I can avoid painful, even costly change. But another part of me is exhilarated by the possibility of becoming more human. So I listen in order to be transformed. Somehow the gospel itself has the power to activate in people that "hunger and thirst for justice" that Matt 5:6 speaks about (whether in the words of Jesus or of a like-minded evangelist). There are people who want to be involved in inaugurating God's domination-free order, even if it costs them their lives. *Respondeo etsi mutabor*: I respond though I must change. And in my better moments, I respond *in order to change*.

Truth is, had Jesus never lived, we could not have invented him.

Notes

* This essay is an abbreviation and revision of Wink, *The Human Being*, 7–16.

Works Consulted

Childs, Hal. *The Myth of the Historical Jesus and the Evolution of Consciousness.* Society of Biblical Literature Dissertation Series 179. Atlanta: Scholars Press, 2000.

Chilton, Bruce. *Rabbi Jesus.* New York: Doubleday, 2000.

Flowers, Betty Sue. "Practicing Politics in the Economic Myth." *The San Francisco Jung Institute Library Journal* 18.4 (2000) 65–86.

Heisenberg, Werner. *Philosophical Problems of Quantum Physics.* Woodbridge, CN: Ox Bow Press, 1979.

MacKinnon, Catherine A. *Toward a Feminist Theory of the State.* Cambridge, MA: Harvard University Press, 1989.

Matt, Daniel C. "'New Ancient Words': The Aura of Secrecy in the Zohar." Pp. 181–207 in *Gersom Scholem's Major Trends in Jewish Mysticism 50 Years After. Proceedings of the Sixth International Conference on the History of Jewish Mysticism.* Eds. Peter Schäfer and Joseph Dan. Tübingen: J. C. B. Mohr, 1993.

O'Collins, Gerald. *Interpreting Jesus.* London: G. Chapman, 1983.

O'Flaherty, Wendy Doniger. "The Uses and Misuses of Other Peoples' Myths." *Journal of the American Academy of Religion* 54 (1986) 219–39.

Poland, Lynn M. "The New Criticism, Neoorthodoxy, and the New Testament." *Journal of Religion* 65 (1985) 459–77.

Rosenstock-Huessy, Eugen. *Out of Revolution: Autobiography of Western Man.* New York: William Morrow & Company, 1938 (reprint 1969).

Stevenson, W. Taylor. *History as Myth.* New York: Seabury Press, 1969.

Stock, Brian. *Listening for the Text: On the Uses of the Past.* Baltimore: Johns Hopkins University, 1990.

Wink, Walter. *Engaging the Powers: Discernment and Resistance in a World of Domination.* Minneapolis: Fortress Press, 1992.

———. *The Human Being: Jesus and the Enigma of the Son of the Man.* Minneapolis: Fortress Press, 2002.

Giving Up the Truth

David Galston

It was very early in the morning, the streets clean and deserted, [and] I was on my way to the station. As I compared the tower clock with my watch I realized it was much later than I had thought and that I had to hurry; the shock of this discovery made me feel uncertain of the way, I wasn't very well acquainted with the town as yet; fortunately, there was a policeman at hand, I ran to him and breathlessly asked him the way. He smiled and said: "You asking me the way?" "Yes," I said, "since I can't find it myself." "Give it up! Give it up!" said he, and turned with a sudden jerk, like someone who wants to be alone with his laughter.

-Franz Kafka[1]

Giving up the truth is not consonant with the American way; after all, as one of my teachers claimed, ours is "the officially optimistic society."[2] Far be it for anyone to sound a depressing note. But "giving up the truth" also has a philosophical meaning that goes beyond pessimism or optimism. Giving up, in effect, is the nature of truth—that is, giving up is the avenue by which "truth" is approached. For in the philosophical understanding, truth is never possessed as a commodity, and in fact to try to possess the truth as a commodity is exactly not to understand it. Being in consonance with truth means letting go because it requires admitting that human life is finite and partial. Life affords only an interpretation—or a perception—of the world and our place within it.

Parables play with the finite nature of being human by playing with interpretation. A parable does not have a definite interpretation, and it cannot have one, because it is about crossing the line of fixed realities and entering the play of flexible realities. Bob Funk called a definite or fixed reality (the way things are) the "default reality" of everyday human affairs, but the parable is about crossing over the default line to see the world from the vantage point of a different order. If one attempts to fix the vantage point gained from the parable in a definite way, then the parable is lost because it is turned back into a default or fixed reality. Instead, the student of the parable, in order to understand the parable, must give it up as the truth and learn to play with it—to take the new perspective almost as a game, but certainly as something characterized by lightness, flexibility, and creativity—even joy. Bob Funk once said, "All my plans are written in water."[3] That saying is from someone who knew both the meaning of parable and the meaning of giving up the truth.

Franz Kafka, although cryptic and difficult, is nevertheless attractive because he tells parables. What he gives with one hand he takes away with the other. It is impossible to know precisely what he means. In the opening lines of the novel *The Castle*, Kafka as narrator describes the scene. The main character, called "K," is looking at a castle in the mist and darkness of evening, but in the course of trying to imagine exactly what this castle looks like, Kafka tells us that there is not even a sign the castle is really there. Kafka opens his book with a parable about a castle and a character who, we learn, is a land surveyor determined to measure what is not a thing but an order of reality. K never learns that he is already in the castle; he never understands that what happens around him is fiction. He isn't able to laugh. In the parable world, one goes on with life because it is gratuitous, and one gives up the truth because releasing that weight is the liberty of grace.

The Weight of Christianity

In contrast to Jesus the teller of parables, Christianity as a religion developed in a rather serious and weighty manner by packing all its truth into creeds. Slowly, over the first few centuries of its history, Christianity converted itself from a practice of life to a confession of creeds. With its new love for confessions, Christianity recast itself as a new default reality. As opposed to a religion of practice, where truth is tied to lifestyle, Christianity became a religion of confession whose truth was used to distinguish between believers and heretics, insiders and outsiders. In simpler terms, within a few centuries the theology of Jesus turned irrevocably into theology about Jesus Christ. The opening words of the Nicene Creed—"We believe in one Lord, Jesus Christ, the only Son of God, eternally begotten of the Father"—resemble neither the words nor the practice of a parable.

I did not grow up confessing creeds, since my religious home was in what now seems a rarity: a liberal church. At the time, liberalism was the main expression of Christianity and the most popular one. But twentieth-century liberalism in Christianity has its own story of conversion, too, which mimics early Christian history; it also is the story of practice converted to confession. Admittedly, liberalism is a hard word to define because it is so widely used. In addition to a religious outlook or a theological persuasion, it can describe politics, economics, or philosophy; it can denote an historical era, an attitude, or a way of life; it can describe a cultural genre or an overly enthusiastic use of spice. We can relate it to and perhaps most easily associate it with nineteenth-century capitalism, colonialism, and free trade (at least it was "free" for the colonial powers). But the story of liberalism and its association with an open-minded attitude can be traced mainly to the French Revolution, during which the notion of the "citizen" was developed philosophically and culturally as it was nowhere else. The shift from identity and civil rights based on religion to identity and civil rights based on citizenship is the remarkable change the Enlightenment brought to the world. In the Enlightenment understanding, I have inviolable rights not because I am Christian or Jewish or Muslim, but because I am a citizen of a particular political state. The idea of the citizen gave birth to the notion of human rights that transcend any cultural, sexual, or ethnic marker my personal history may carry.

The lingering influence of the Enlightenment ideal in twentieth-century North American theology was the social gospel. It was as if the extension of the gospel to society necessarily involved the priority of human rights. As Walter Rauschenbusch (the key figure of the social gospel in the United States) poetically stated, Christianity is not about "getting individuals to heaven" but transforming life on earth into "the harmony of heaven."[4] As a political movement the Enlightenment promoted universal education, laws against child labor, basic rights for the working poor, and equal access to health care. All of these ideas rested on the assumption that government exists for the betterment of the citizenry. The social gospel claimed that these ideals in effect represented the character of Christian practice. Christianity is not about believing things, but about a revolutionary effort to change the world. As Rauschenbusch claimed, ". . . the spirit of primitive Christianity did not spread only sweet peace and tender charity, but the leaven of social unrest."[5]

Rauschenbusch was an extremely influential thinker, one who inspired Mahatma Gandhi and Martin Luther King, Jr., but even his strong voice in favor of a social imperative could not stop liberal churches from moving to a confessing imperative. That new stance took the form of what is commonly called neo-orthodoxy. And that is the type of church I grew up in: liberal but neo-orthodox.

It is not possible to talk about neo-orthodox theology without talking about the great twentieth-century theologian who continues to be a strong influence in Christian thought today, Karl Barth (1886–1968). Originally his theology was identified with two terms, crisis theology and dialectical theology. The inspiration for Barth and many of his generation was Søren Kierkegaard. Crisis in Greek means separation and, like the word dialectic, refers in this theology to the separate realms of the divine and natural worlds. The relation between these two worlds is, Barth insisted, not a natural point of contact, but discoverable only in revelation. Barth's contempt for so-called natural theology was displayed in *Natural Theology*, a book he wrote with Emil Brunner in 1946. In a few decades crisis theology became better known as neo-orthodoxy. The crisis of Barth's time was the First World War, when his so-called liberal teachers failed to voice their opposition to the German war effort. Instead, theologians like Adolf von Harnack, particularly noted by Barth, signed the "Manifesto of the Ninety-Three German Intellectuals to the Civilized World" (a document defending Germany's invasion of Belgium in 1914). Barth felt that his teachers effectively cancelled the independent voice of the Christian gospel by merging it with what was clearly political ideology. To call upon Christianity to justify a war is to say not only that God takes sides in a war but that the truth of God is the same as the truth of a culture; and against such notions Barth flung an overwhelming "No!" We cannot equate our cultural assumptions and values with the divine. "The Gospel is not," he wrote, "a religious message to inform [hu]mankind of their divinity or to tell them how they may become divine."[6] Rather, the Christian gospel originates outside the human historical experience and breaks into history as the Word. Since it comes from beyond the human realm, it is known only through its absence in human experience. Ironically it is the gospel's absence that enables it to be present as the proclamation or *kerygma* of grace. But the absence of the gospel, and therefore its grace, cannot be known if the gospel is reduced to or equated with a philosophical movement, a cultural ideal, a scientific breakthrough, or any other human construct. The gospel is always the outside and the unknowable that is at the same time the Word breaking into the world. The "Word" for Barth is always grace, but the content of grace, since it is beyond us and is God, is judgement as much as it is peace.

That was how Karl Barth understood the Christian gospel, and it is easy to see how in the context of the First World War his theology stirred critical voices against government propaganda and a few decades later laid the foundation for Christian resistance to Nazi Germany. Yet it is also easy to see how this very stubborn theology could, following the war years, inspire new imperatives for obedience and fixations on confession. If God is unreachable and unknowable, if the Word of God is exactly what stands outside and against humanity—and is the darkness that breaks into the world as light—then its presence can be grasped only symbolically through communal forms of mediation that represent the transcendent power of the Word. And despite Barth's amazing appeal, the gospel was soon back in the exclusive hands of its mediators: professional theologians with their ecclesiastical creeds. (I say "creed" here whereas Barth would probably say "The Resurrection"; but after all, the resurrection is the first Christian creed.) The unbrokered wisdom of Jesus the parable teller became brokered once again. The power of neo-orthodoxy lay not simply in its appeal to the outside, but also in its ability to crush the inside—the unbrokered human spirit. After neo-orthodoxy, the Kingdom of God that the social gospel had located in this world of human life was returned to the "no-place" of the Christian utopia called heaven. "The world" may be of some interest insofar as it is that against which the kerygma is cast, but otherwise the world is no place for a theologian to rest his or her head.

The church I grew up in was the liberal neo-orthodox church whose history was social action, but whose direction from about the 1970s decidedly turned to confession. It became a matter of believing the unbelievable, confessing sin, and then redoubling one's effort to live in faith. Yet, after all the fuss, everyone returned to church just one week later to confess sins again and to start the cycle anew. To be sure, the church I grew up in seldom recited the Nicene Creed, but when it did that rite always marked a particularly special occasion and demanded a standing observance. I discovered in my early teens that almost no one believed a word of the Nicene Creed, yet remarkably that was exactly the point. "Not believing" is a valuable neo-orthodox tool: it is the experience of the darkness that Barth was so fond of that delivers us to the helpless state of confession. In the neo-orthodox understanding, I am asked as an act of faith to override my subjective certainties and doubts. It is as if I were mimicking the father in Mark 9:24 who, unable to believe in a miracle, cried out, "I believe; help my unbelief." The natural human spirit of suspicion is suppressed, even dismissed, so that the darkness of God can be fully enlightening. Beliefs are not factual. The resurrection, biblical miracles, and virgin birth are not literal. Nevertheless, they are confessed as an act of what Rudolph Bultmann called, *sacrificium intellectus* to discipline one's faith and override one's ego. It might be added that Bultmann, too, claimed to be neo-orthodox; but he did ask a crucial question that marked a turning point in my development as a student: "Is it possible to expect that we shall make a sacrifice of understanding (*sacrificium intellectus*) in order to accept what we cannot sincerely consider to be true—merely because such concepts are suggested by the Bible?"[7] In neo-orthodox understanding, faith is the contradiction of reason precisely because its goal is to mark the distance between God and the world. "It is certain because it is impossible" is how Tertullian described the resurrection.[8] It could also describe the presuppositions of neo-orthodox theology.

In the preface Bob Funk highlighted the disjunction between what I know (or think I know) and what I am asked to confess. Then he pushed the question further: at what point is the disjunction so acute that "my personal integrity is at stake." I like to put the question a bit more pointedly: to what extent am I prepared to lie? This acute problem is exactly the "weight" of Christianity, and really any religion, when its practice is primarily the demand for confession. At a certain point the insightful lessons of darkness in neo-orthodox theology are transformed from an act of self-annihilation to one of self-deception. As a minister, I participated in the theology of self-annihilation many times. I wore an alb and stole (garments that subtract from the individual identity and represent the community at large) and I recited the Nicene Creed weekly with a congregation—not as an act of stating common beliefs but as one that eliminated individual interpretation. I guarded the formulas of the church particularly related to baptism and the Eucharist not because I was against the laity but because the formulas held a transcendental integrity. That was the heavy nature of a neo-orthodox faith I was taught in seminary and confessed in the church.

I do not condemn neo-orthodox theology; it can be effectively deployed in critical relation to the latest cultural fashion or political manifesto and in this way can exert a great and salutary power. But it consistently collapses into superciliousness when the cracks in its mighty exterior finally reveal an interior concern for authority, obedience, and guarded privileges. Neo-orthodoxy gives to Christian leaders renewed fascination with the theatrical gestures of worship and invested certitude in oblique theological pronouncements, but in doing so creates a false and ultimately pernicious divide between the sacred and profane. At some point, when profane knowledge holds a certainty that no confession can overcome, that crossroads Bob Funk so neatly voiced becomes a crisis. A thoughtful theologian cannot ignore the well-tested conclusions of science, history, literary studies, cultural anthropology, linguistics, and any number of other modern disciplines. What we come to know—or with reasonable certainty think we know—by way of the profane eventually overwhelms what we are asked to state in the context of the sacred. The confession becomes too heavy; the weight is crushing. The only alternative is to reject the sacred world for the profane or in some way to integrate the two with intellectual integrity. And integrity requires consonance between what I believe and what I think I know.

When, in the face of this disjunction, a credible historical Jesus appeared on the scene, I had what might be called an epiphany. My experiences in seminary had convinced me that the historical Jesus was a useless construct best left to the fanciful dreams of nineteenth-century scholars, and in graduate school I was too absorbed in philosophy to worry much about what was going on in biblical studies. When I did hear about the Jesus Seminar and finally in 2000 had time to check it out, the discovery of the "voiceprint" of the historical Jesus made an otherwise anticlimactic millennium remarkable to me. The simple insight concerning the centrality of Jesus' aphorisms and parables meant a world of difference. No cross, no Christ, no confession, and really not even God are the subject of concern for that voice. Parable displaces confession. Neo-orthodox insistence that the historical Jesus must be rejected in favour of the divine revelation gets turned inside out. Instead of the historical Jesus, it is the divinised Christ who gets rejected; death is set aside in favour of life. Parable is life-centred theology whereas Christ is God-centred confession. The immanent trumps the transcendent; the practice of life takes priority over the confession of idealised propositions.

The historical Jesus enabled me to fall into life, to engage the immanent, to practice the present; to put it in theological terms, the choice is between the parable and the revelation, between a human being and the Son of God, between life and Empire. Whatever Christianity might mean by revelation and whatever revelation can be understood to mean, it certainly does not mean parable. Great Christian theologians like Barth call us to seek justice because it is what God wants; others like Dominic Crossan, because Jesus endorsed it. But the voice of the historical Jesus is not one of personal assurances or divine sanctions. Instead, we practice justice only because we can; meanwhile, questions of God and the Son of God fall away. There is no need for God inside a parable.

The Jesus of history is a human being like anyone and not God's revelation of the Word. Indeed, with the historical Jesus the Word comes crashing to the ground. If I may play with the image for a moment, allow me to call theology with the historical Jesus "fallen" theology and the theologian who employs this model the fallen theologian. Such a "fallen" faith does not divide the sacred from the profane, confess the incredible despite contrary evidence, or proclaim the Word over against the world. Rather, it involves something like taking hold of a vision and becoming that vision by the very manner in which one chooses to live one's life.

The Fallen Theologian

In the course of my academic life, I have moved from neo-orthodoxy to a new form of existentialism (that is, immanence) that in church circles I call "Jesus following." It consists, as I have stated, of a fall to radical presence in the world. This fall from transcendence into immanence retains the basic characteristics of what we can still call faith, but can it still be called "Christian"? This is the debate in which I presently find myself engaged, and the one with which I'd like to conclude.

"Falling" into the world is an expression that recalls many of the radical "Death of God" theologians from the 1960s. Though I need to distinguish my "fallen" theologian from this group, in many respects they had it about right. They abandoned so-called classical Christian beliefs in favour of what they variously described as "the full meaning and reality of the world."[9] My break from neo-orthodoxy was pinned on the historical Jesus and based on the real world. Death of God theologians achieved almost the same thing, except for one minor variant: in the Death of God movement there remained a resolute intolerance for a strictly human Jesus.

William Hamilton, who along with Thomas J. J. Altizer founded the Death of God movement, had concluded by 1993 that the only good Jesus is a fictional Jesus.[10] Yet it seems that he never understood exactly what he was implying. While it is true that the Jesus of history will always be a stranger to us—since his form necessarily emerges in part from our own interpretive bias—this is due not to Jesus or problems of biblical studies, but the nature of history as such. History is exactly about what is unknown to us. We may have more data concerning someone like the Roman emperor Octavian or Marcus Aurelius, but that does not mean they are any less "strangers" to us than the historical Jesus.[11] Ironically, perhaps, the writing and thinking of history is what "history" means: that is to say, history is the re-creation of memory. It has no other meaning outside of how it is represented—how it is "fictionalized," if you like—by its recording and interpretation. The task of the historian is not to determine a final picture. History inevitably involves receiving the past as a stranger whose outline we attempt to discriminate from a background of darkness and jumbled memories. The historian's task is to assemble an interpretation that balances evidence with credibility.

I face the same problem with Jesus as I do with my great-grandmother. And since unlike the gospel writers my family did not record her quips and comments, I can say with integrity (even having met the woman several times as a young boy) that I actually have better records for Jesus. Therefore, while it is true that our knowledge of the Jesus of history pales by comparison to our information about Roman emperors, Hamilton's radical conclusion—that the historical Jesus is a stranger and that accordingly we must be content with the Jesus of fiction—actually holds little water. Every figure of history is a stranger and a fiction. It's just that some among them wrote books and some employed government bureaucracies. Those who were illiterate and who relied on wit and parable may be less clearly recorded, but they are not therefore less real or less important.

The Death of God movement, then, did not provide much help to me when as a fallen theologian I moved forward with the historical Jesus. In fact, it became increasingly clear that the Jesus of fiction advocated by the Death of God faction ended up being the eschatological revelation of God: the God who is outside of time but who breaks into time wholly yet surreptitiously as the crisis of decision. How then could radical Death of God theology become a poetic form of neo-orthodox teaching? The answer is it could because the consequence of dismissing historical criticism is like releasing the anchor of reality: without historical criticism the relationship between what we create out of history and our responsibility for history falls apart. The tension between fiction and reality, a tension normally called accountability, is cancelled. In the academic world that account-ability is called "evidence." The Jesus of history is never simply fiction, but rather *accountable fiction*. His, like history itself, is the type of fiction that requires evidence when it is told. Anything less is a disservice to the one thing we can say about Jesus absolutely: that he was a human being. When it came to the historical Jesus, the Death of God theologians dismissed his-tory as useless and claimed that "Jesus is inaccessible by historical means."[12] Thus, they inadvertently made Jesus non-historical and thereby made him non-human—bypassing the requirement of evidence and returning theol-ogy to the chase of fiction.

The fallen theologian, I propose, is a truth teller rather than a story teller mainly because he or she deals exclusively with humanity and explicitly with a human Jesus. However sketchy the recorded memories of Jesus, they still rest on the indisputable fact of his humanity. There was nothing more astounding about him than there can be about anyone else. This point seems too easy, yet when taken seriously it changes the question entirely. Unlike the Death of God theologians who concluded that in the fiction (of Jesus) there lies some truth (about God in the world), the fallen theologian concludes the opposite: in the truth (of Jesus) lies the fiction (of God in the world). God is the fiction, not Jesus, and that is a very different point. The truth about the historical Jesus is that he created fiction. The truth-telling of the fallen theologian is that fiction is to be lived. The seriousness of the Death of God theologians, and with them the neo-orthodox seriousness about God, lies in their burdening of fiction with the pressing weight of truth. By contrast the fallen theologian is the theologian of lightness.

The simple but resolute decision for the humanity of Jesus inspires a second and major one: the very truth about the humanity of Jesus requires the fallen theologian to deny the fiction of Christ. This particular form of argumentation might be taken to mark a genuine break from Christianity, which after all is traditionally defined by a string of confessions about Jesus Christ, Lord, Son of God, Saviour, risen from the dead, etc. But the Christ image is thematic or a-historical; and being first and foremost a confession, it has little to do with reality. "Christ" is primarily an heroic figure, and as an image has far more in common with ancient (and modern) hero worship than it does with life. Neither does it take long to display Christ as both myth conveying and life denying. Here we can rely on two monumental thinkers whom theologians too seldom consider: Carl Jung and Joseph Campbell.

It was Jung who developed the notion of the archetype, a defining example or primary pattern for certain traits, virtues, and vices. Of particular
interest is Jung's "hero," an extremely powerful image that embodies cultural ideals. Among other things, Jung associated the hero with restoration
(salvation), self-sacrifice, vindication, innocent suffering, and retribution.
He saw that "[t]hrough the [hero's] act of deliverance what was inert and
dead comes to life."[13] Naturally it is easy to point to heroic acts in the Bible,
whether by Jesus or the Prophets or God. Jung liked the Greek phrase in
Acts 3:21 ("restoration of all") that he claimed indicates an early Christian
motif of God as a cosmic hero. Meanwhile, the heroic image that seems
almost universally present is the slaying of a sea monster or serpent (the
Bible's Leviathan), of which Isaiah 27:1 is an excellent example. The image
of slaying a "beast" in one form or another is everywhere: Egypt, Sumer,
Greece, Rome, and virtually all other ancient cultures including aboriginal
nations of North America. Here we see not one group copying another, but
rather the common hope of chaos being defeated and life triumphant over
death. Joseph Campbell called the cycle of heroic narrative a "cosmogonic
cycle" and claimed it was present with "astonishing consistency" on all
continents.[14] It is simply impossible to deny, unless we simply refuse to see,
that the Christian Christ is the heroic transmogrification of the historical
Jesus. Jesus as the Christ is Jesus as an epic. Even if Crossan is right to say
that the Christian epic is exceptional because it concerns a Galilean peasant set against the normalcy of Roman "civilized" violence, we are still left
with a bitter conclusion. Casting Jesus in an anti-Roman epic that borrowed
the language of Roman imperial theology was early Christianity's mistake.
In place of parable and humanity the Church offered splendor and impe-
rialism. Jesus remained buried somewhere under Christ, but no amount
of academic apology or justice-language defence can liberate his memory
from that weight. The historical Jesus was neither the Christ who appeared
in opposition to Caesar nor the Christ whom Christianity converted into
Caesar. The historical Jesus is the memory of a voiceprint available to who-
ever has ears to hear.

To a fallen theologian, an heroic Christ may be an admirable figure, but
cannot appear in human form; even Campbell was aware of the impasse.
When an historical being is swallowed by an epic, the person is dehuman-
ized and becomes an archetype. The historical individual is now "the whole
meaning of the universe";[15] and although we could argue that the "whole
meaning of the universe" is in all of us (for we are all children of the universe), that claim cannot fall within the purview of history. The fallen theologian, as I imagine him or her, gives up the fiction of Christ for the voice
of the historical Jesus, abandons the infinite for the finite, and renounces
the epic for the parable.

To a fallen theologian, the epic and the parable are at loggerheads. Indeed, an epic superimposed on a parable destroys it, for the interpretive force of the epic is allegory. And as allegory, the epic deploys the forms of another world, the world of transcendental ideals represented in both characters and settings. The parable, on the other hand, employs metaphors taken from common life to subvert the common view of life. A police officer is supposed to give directions, a father is supposed to be a paragon of respectability, a Samaritan is supposed to be an enemy. But in Kafka and Jesus, characteristic expectations are transformed without leaving this world. Instead of giving directions, a policeman denies the meaningfulness of life; a father responds to a wayward son with traditional maternal behaviors (worries, runs, hugs, kisses, feeds); and a Samaritan, a despised enemy, saves the life of an unfortunate Judean traveller. Interpreting these images according to epic protocols would transform them from metaphor to archetype. The elusive nature of a parable is lost: the archetype becomes its default interpretation. That is exactly the temptation to which gospel writers and Christian preachers surrender: the prodigal child is the archetypical human sinner, the traditional father is the archetypical divine Lord, and the banquet at the end of the prodigal story is the archetypical heavenly promise. For centuries the epic gospel of Christ was Christianity's message, but from my perspective after the fall it seems more like Christianity's blunder.

In short, Christ is an epic image that has converted the historical Jesus into an allegory. Those who pursue this interpretive path have to look into the Christ fiction for a truth, some truth that can make the crucifixion more than tragedy and the title "Son of God" more than a joke. Here, of course, I am being somewhat critical of Crossan's *God and Empire*, a book I admire; but the belief that Christianity can be reformed by the rectification of Jesus' names seems to me misdirected. Increasingly, the challenge of the historical Jesus involves leaving Christianity—letting the dead bury the dead—for the vision of the parabolic world. This vision, however, cannot be achieved as long as Christ remains the confessional truth of a serious religion named Christianity. The claim of the fallen theologian is that all the seriousness in the world misses the point, for a parable is about the lightness of being that arrives when life is reconceived as fiction.

Parables start with the serious or default world but, unlike an allegory, stretch the default world into another truth. In effect, a parable uses fiction to change reality. Allegory, on the other hand, poses the default world as a series of clues to a deeper level of reality, a world of transcendental ideals. That essentially Platonic modality informed much early Christian theology and has persisted into the present. Nor have progressive Christians significantly changed the picture, for the touted new Christianity often remains encumbered by promises of salvation and fictions of Christ and God—combined with a few inoculations of modern truth. But the fallen theologian, with the historical Jesus, opts for the parable. The parable breaks truth into fiction, and this is its grace, its call to awaken.

The default world, and with it default theology, are unreal in the parabolic framework because they try to be too real: they turn the parable back into allegory by exchanging common reality for the transcendental ideal. The ideal, as Don Cupitt reminds us, is then posed as the hidden "really real" against the pale shadow of the obvious but "falsely real" world. In the parables of Jesus, the whole thing works differently.[16] The real world takes us to the edge of itself, to the place where the vision is not an ideal but an alternative. There is no pretence here and no hidden agenda. Once the fallen theologian returns his or her feet to the ground, the curtain of allegory is parted and parable reveals the world as it is. Surprisingly, the content of the revelation can be anything, provided the truth of the matter is fiction. To live one's life fully is to live it as fiction. That's the inherent paradox of the parable but also its remarkable promise. One does not have to be the default Samaritan or the default police officer. The option to change is not a mystery but a simple step sideways—or perhaps a leap, as Kierkegaard might say. The Samaritan moves off the well-trodden path of social prejudice. Can the hearer of the parable do the same? The police officer cashes in the role of authority for a gesture of wisdom. It happens all the time, but still can the hearer do the same? The challenge in parable is to recreate the world out of the truth it presently is. The parable is not the dream of an unreal world, but an invitation to live at the edge of the world you are in. My bet is that only the fallen theologian can live up to the challenge of the parable because only the fallen theologian has nothing to lose.

The Practice of the Fallen

"We must begin by giving Jesus a demotion," Bob Funk declared. "He asked for it, he deserves it, we owe him no less."[17] If the first priority of a fallen theologian is to affirm a strictly human Jesus, then it is evident that the second priority is for Jesus to fall too. That is his demotion. It gives him back his humanity.

Why has it been difficult even for the scholars of the Jesus Seminar to give Jesus a demotion? The reason, I suggest, is that the death of Jesus gets in the way. There must be a reason why he died. A regular theologian is bound to feel that a lack of explanation here will leave a void in argument that needs to be filled. Jesus must have had a program or been a prophet or thought the world was about to end. Somehow, he threatened Roman authorities to such a degree that an example needed to be made of him.

But the fallen are free from a needed explanation, for, like the Q people, they find the point in the voice of Jesus and not his death.[18] We forget, after all, that hundreds of thousands were crucified in Roman times—and often enough, no doubt, as a result of mistaken identity. It could be that novelist Nino Ricci is right in concluding that the crucifixion of Jesus was a matter of being in the wrong place at the wrong time.[19] A fallen theologian, therefore, must ask whether Jesus is to be followed because he died. That would be epic rather than historical reasoning. Is not the better option to follow Jesus because he lived? If so, then the focus returns to the gifts of his life: aphorisms and parables. E. P. Sanders was right to say that at this level Jesus is not unique,[20] but he overlooked the crucial fact that at this level Jesus is unequivocally human.

One other element should be mentioned before we examine several aspects of Jesus following—the fallen route—which is distinct from Christ confessing, the traditional Christian route. Unlike Gautama who was called Buddha, Jesus who was called Christ did not live very long. Gautama lived approximately 80 years and left behind him an established *sangha* or association with well-tried rules of practice. The historical Jesus had no such luck. Like John the Baptist, he died too early to develop any lasting organization. Concerning his brief career, Bob Funk made another important point: he left only fragments to work with.[21] Too quickly the organization that developed after Jesus created his epic status by attaching to his peasant garments royal insignias and to his common name imperial titles. Confessing Jesus Christ as Son of God, Redeemer, and Lord in the Roman Empire context, as Crossan says, may be "low lampoon or high treason" (personally, I choose lampoon), but in either case the confessions are not the teaching of Jesus.[22] The parables are teachings that play with reality, stretching it somewhat out of shape, but not allowing it to escape from the world into the realm of ideals; they open a path to re-imagined life. The fragments that echo the voice of Jesus do not offer a great deal, but they do give parable.

The main practice of Jesus following is to understand oneself un-seriously. That statement is based on the surprises found in the parables: most figures or acts, despite appearances, are not what they ought to be. Parables give their actors a type of self-government—they express or carry out the unexpected. They do things that ordinary persons of the same status or in the same situation would not think to do. That's the autonomy of the parable form. A dinner party is a party of nobodies, for those invited do not show up; the mustard weed is given the characteristics of a cedar tree; a loser son comes home to a winner's celebration. If one tries to explain the parable too precisely, the vision is lost. Comedy is a necessary ingredient, but it comes only when one is freed from the seriousness of self and world and thereby enabled to see for the first time the strangeness of the usual.

Many complain that it is impossible to formulate a definite picture of the historical Jesus. The argument is well worn: the evidence is so slim that our methods of investigation invariably create the historical Jesus rather than find him. The fallen theologian cannot solve this problem but only play with it. The very situation is indeed a type of parable. Yet what if instead of seeking the specific meaning of every parable, we simply admit that Jesus used them? Would not his use of parables say something about the spirit of the one who employed them? Since such elusive vignettes are readily misinterpreted, someone who uses parable as a form of teaching cannot be a literalist. His aim must be at generating a new level of consideration. As Northrop Frye once remarked, to answer a question directly is to support the foundation upon which the question is asked. A direct answer to a question is good if the question concerns how to get to a local restaurant or other destination. But if the question concerns life, a teacher fails a student if the answer only confirms prejudices implicit in the question. The point of teaching is to invoke wonder (which is the main ingredient in the art of wisdom), and the parable form is indeed highly suited to this task. The fact that Jesus used parable says something about him as a teacher. He did not make proclamations and surely did not have a specific program. Jesus and Gautama employ elusive and allusive teaching methods because their point is not program but enlightenment. According to Mark 4:12, Jesus said he taught in parables so that people wouldn't understand him. The Jesus Seminar voted that saying black, but it strikes me that only a true teller of parables could come up with a response like that!

In the parable world the main thing is not to be direct. The default reality is not allowed to dictate, but only to serve as an access point to re-assessed living. In the parable world, a winner isn't a winner and a loser isn't a loser; the sense of that dichotomy is overturned. The sower is a failure who does not fail (Mark 4:3–8); the steward is a fired person whose advantage is that he was fired (Luke 16:1–8a); a woman finds emptiness when setting down what had been a full jar (Thomas 97). The essence of parable is that it says more than its narrative content and thereby reflects an attitude toward or a way of envisioning life. Parable is the gleam in the eyes of those who see life afresh; it is the practice of life as art. That Jesus told parables says at least this much about Jesus: his teaching was not discursive, directive, or specific. For a fallen theologian who remains a Jesus follower this is permission enough to change from confessing the status of Christ to adopting the technique of Jesus.

The practice of the fallen is to hold to qualities of life rather than specific directives for living. Admittedly the qualities are elusive, indefinite, and somewhat comical. They involve a refusal to see the world in the packaging of class or privilege or wealth, but instead to employ the liberty of transformation. The fallen take things as they are, for that's the only place where the journey can begin. But in life as in parable, what is, is also what is to be created. If life is not taken personally, if social standing is not taken seriously, if the truth is not taken definitively, then the world can be taken parabolically. That is the challenge of the historical Jesus. To be sure, it is the challenge for the fallen who refuse to confess, but for the confessors who refuse to fall it is only a parable.

"Why such reluctance? If you only followed the parables you yourselves would become parables and with that rid of all your daily cares. Another said: I bet that is also a parable. The first said: You have won. The second said: But unfortunately only in parable. The first said: no, in reality: in parable you have lost."[23]

Notes

1. Kafka, *Complete Stories*, 456.

2. Hall, *Lighten Our Darkness*, 43.

3. Funk, *Just Call Me Bob*, 163.

4. Rauschenbusch, *Christianity and the Social Crisis*, 65.

5. Rauschenbusch, 139.

6. Barth, *Epistle to the Romans*, 28.

7. Bultmann, *Jesus Christ and Mythology*, 17.

8. Tertullian, *De Carne Christi*.

9. Altizer and Hamilton, *Radical Theology and the Death of God*, 20.

10. Hamilton, *A Quest for the Post-Historical Jesus*, 20.

11. Jesus as the enigma and stranger of history is Albert Schweitzer's conclusion in 1906, and Hamilton repeats it almost as if nothing of substance has since occurred, *A Quest for the Post-Historical Jesus*, 18.

12. Hamilton, *A Quest for the Post-Historical Jesus*, 19.

13. Jung, *Psychological Types*, 263.

14. Campbell, *Hero with a Thousand Faces*, 39.

15. Campbell, 386.

16. See, for example, Cupitt, *Radical Theology*, 115–20 and *Is Nothing Sacred?* 33–45.

17. Funk, *Honest to Jesus*, 306.

18. The Q Document, which consists of the sayings common to Matthew and Luke, does not have a passion narrative. In fact, it makes virtually no reference to the death of Jesus. For the importance of the voiceprint, the best review is Bob Funk's *Honest to Jesus*, especially pages 158–63. For commentary on Q and the Q community, the technical but important books for me have been Kloppenborg, *The Formation of Q*, and Vaage, *Galilean Upstarts*.

19. Ricci, *Testament*. This novel develops an interpretation of Jesus from the vantage point of his various followers, but the crucifixion of Jesus follows from an arrest in the temple courtyard that occurs in the midst of a mix up (416–17).

20. Sanders, *Jesus and Judaism*, 319–20.

21. See Introduction to Funk, *A Credible Jesus*.

22. Crossan, *God and Empire*, 141.

23. Kafka, *Complete Stories*, 457.

Works Consulted

Altizer, Thomas J. J., and William Hamilton. *Radical Theology and the Death of God*. New York: The Bobbs-Merrill Company, 1966.

Barth, Karl. *Community, State, and Church*. Gloucester: Peter Smith, 1968.

——. *The Epistle to the Romans*. New York: Oxford University Press, 1976.

Barth, Karl, and Emil Brunner. *Natural Theology*. London: The Centenary Press, 1946.

Bultmann, Rudolph. *Jesus Christ and Mythology*. New York: Charles Scribner's Sons, 1958.

Campbell, Joseph. *The Hero with a Thousand Faces*. Princeton: Princeton University Press, 1973.

Crossan, John Dominic. *God and Empire*. New York: HarperSanFrancisco, 2007.

Cupitt, Don. *Radical Theology: Selected Essays*. Santa Rosa, CA: Polebridge Press, 2006.

——. *Is Nothing Sacred?* New York: Fordham University Press, 2002.

Funk, Robert W. *A Credible Jesus*. Santa Rosa, CA: Polebridge Press, 2002.

——. *Honest to Jesus*. New York: HarperSanFrancisco, 1996.

——. *Just Call Me Bob*. Ed. Andrew D. Scrimgeour. Santa Rosa, CA: Polebridge Press, 2007.

Frye, Northrop. *The Great Code*. Toronto: Academic Press, 1982.

Hall, Douglas John. *Lighten Our Darkness*. Philadelphia: Westminster Press, 1976.

Hamilton, William. *A Quest for the Post-Historical Jesus*. London: SCM Press, 1993.

Jensen, Robert W. "Karl Barth," *The Modern Theologians*. Ed. David F. Ford. Cambridge: Blackwell Publishers, 1997.

Jung, Carl. *Psychological Types*. Princeton: Princeton University Press, 1977.

Kafka, Franz. *The Complete Stories*. New York: Schocken Books, 1976.

Kloppenborg, John S. *The Formation of Q*. Philadelphia: Fortress Press, 1987.

Rauschenbusch, Walter. *Christianity and the Social Crisis*. New York: Macmillan Company, 1907.

Ricci, Nino. *Testament*. Scarborough, ON: Doubleday Canada, 2002.

Sanders, E. P. *Jesus and Judaism*. Philadelphia: Fortress Press, 1985.

——. *The Historical Figure of Jesus*. London: Penguin Books, 1992.

Tertullian. *De Carne Christi*. "On the Flesh of Christ." http//:www.earlychristianwritings.com.

Vaage, Leif E. *Galilean Upstarts*. Valley Forge, PA: Trinity Press International, 1994.

Min(d)ing God

Darren J. N. Middleton

Introduction

"Faith" is the word I use to describe how and why people construe the world theistically. I am a person of faith, someone who calls himself "Christian" actually, and from this position I practice disciplined theological inquiry to articulate my sense that life mediates God-in-Christ. In my judgment theological analysis amounts to the unblinking scrutiny of God, and the many makers and re-makers of the Christian theological tradition would seem to support this approach. On this view, "Christian theology" is an imaginative, thoughtful attempt to grasp the significance of God's gracious Self-Offer through Jesus of Nazareth. The burden of this essay is to show how such an understanding informs my faith profile. I must confess that after many years teaching in the academy and serving in the church, it is God, not Jesus, who remains my mind's real focus and my persistent spiritual concern. Talking about God makes sense to me, at least sometimes, and I want to show how. In this way I hope to contribute to this book's overall aim of illustrating how various scholars comprehend, and even recast, the old traditions in the contemporary world.

After outlining how I see theology's nature and task, I propose three criteria for evaluating different models of divinity, and show how such criteria apply to the way I speak of God, namely, as One marked by "process" and "relationality." I abandoned *classical theology* many moons ago, disquieted by its strangely unmovable divinity, and these days I uphold *process theology* or *process panentheism*, which accentuates the interconnectedness of an evolving God and our emerging world. I find this way of thinking compelling, at least for now, because it incorporates the divine as an integral part of a contemporary scientific understanding of the cosmos, and it thus takes its place in a long line of liberal apologetic systems. Unlike most Christians who sympathize with process theology, however, I have tried to move beyond its explicitly rationalistic approach to God. Metaphysical speculation takes me only so far. I prefer subtle or intuitive thinking rather than precise or nonfigurative thinking, and this explains why I have spent the last decade studying how "the process God" appears in poetry, short fiction, novels, and memoir. Subtle or intuitive thinking tends to celebrate the way literary devices, or tropes, help us to see the world—imprecisely, ambiguously, yet creatively and open-endedly. Using this approach I have spent the last decade addressing the process theology of Nikos Kazantzakis. I conclude my profile of faith with some concrete examples of how literature influences my own evolving theology and spirituality.

Digging Theology

A coal-miner's son from the English East Midlands, I came to the Christian faith at a youth revival held slightly north of Nottingham's city center, autumn 1982. I had recently turned 16. Like October's furious winds that raged against the night outside, the charismatic Methodist preacher spun around the stage in front of us, proclaiming theological truths—God's sovereignty, our original sin, the substitutionary theory of the atonement, and an imminent judgment—that made sense back then. I felt convicted. And so I got up from the pew and walked to the front of the church, prayed the sinner's prayer, and then invited Jesus to come into my heart. Behind the scenes I met with a man whose kindness I have not forgotten, even if his name eludes me today. He advised me to find a faith community, one that would help me take my first steps on the discipleship road; I joined the Mansfield Road Baptist Church two days later. From there I asked the questions that would make any self-respecting Non-Conformist, Free Church Christian proud: Does God speak through the Bible? Is it possible to have an event that is religiously true but not historically true? What is the heart of the Christian message? Several congregants soon took me aside and put me on to Rudolf Bultmann, one of the last century's finest New Testament critics, and a fresh life unfurled before my eyes.

Not everybody at Mansfield Road was pleased with my new direction. Before I left Nottingham to attend a Baptist theological seminary in Manchester, for example, I preached one last time. Shortly after the service, and in full view of several deacons, a man called Jack approached and begged me to listen to his "word from the Lord." Briefly, he informed me that God was using him to warn me of the perils of formal study. The essence of the gospel, according to Jack, is not found by reading and thinking theologically, but in the feeling and experience of "being redeemed" by the person and work(s) of Jesus Christ. Our minds cannot stretch as far as *reasoning* about a holy, saving presence, he said. For believers like Jack, the kingdom of God is an intensely personal issue. And to live by its light requires a confident profession of belief. Thus, it is little wonder that such folk declare: "I do not have a theology; I have a faith." Like Desiderius Erasmus, the fifteenth-century Dutch satirist, they have a sense that "it would be better to pass silently over the theologians . . . they attack me with six hundred arguments and force me to retract what I hold, for if I refuse, they will immediately declare me a heretic."[1]

In retrospect reading theology has worked wonders for me. I would not be half the man I am today without appreciating, say, *The Prayers and Meditations of Saint Anselm*, especially the way it indicates that faith and reason are part and parcel of our universe. Then there's Søren Kierkegaard, the nineteenth-century Danish Lutheran who, throughout his writings, but especially in *Philosophical Fragments*, speaks to me of truth and subjectivity. We cannot confine our existence in a merely rational system, he says; instead, we must look to our own experiences as a drama out of which to fashion our way of talking about God. After reading Anselm and Kierkegaard, I cannot *not* think for myself. Because of them, and others, like the English radical theologian Don Cupitt, I remain committed to posing those questions whose answers do not come easily, if they come at all. Cupitt's book *Taking Leave of God* repays close attention, particularly for the way it problematizes our apparent need to speak of God in objective or cosmic terms.

Independent thinking is but one way, albeit an urgent, unending way, to make sense of the old traditions in our contemporary world. The history of Christian thought is not something I downplay or ignore; for me, there is much in its deep, rich veins to unearth—multiple models of God to mull over, contrasting Christologies to contemplate, different dimensions of discipleship to discuss, and so on. I never went down into the mines to work for a living, like my Dad, but I like to think I am mining in my own way, quarrying Christianity and digging (for) theology.

Theology's Nature and Task

When I attended university, Karl Rahner's "transcendental Thomism" pulsated at the heart of several classes I took. And I am as fond of it today as I was when I first encountered it. Very generally, Rahner declares that an inquiry into the characteristics of our existence yields the basis for talking about God. Our primary trait is something he calls "spirit" or "openness," and the initial elements of such are

> . . . the experience of infinite longings, of radical optimism, of unquenchable discontent, of the torment of the insufficiency of everything attainable, of the radical protest against death, the experience of being confronted with an absolute love precisely where it is lethally incomprehensible and seems to be silent and aloof . . . these elements are in fact tributary to that divine force [God] which impels the created spirit [us]—by grace—to an absolute fulfilment.[2]

These "elements" constitute the "supernatural existential," Rahner says, for they are aspects of our lives (hence, "existential") that do not explain themselves; instead, they both originate in and point toward some transpersonal or trans-historical ("supernatural") source. Being human involves sensing that life raises questions (*fragwürdigheit*); and as finite, questing spirits thirsting for meaning and value, we exist within an infinite horizon that, for primordial reasons, Rahner calls "God." We are inescapably religious because we are both constituted by and directed toward an all-embracing Mystery. My Texas Christian University colleague, C. David Grant makes a similar point when he argues that we are hard wired for meaning. And on this view, theology represents an attempt to grasp what it means to live in light of such Mystery.

All theologies are constructive activities. Those who commit themselves to grasping God often use their own experiential and conceptual building blocks to make sense of the world around them. Religious theorist Mark C. Taylor puts it this way: "*What* one thinks is deeply conditioned by *where* one thinks."[3] In other words, theologians habitually use their society's cultural resources, and commonly find ways to forge links between their everyday lives and talk of God. Consider how and why the Church Fathers turned to Greek philosophy—*the* intellectual material in their own day—to assist them with those problems that had no evident solution in Scripture (for additional details see Evans, *The First Christian Theologians*). And ponder last century's liberal theological emphasis on "enculturation," that is, the notion that people always read, think, and understand from their particular place on the planet. Then mull over the many and diverse ways enculturation has inspired new theologies (Latin and South American liberation theology, feminist theology, Asian theology, womanist theology, and so on) that have emerged to dispute Christian theology's so-called Western, white, and male default mode. Last century's theological thought is a bewildering field of study for the beginner. I recommend Ford and Muers, *Modern Theologians* (esp. pp. 427–552).

Sometimes such constructive theologies resemble cathedrals of the mind, and sometimes they take the shape of mental meeting-houses—either way, whether they are ordinary or extraordinary, all theologies are humanly constructed, and in time they often find themselves subject to deconstruction and reconstruction. Sallie McFague puts it like this:

> Theological constructions are "houses" to live in for awhile, with windows partly open and doors ajar; they become prisons when they no longer allow us to come and go, to add a room or take one away—or if necessary, to move out and build a new house.[4]

This fate is understandable. After all, if theologies are not divinely revealed but, rather, bubble up from our own, frequently quite precise and always shifting cultural contexts, then all theologies are subject to change as we are subject to change.

In light of this understanding that theology is a form of imaginative, human construction, I want to acknowledge certain characteristics as appropriate to theology's work, although they are not always seen in that light. By working with the sense that all theologies are shaped by our contexts, it seems appropriate to view *tentativeness* as a proper characteristic of our God-talk. As the fallible, human attempt both to understand and respond to the Transcendent Mystery, theologies are best seen as provisional and partial. They do not offer direct windows onto reality; they are not final Truths. "Religious and theological integrity is possible as and when discourse about God *declines the attempt to take God's point of view* (i.e. a 'total perspective')," Archbishop Rowan Williams says.[5]

In being partial and provisional, theologies are also *inadequate*. They can reflect only our understanding at any one time. But this observation need not entail that all theologies are merely useless, self-indulgent fictions. Indeed, perhaps theological understanding needs something comparable to "critical realism" in the philosophy of science. The critical realist recognizes, for instance, that scientific models emerge from our mind's creativity and are, as a result, best seen as open-ended, exploratory yet serious candidates for reality. Such is the case with the so-called "string theory" for making sense of everything. Likewise, theological models may be viewed as reality depicters without our ever having to view them as literally true. The perceived inadequacy of any theological model highlights both the anthropological character of theological construction, and the need for further responsible, but again contextual, theologizing to prevent the initial model becoming irrelevant at best and idolatrous at worst.

We can deal with such potential irrelevance and idolatry by stressing theology's *revisability*. When we problematize our own profiles of faith and question the beliefs of others, we insure that no *one* theological model prevails. Revising our faith through regular and candid inquiry enables us, at least on this view, to uphold the Transcendent Mystery's complexity; and it recognizes, perhaps even celebrates, the many and varied ways in which people construe the world theistically.

I seek continually to ensure that my own constructed theology, my profile of faith if you will, models these characteristics. That said, there remains one other item that I consider integral to the theologian's vocation: practical human needs are an extremely important criterion for the selection of certain theologies, or models of God, at any particular time. Let me elaborate on this issue with reference to the work of Gordon D. Kaufman, one of America's leading theologians. He notes in several places, for instance, that we need to re-conceive the concept of God in light of the nuclear age in which we now find ourselves. Kaufman finds fault—rightly, in my view—with the two main models of God associated with what he calls "apocalyptic fundamentalism." One model suggests that a nuclear war—if one were to happen—would be God's supreme will for history's end. And we would be required, on this view, to accept the fallout in faith. Another model proposes that even if we rebel against God, and sinfully wage nuclear war against each other, God can, nevertheless, be relied upon to intervene in the world and exercise God's providential care to avert global destruction. Kaufman questions the practical implications of such "nuclear eschatology" and claims that while such models uphold the traditional notion of God's sovereignty, they do so by severing the "nerve of human responsibility" for our planet's health.[6] Notice how human needs—nothing less than our survival in fact—inspire Kaufman's remarks. He knows, as many of us do, that all theological models feature a valuational component—they affect our actions, foster our feelings, and shape our sentiments. And Kaufman favors those ways of thinking about God and life that nurture a relational vision—one where the divine and human beings are seen as co-creators in developing new possibilities for human togetherness, ecological sensitivity, and conversion to the love of God. An ecological sensitivity is essential to a well-rounded theological model; for theologies ought to be judged according to how far and to what extent they satisfy the "practical human needs" criterion of truth. If truth be told, we are part of nature, and creation's need is our need.

These days I think our models of God are related to human need, and I therefore sympathize with Kaufman's approach; but to guard ourselves against the accusation that our theologies are based *only* on the needs they address, I also think we should introduce additional criteria for assessing the adequacy of talk about God. In addition to the pragmatic criterion, which we might call the criterion of *existential fruitfulness*, I propose two others. And in the next section I outline what they are and how I employ them to commend what is, for me, today's most promising relational vision, namely, process theology. Process theology (also described as process-relational theology or process panentheism) is a branch of modern theological inquiry. Its origins and at least one of its central tenets are explained in the following section, but a full explanation falls outside the scope of this paper.

Evaluating God-Talk

First, the criterion of *critical plausibility* judges our theologies on their ability to provide a coherent and reasonable fit with our understanding of reality in general. In other words, does our God-talk take seriously our world-talk? On this view theologies fail when they overlook or resist the major turning points in our understanding of how life goes. And second, the criterion of *theistic relevance* recognizes that any model of God must have religious value, where religious value denotes a model's "power to express and enhance reverence or worship on a high ethical and cultural level."[7] A model of God becomes theistically relevant, in other words, when it upholds the worshipfulness of the divine; for this is, arguably, where God's real power exists, namely, in the adoration and love God inspires.

Now, I think something like *fundamentalism* fails, at least with recourse to the aforementioned criteria, because (a) it neglects or demonizes evolutionary theory, and thus seems ill-fitted to current models for explaining reality; and (b) it sponsors a spirituality of fear, even timid obsequence, for its God comes across as an officious Celestial Ethicist who lays down a fixed and unalterable code for us to follow unthinkingly; and (c) its vision of a predisposing God, who determines our universe's every cosmic detail, especially its imminent final judgment, undercuts our creativity. Despite my impressionistic sketch of fundamentalism's beliefs and practices, I do take fundamentalism seriously, as should every thoughtful Christian. Against fundamentalism's theological outlook, which I deem critically implausible, theistically irrelevant, and existentially fruitless, I favor process theology. It has been and continues to be an integral feature of my faith profile; let me outline how and why.

Emerging in the early decades of the last century in the philosophical writings of Alfred North Whitehead and Charles Hartshorne, process theology complains that traditional Christian theology remains yoked to the ancient Greek philosophical idea of the One and the Many, or permanence and change, and so presents God as the fixed and passionless Absolute. On this view whatever changes, decays, to state the issue briefly, and so the ancient Greeks not only equate change with imperfection, they think of the perfect God as changeless. Thomas Aquinas, the Scholastic theologian, embraces this logic and describes God as the Unmoved Mover—capable, that is, of initiating change in others but remaining unchanged in Godself. Such is traditional Christian theology's presiding model of God, and I have heard it preached in church and taught in the classroom, yet process theologians challenge it fiercely.[8] They point out that this Unmoved Mover remains essentially unrelated to us; and I agree. For me, authentic Christian theology speaks of God's love for our world, of faith as our response to the Divine Self-Offer, and it notes that both "love" and "faith" are relational and processive concepts.

We are not islands alone unto ourselves. Our actions matter or at least they ought to matter to every one of us. Think about it. We are not inflexible entities that trek unchanged through time. Rather, we are the many experiences and changes we have had; therefore, we are relational and processive. The same is true of God. And to say anything less horrifies me religiously. If our tears twirl humanity's water mills, for example, but fail to move God, then I find myself forced to wonder whether this passionless Absolute is really, truly worthy of our worship. In my faith profile, to put things succinctly, God is subject to change as we are subject to change. And so these days I think the divine is actually part of life's insubstantiality, and intimately involved within our world, sometimes to the point of being affected by what occurs within it. This position is sometimes called process panentheism, which should not be confused with *traditional theism* (as defined above) or *pantheism* (thinking of God *as* nature without remainder). Panentheism is the theory that God includes all created life *within* God's life. What happens to the world happens to God. American writer Annie Dillard puts it this way:

> [As] Rabbi Menachem Nahum of Chernobyl [said]: "All being itself is derived from God and the presence of the Creator is in each created thing." This double notion is pan-entheism—a word to which I add a hyphen to emphasize its difference from pantheism. Pan-entheism, according to David Tracy, theologian at the University of Chicago, is the private view of most Christian intellectuals today. Not only is God immanent in everything, as plain pantheists hold, but more profoundly everything is simultaneously in God, within God the transcendent. There is a divine, not just bushes.[9]

I commend process theology, or process panentheism, because it uses current understandings of the way the world goes—evolutionary theory—to form a new, critically plausible and theistically relevant God-talk. In process thought, that is, a processive conception of the divine, as opposed to a substantial model of God (i.e., the Eternal Absolute), more adequately grounds evolution, and may even inspire evolution's many world inhabitants both to proceed toward and adore Spirit. The valuational component in this theology—its existential fruitfulness, if you will—lies in the arresting notion that if the future is the future for God, not simply for us, then life itself is nothing less than an adventure of the spirit. American theologians Clark M. Williamson and Ronald J. Allen summarize the process vision as follows, and this statement best represents my own view:

> A process spirituality will seek to encourage people to enhance their God-given creativity and capacity to envision the new way in which God now calls us to walk. It will help people with the difficult intellectual and moral reflection involved in figuring out in what ways faithful people should understand and act in the situation in which it is given us to live. It will recognize that not all new possibilities are from God (novelty is not to be deified), but that some are. The good role that conservatives play is that of forcing the rest of us to test the case that is made on behalf of any given possibility. An authentic spirituality will provide for us the strength and reassurance to take the heat that comes from being willing to leave Ur of the Chaldees and venture forward with the God of the ahead.[10]

Being religious in a relational and processive world involves responding to the God who agitates, stimulates, and sways us in our restlessness by seeking creation's flourishing. Everything matters. And our awareness that our struggle to seek personal and systemic transformation, higher goals, and ever new possibilities truly matters to God can serve to foster our commitment to a lifestyle that nurtures and sustains human togetherness and ecological sensitivity. Genuine faith and its practical outworking, that is, spirituality, thus flows out of a discernment of the part we play as co-creators with the divine in the evolutionary process. And theology is the unblinking scrutiny of it all: Min(d)ing God.

God, Literature, and Process Theology

I've been using fiction as a lens through which to view and investigate God ever since I received my doctorate in literature and theology from the University of Glasgow in 1996. And I appreciate this approach not simply because it appeals to academics but because local church folk with whom I often work find it so fascinating. It's not hard to see why. Telling and hearing stories is as natural to us as breath and circulation of the blood. We all seem to love a good yarn. Here are two suggestions: I consider these two books the best of the many texts that have stimulated discussion whenever and wherever I have assigned them: Jack Miles, *God: A Biography* and Franco Ferrucci, *The Life of God (as Told by Himself)*.

I commend Jack Miles's *God: A Biography*, which won the Pulitzer Prize in 1996. This is not a work of fiction, to be sure, but its sparklingly clear and deeply evocative prose makes it feel like the best art. *God: A Biography* focuses on the Lord God as a literary character, the central protagonist who undergoes development and succession in the course of an extended story, the Hebrew Bible, and Miles offers excellent examples of how the many and varied scripture writers think of divinity in process:

> "Jesus Christ is the same yesterday and today and for ever," the New Testament reads at Hebrews 13:8; but that one late and questionable verse aside, there is virtually no warrant in the New Testament for any claim that God is immutable, and there is equally little in the Hebrew Bible. The origin of this view lies presumably in Aristotelian philosophy, with its view of God as the unmoved mover, existing in a single, eternal moment. True, the Lord God of Israel is the creator and ruler of time, and the Psalms delight in repeating that he lives forever. To that extent he is like Aristotle's unmoved mover. And yet, contradictory as this must seem, he also enters time and is changed by experience. Were it not so, he could not be surprised; and he is endlessly and often most unpleasantly surprised. God is constant; he is not immutable.[11]

Miles's provocative conclusion that God is a sort of cosmic Hamlet, internally divided, marked by ceaseless becoming and not static completeness, captures a book that displays real insight and, dare I say it, even Updikean panache. I am often unable to say the same of the weighty, ponderous process theological texts out there, even if some exceptions, such as the work of Lutheran theologian Ann Pederson, disprove the rule.

Although on the surface Franco Ferrucci's *The Life of God (as Told by Himself)* seems like a quirky novel in which God functions as an omniscient narrator of God's own story, one that charts the demise of the Divine from creator to semi-retirement in the celestial equivalent of West Palm Beach, its frequent flashes of narrative and theological artistry reveal an author struggling with a traditional model of God:

> It had already occurred to me [God] that my constant shuffling from one condition to another, from season to season and realm to realm, was a manifestation of my complex nature. In certain climates I would know only summer and long days, in others I would bury myself deep within icebergs. In a single day I would go from morning to noon, from afternoon to twilight, repeating the succession of childhood, youth, maturity, and old age. Everything mirrored my mutable character.[12]

At one point in Ferrucci's story, as God hurtles through time and takes respite during the Middle Ages, God seeks an interview with Aquinas who, by the time God meets him, "was already thinking about his arrival in the immutable realm of eternity, where a still and silent God would preside over a world motionless in its perfection."[13] Also, we are told that Aquinas encounters God during Mass in a Neapolitan church, and that "he [Aquinas] had finally seen me [God] for what I was, bustling and impatient, and at that moment his philosophical castle seemed to collapse before him."[14] Enlightening and amusing, particularly for the way it discusses God with a familiarity that in an earlier age would have been condemned, Ferrucci's novel transforms the way we think about the divine—as a very active verb, and not as a noun. Along with Miles's literary criticism, I commend *The Life of God (as Told by Himself)* for the way it brings "the process God" to life.[15]

Conclusion

Christian theology involves min(d)ing God—the unblinking scrutiny of whatever we quarry from Christianity's rich, deep veins of tradition. And this dual process is entirely democratic. All of us are invited to roll up our sleeves, mine the mother-lode, and pay close attention to what we unearth along the way. This is faith's word for us today; thanks be to God.

Notes

1. One of my undergraduate professors made this remark. While it certainly fits Erasmus's satirical tone, I have not had much luck locating it precisely.

2. Rahner, *Theological Investigations*, vol. 4, 183.

3. Taylor and Lammerts, *Grave Matters*, 40.

4. McFague, *Models of God*, 27.

5. Williams, *On Christian Theology*, 6.

6. Kaufman, *Theology for a Nuclear Age*, 8.

7. Hartshorne, *The Divine Relativity*, 1. This point is detailed in Williamson and Allen, *Adventures of the Spirit*, 61–88.

8. See Suchocki, *God-Christ-Church*, 3–45.

9. Dillard, *For the Time Being*, 176–77.

10. Williamson and Allen, *Adventures of the Spirit*, 60.

11. Miles, *God*, 12.

12. Ferrucci, *Life of God*, 16. Later, Ferrucci's God complains of being "disfigured" by those Greek philosophers who "set me on high, unseizeable and perfect, far from the world's cares" (100).

13. Ferrucci, *Life of God*, 188.

14. Ferrucci, *Life of God*, 189.

15. Numerous creative writers address process theological themes in their work. For a selection, see: Graham Greene, D. H. Lawrence, and David Lodge.

Works Consulted

Aquinas, Thomas. *Summa Theologica*. 5 vols. Notre Dame, IN: Christian Classics, 1981.

Anselm. *The Prayers and Meditations of Saint Anselm*. Harmondsworth, Middlesex: Penguin Books, 1973.

Bracken, Joseph A. *Christianity and Process Thought: Spirituality for a Changing World*. Philadelphia and London: Templeton Foundation Press, 2006.

Bowman, Donna, and Jay McDaniel, eds. *Handbook of Process Theology*. St. Louis, MO: Chalice Press, 2006.

Carlson, Paula J., and Peter S. Hawkins, eds. *Listening for God: Contemporary Literature and the Life of Faith*. 3 vols. Minneapolis, MN: Fortress, 1994, 1996, 1999.

Charry, Ellen T., ed. *Inquiring After God: Classic and Contemporary Readings*. Malden, MA: Blackwell Publishers, 2000.

Cobb, John B. Jr., and David Ray Griffen. *Process Theology: An Introductory Exposition*. Belfast: Christian Journals, 1976.

Cobb, John B. Jr., *Becoming a Thinking Christian*. Nashville, TN: Abingdon Press, 1993.

Cooper, John W. *Panentheism: The Other God of the Philosophers*. Grand Rapids, MI: Baker Academic, 2006.

Culbertson, Diana, ed. *Invisible Light: Poems about God*. New York: Columbia University Press, 2000.

Cupitt, Don. *Taking Leave of God*. London: SCM Press, 1980.

Curtis, C. Michael, ed. *Faith: Stories*. Boston and New York: Houghton Mifflin, 2003.

———, ed. *God: Stories*. Boston and New York: Houghton Mifflin, 1998.

Dillard, Annie. *For the Time Being*. New York: Knopf, 1999.

Evans, G. R., ed. *The First Christian Theologians: An Introduction to Theology in the Early Church*. Malden, MA: Blackwell Publishers, 2004.

Ford, David F., and Rachel Muers, eds. *The Modern Theologians: An Introduction to Christian Theology since 1918*. 3d ed. Malden, MA: Blackwell Publishers, 2005.

Ferrucci, Franco. *The Life of God (as Told by Himself)*. Chicago: The University of Chicago Press, 1996.

Geering, Lloyd. *Christianity without God*. Santa Rosa, CA: Polebridge Press, 2002 (esp. pp. 54–55 on panentheism).

Gnuse, Robert K. *The Old Testament and Process Theology*. St. Louis, MO: Chalice Press, 2000.

Grant, C. David. *A Theology of God's Grace: Life, Faith, and Commitment*. St. Louis, MO: Chalice Press, 2004.

Greene, Graham. *The Honorary Consul*. London: Book Club Associates, 1973.

Hick, John. *An Interpretation of Religion: Human Responses to the Transcendent*. New Haven: Yale University Press, 1989.

Hartshorne, Charles. *The Divine Relativity: A Social Conception of God*. New Haven: Yale University Press, 1948.

Jennings, Theodore W. Jr. *The Vocation of the Theologian*. Philadelphia, PA: Fortress Press, 1985.

Kaufman, Gordon D. *Theology for a Nuclear Age*. Manchester, England: Manchester University Press, 1985.

———. *The Theological Imagination: Constructing the Concept of God*. Philadelphia: The Westminster Press, 1981.

Kelly, Geffrey, ed. *Karl Rahner: Theologian of the Graced Search for Meaning*. Minneapolis, MN: Fortress, 1992.

Kierkegaard, Søren. *Philosophical Fragments*. Princeton: Princeton University Press, 1985.

Lawrence, D. H. *Lady Chatterley's Lover*. London: Penguin Books, 1990.

Leaves, Nigel. *The God Problem*. Santa Rosa, CA: Polebridge Press, 2006.

Lodge, David. *Paradise News*. London: Secker and Warburg, 1991.

Maney, J. P., and Tom Hazuka, eds. *A Celestial Omnibus: Short Fiction on Faith*. Boston: Beacon, 1997.

Marsden, George M. *Fundamentalism and American Culture: The Shaping of Twentieth-Century Evangelicalism, 1870–1925*. Oxford and New York: Oxford University Press, 1980.

McFague, Sallie. *Metaphorical Theology: Models of God in Religious Language*. London: SCM Press.

———. *Models of God: Theology for an Ecological, Nuclear Age*. London: SCM Press, 1987.

Middleton, Darren J. N., and Peter A. Bien, eds. *God's Struggler: Religion in the Writings of Nikos Kazantzakis*. Macon, GA: Mercer University Press, 1996.

Middleton, Darren J. N. *Broken Hallelujah: Nikos Kazantzakis and Christian Theology*. Lanham, MD: Lexington Books, 2007.

———, ed. *God, Literature and Process Thought*. Burlington, VT; Aldershot, Hampshire: Ashgate Publishing, 2002.

———, ed. *Scandalizing Jesus?: Kazantzakis's* The Last Temptation of Christ *Fifty Years On*. London and New York: Continuum, 2005.

———. *Novel Theology: Nikos Kazantzakis's Encounter with Whiteheadian Process Theism*. Macon, GA: Mercer University Press, 2000.

———. "Sing Praise with the Mind: Reflections of a Baptist Theologian-in-Residence." *Baptist History and Heritage* 37.2 (2002) 73–86.

Miles, Jack. *God: A Biography.* New York: Random House, 1995.

Muilenburg, Greg. "In Praise of Subtle Thinking." Pp. 38–56 in *Translucence: Religion, the Arts, and Imagination.* Eds. Carol Gilbertson and Greg Muilenburg. Minneapolis, MN: Fortress Press, 2004.

Pailin, David A. *God and the Processes of Reality: Foundations of a Credible Theism.* London and New York: Routledge, 1989.

———. *The Anthropological Character of Theology: Conditioning Theological Understanding.* Cambridge, England and New York: Cambridge University Press, 1990.

Pederson, Ann. *God, Creation and all that Jazz: A Process of Composition and Improvisation.* St. Louis, MO: Chalice Press, 2001.

———. *Where in the World is God? Variations on a Theme.* St. Louis, MO: Chalice Press, 1998.

Rahner, Karl. *Theological Investigations.* 4 vols. Trans. Cornelius Ernst. Baltimore, MD: Helicon Press, 1961.

Suchocki, Marjorie Hewitt. *God-Christ-Church: A Practical Guide to Process Theology.* New York: Crossroad, 1986.

Taylor, Mark C., and Dietrich Christian Lammerts. *Grave Matters.* London: Reaktion Books, 2002.

Whitehead, Alfred North. *Process and Reality: An Essay in Cosmology.* Corrected ed. Eds. David Ray Griffin and Donald W. Sherburne. New York and London: The Free Press, 1978.

Williamson, Clark M., and Ronald J. Allen. *Adventures of the Spirit: A Guide to Worship from the Perspective of Process Theology.* Lanham, MD: University Press of America, 1997.

Williams, Rowan. *On Christian Theology.* Malden, MA: Blackwell Publishers, 2000.

Wiles, Maurice F. *Faith and the Mystery of God.* London: SCM Press, 1982.

Coming to Jesus, Coming Through Jesus

Susan M. (Elli) Elliott

Introduction

As I come to this reflection, I am at a new crossroads in my faith. When I started to write this essay, I reflected on how my beliefs have unfolded since childhood. Over the years I have rejected various portions of the traditional language of the faith in which I was raised. Yet I find that each time I reject some part of the language of traditional faith, a deeper foundation emerges from that same faith. I am now in the midst of another reconsideration of my beliefs. The original title "Coming to Jesus" was meant to reflect a journey from a God-centered faith to an understanding of the faith centered in Jesus. The addition, "Coming Through Jesus," reflects a return to the God-centered faith I was blessed to receive as a child. I cannot offer you a list of my beliefs. I hope never to do so. A list of beliefs is not the nature of faith for me. I can only tell you about the spiral of the journey so far. What has become real for me is the deepening and widening of my faith, which is emerging just as the forces of life crack the seed's shell, as roots spread more deeply into the soil of history and into the far reaches of the soul, as life grows and strengthens in wisdom and courage in the light, and as fruit ripens for nourishment and seeds fall to begin again. Just so is the nature of my faith.

The headings for the different sections of this essay are themes that grow out of my spiraling faith journey as I explore a changing world. I offer no propositions to be voted on by the Fellows in order to record "what the Fellows really believe." This essay attempts only to track the unfolding story of my own faith. What I "really believe" is that truth is "embodied truth." That is to say, we tell the truth in a living narrative more fully than we can in propositional belief statements. What I "really believe" is that truth is never finished. There is always more truth unfolding. In other words, the truth we live counts more than the truth we think. This position is true to the tradition in which I was raised: as John Robinson said in his speech to the Pilgrims boarding the Mayflower, "The Lord hath yet more light and truth to break forth from His [sic] word." What I "really believe" is that truth unfolds in our telling and hearing together, and we are all part of its unfolding.

Bible

I cannot remember a time when I took the Bible literally. In childhood I was unaware of the issue of literalism as I learned the stories in liberal Christian congregations of the United Church of Christ where my father was minister. His Congregationalist mother had sent him off to college with a stern warning not to be deceived by the teaching of evolution. In his first semester, however, he took a biology course that convinced him that evolution was the most reasonable explanation of creation. When he met my mother, the process philosophy that she had learned in her American Baptist young adult discussions helped to reframe his thinking. In the congregations in which I was raised, ideas were interchanged in an accepting atmosphere that included Fundamentalists and conservatives along with many mainline liberals, as well as Unitarians, Friends, Mennonites, and others from the Christian stream.

Growing up in these United Church of Christ congregations, I absorbed as if by osmosis what I now recognize as a covenantal framework of biblical understanding. By "covenantal framework," I mean that the Bible mediates a dynamic relationship shared among several participants: our forbears in faith, the generations who will come after us, us in our own generation interpreting the Bible from different points of view, and the ultimately unknowable God who is present in all time and beyond time.

In this covenantal framework the preaching in worship, the church school teaching, and the study group discussions all assumed a historical-critical method of interpretation without labeling it as such. I recognize this orientation of the congregations only in retrospect, however. I knew that the Bible was a product of stories that people had told that were written down much later and collected. I knew these were stories worth hearing, thinking about, and then repeating. I knew the Bible contained poetic words of great beauty, and powerful parables, and set out in Jesus' life a challenging model for our lives. Whether or not it was "fact" was not much of an issue for me then. The Bible was part of an immense world of understanding of the unimaginably vast and ancient universe. The texts of the Bible were wonderful because they connected us short-lived humans with an ancient past spanning thousands of years. Yet, even the Bible's time span was short considering the time required for granite to form in the depths of the earth and to be lifted by slow geological processes into towering mountains.

Today, as a scholar, I find that the study of these texts is both an opportunity to explore in more depth how they began and evolved and an exercise in humility about what we can say for certain about them. Scholarly study has given me an ever deeper sense of reverence for this collection. Looking into the faces of third-graders while presenting them with Bibles on Bible Sunday, for example, I stand in awe. I think of the diversity of the collection and the thousands of years of an unfolding relationship with God to which these texts witness. I consider the different points of view reflected among the texts and the tales of terror that must be explained. I wonder at some of the distasteful images of God with which we must struggle. I ponder the violence and jealousy in these images and how these texts call us to deep acknowledgement of the full range of reality, human and divine. I remember the stories of betrayal and forgiveness that the texts contain, followed by more betrayal and consequences—and forgiveness. I recognize the messy process that has given us this particular set of texts as the canon, and appreciate the scribes who ruined their eyes and spent their lives copying and recopying these texts. I remember that people died to defend these texts in times of persecution. I respect the ability of common folk to read and interpret these texts in many different ways and to be challenged by them. I sense the transformative power present when we read and share these texts, the power that changes lives and changes the world. I pass out the books with reverence.

The more I know about the Bible, the deeper my understanding becomes, the more I hold the Bible in reverence, and the more I respect the variety of interpretations of all those hungry hearts approaching it with faith. Analytical study has deepened my apprehension of the sacredness of the mysteries we approach together through these writings. The mystery unfolds in a complex relationship traditionally called "covenant."

Covenant

The covenantal framework for interpreting the Bible is part of an understanding of faith itself as covenant more than as "belief." In the new church start in Montana in which I was raised, I do not recall repeating ancient creeds in worship. We learned the Statement of Faith of the United Church of Christ in confirmation, and occasionally recited it during worship. I also recall on one occasion re-enacting in Sunday school the debates leading to the Nicene Creed. We were not a "creedal church." Instead, following our Congregationalist tradition, we "owned" the covenant of our local church, Mayflower Congregational United Church of Christ of Billings, Montana. Founding members of the congregation composed the first stanza using models from other churches in the tradition of the Salem Church Covenant of 1629; the second stanza is from Eph 3:17–29. The Rev. Thomas Hall assisted me in recovering this text from the current constitution of the congregation. It has been updated with inclusive language. This covenant has been one of the most important guiding texts in my life and thought:

> Here before God and in God's holy presence, we covenant together to be
> a church in this place, a people of God and do solemnly bind ourselves to

God-in-Christ, and to each other, to walk faithfully and obediently as servants of Christ our Lord, in all his ways, made known or to be made known to us, through the blessed word of truth, whatever it shall cost us, the Lord assisting us.

May Christ live in our hearts through faith, that we, being rooted and grounded in the love of Christ, may have power to comprehend with all God's people what is the breadth and length and depth and height of the love of God, and to experience God's love, though it is beyond understanding.

Now to God who is able to do exceeding abundantly above all that we ask or think, according to God's power at work among us, to God be glory in the church by Jesus Christ throughout all ages, world without end. Amen.

Owning this covenant did not mean giving intellectual assent to a set of beliefs nor did it mean pledging allegiance to beliefs in a way that bound us to defend our beliefs from others' beliefs. Owning this covenant meant a holistic commitment to a way of life in community with one another and with God, a commitment to an ongoing exploration of our relationship as a community with God (i.e., following the covenant: "in all [God's] ways, made known or to be made known..." and "whatever it shall cost us"). Truth was something to be explored, lived, and celebrated with others, not something to be determined and possessed for one's own self-satisfaction. This local church covenant introduced me to life in covenant.

Life in covenant means a commitment having an acknowledged cost, a commitment to a different standard for our lives than the standard of life lived only for ourselves. I learned this as the way of discipleship, the way walked by followers of Jesus who knew the consequences of living in the way of the cross. A life-sized empty cross (the cross of the Reformed tradition) hung on the cement block wall of the sanctuary—which did double-duty as a fellowship hall—and it simultaneously symbolized the reality the Jesus' death on the cross and the resurrection power revealed through it.

As I came to adulthood, the cost of life in covenant became apparent in social struggles: for civil rights, against the Viet Nam war, for the protection of the environment, and for low-income housing. Our covenant meant we stood for something. We stood for a vision of life on earth rooted in God. How to work out that vision in practical day-to-day living, however, was always under discussion. I learned that covenant with God is more than "being a good person" and living an ethical life as a solitary individual. Covenant involves a commitment to life in community lived for the greater good, to something I now label "God's ongoing social project"; this project is that elusive vision Jesus proclaimed, which is traditionally translated as the "kingdom of God," the "imperial rule of God" or "God's power as it rules."

God

If we are in covenant with God, who or what is God? To speak of covenant as a relationship with God poses a logical difficulty. If we understand God as a Being-in-relationship, we cast God as a character in our human drama. By our use of language, we make God a member of our human society on some level, understandable on our terms. Life in covenant, however, makes us responsible for how we speak about God and how we relate to God. In a covenantal relationship that responsibility includes at least the other people and living beings on our planet. How we speak about God and how we include God in our social and environmental relationships affects others. Yet we form a relationship with God filtered through the language and images that others give us and through our very human experiences.

As a child of about four, I imagined God as an enormous male college student, perhaps fifteen feet tall, dressed in a long-sleeved blue and white striped T-shirt and sailor trousers. Later, in a first grade Sunday school class, we decided to draw pictures of God. In two short years my God had grown much larger; he had ascended into the sky, and aged. I drew him as a kindly old man whose billowy white beard was visible to us as the clouds. Another child in the class, Lynne Soper, drew a picture that helped me to see the God that I have known for the rest of my life. She drew a picture of mountains and flowers and houses—a whole page full of world. She showed it, saying, "None of these things is God, but God is here." I looked at my picture, looked at hers, and then I looked out the window realizing she had pointed me to the real God. After that, God was not, and still is not, a supernatural being, a deity made in a human image as "the guy upstairs." These human images of God emerge in our minds as we sing hymns, read the scriptures, and pray; but for me God's presence now is always more expansive, and cannot be contained in any one place or limited to any one image.

I was probably in second or third grade when I learned Christina Georgina Rossetti's poem "Who Has Seen the Wind?" It made a profound impression on me:

Who has seen the wind?
Neither I nor you:
But when the leaves hang trembling
The wind is passing thro'
Who has seen the wind?
Neither you nor I:
But when the trees bow down their heads
The wind is passing by.

I recall watching trees tossed in an autumn wind and thinking about this poem and considering how the evidence of God is seen in people who live reverently. Through the years God's presence was mediated to me in the lives of my teachers and mentors in the church. They helped me see the divine in the wonder and mystery of creation and the immense unfolding universe, in the love they showed one another, and in their concern and hard work for people beyond their own families and our church. They revealed God in their forgiving and understanding hearts, in the way they worshipped together, in their integrity as they stood up for the courage of their convictions, and as they sought the best even when fighting with each other. Dedicated teachers and youth leaders shared the presence of God in our intellectual discussions as they taught us about ecology and social justice, and introduced us to writers like Teilhard de Chardin and Loren Eiseley. They showed God in creative activities of all kinds and in the joy of potlucks and outbursts of silliness. Through these experiences, I came to know myself as one of those people-in-the-presence-of-God, and thus to know God's presence internally as well. In these experiences, I learned about life in covenant with God. Yet what or who is this God with whom we are in covenant?

Connecting to God

I speak to God as if God is a Being who can hear my words. In public worship and with people in times of crisis, such prayer evokes awareness of a Listening Presence. Perhaps this Presence is only an epiphenomenon of our joint attentiveness to the moment. Perhaps we are really only aware of one another all being aware together. Perhaps our joint listening creates the presence of a greater Listener. Nevertheless I know this Presence as a real Sacred Presence. I know this Presence as God. I choose to believe that this Sacred Presence is something more than a byproduct of human experience. I have no external demonstrable proof, however, only experiences of mystic apprehension. Even if this Listening Presence is "only" a socially constructed reality, we still do well to pay attention. When we listen to this Presence in individual or corporate silent meditation and in serious conversation with others, we hear and know that we are not alone. The Presence preceded us and will endure after us. That Presence is known in many different ways and attested to by many different religious traditions.

Attending an experimental college, Prescott College in Arizona, gave me an appreciation for the wide variety of responses to the Sacred Presence. Discussions with Baha'i friends showed me both the value of their community and, in contrast to their views, helped me to understand my own commitment to an open-ended view of time and the capacity of human beings to be co-creators with God. During an eye-opening internship in Denver, I temporarily took up with a community of followers of Sun Myung Moon and learned enough about them to take a much dimmer view of the motivations behind their religious community. I learned still more about responding to God from practitioners of Sufi mysticism and various kinds of yoga, from Catholic Pentecostals, and from participation in Spiritualist church services. On one occasion I experienced the instantaneous healing of a splitting headache lifted from my head by a faith healer's hand. That experience taught me not to limit my understanding of reality too narrowly. Readings from that time that continue to influence me are writings of Antoine de Saint-Exupéry, the poetry of Marge Piercy, and Hopi stories of their people's journey guided by the figure of *Gogyeng Sowuhti*, the spider grandmother. I learned meditation practices associated with creative movement, visual arts, and music that have been part of my experience of Sacred Presence, with and without Christian symbolism. These varied experiences convince me of access to the transformative potential of parts of our consciousness not usually engaged during our regular daily activity.

A primary connection to God also emerges in activist practice. "Praxis" is the simultaneous process of world transformation and personal transformation. Our praxis shapes our connection to and understanding of Sacred Presence. My understanding of "praxis" comes from Karl Marx's deceptively simple *Theses on Feuerbach*. To use these little guideposts for a transformation of thought does not imply being "Marxist" in a political sense. The concept of praxis challenges us, however, to think relationally rather than in our personalized and individualistic patterns, and to live from a more holistic perspective. Consciously and intentionally living out of the "kingdom of God" means living in Covenant with God, knowing ourselves relationally, and thinking critically about the world and our role in it. Living covenantally is itself a way of life and a spiritual practice, a call to transform the world and to be transformed in the process. It is the spiritual practice I choose.

I worked for a while as a community organizer in Arkansas. After organizing drives in several locations, I began to realize that the activity of community organizer was more like selling an organization door-to-door than organizing a community. I realized that I did not want to promote this vision of community. One afternoon I sat in my tiny rented aluminum trailer home by a chicken plant and wrote about the kind of community I wanted to be organizing. I described a lifelong learning community that stood for peace and justice, and that included people equally regardless of their social status. As I wrote, I came to recognize simultaneously both the church that had raised me and my own call to ministry.

So, inspired by the heady mix of liberation movements in the mid-70s, I attended seminary in Chicago, where I participated in a "reflection group" comprised of students from several Chicago seminaries who were working among the poor or who had entered seminary after living in the third world. We discussed the complex dynamics of the struggle for liberation both in social structures and in personal relationships. Many liberation and feminist thinkers influenced us. The work of Paulo Freire and the poetry of Pablo Neruda continue to influence me.

I became part of the feminist movement in theology in those years and we questioned everything. As we broke from thinking and speaking of God as male, I discovered that God was still present but more powerfully. It was as if the male language had been containing a Presence far more powerful than words, and without the male language, a new awareness of the Sacred Presence surged upon me. Freed from entrapment in dominating masculine images, God became a real Presence for me. It was as if God had emerged again from Lynne Soper's crayon picture of the magnificent world where no single thing is God, but God is there. The image of the Old Man in the Sky became a pathetic little deity by comparison.

Commitment to embodiment was an important part of feminist transformation, both social and personal. Choreography by group improvisation in a liturgical dance group may have taught me as much theology as the mental activities of reading and intellectual discussion. More recently I have participated in a practice known as InterPlay, an activity that incorporates creative movement, story-telling, and free vocalization as a body-centered group practice. The theme of embodiment also infuses activist spiritual practice as we seek to live out our commitments with authenticity and integrity. How we think is also rooted in bodily reality and social relationships. More recently, I have found linguist George Lakoff's work helpful to understand how embodied or metaphorical logic operates more powerfully than propositional logic. My current work is based on his analysis of how the family metaphor operates in contemporary political discussion.

Following seminary, I was ordained in Montana and served for a number of years in justice-oriented ministries and with low-income people in Chicago and Mexico. For example, I assembled delegations of church people to speak with prison officials and engaged in non-violent civil disobedience against United States support of governments and paramilitary groups in Central America that were slaughtering hundreds of thousands of peasants. I managed small employment ventures with urban youth and aided abused women to find safety from their abusers. In these activities I encountered Sacred Presence not so much in a consuming conviction of the righteousness of a cause (a tendency certainly present in all this work) but in a deepening love for people who are hurting, a love that seeks solutions and encourages hope. There were many moments of clarity when I was aware of Sacred Presence. For example, when a Regional Director of the Immigration and Naturalization Service withdrew his hand, cowering as I offered a handshake; I saw his heart-breaking fear of connection to the suffering his office was inflicting. On one occasion when I spent an overnight in a police lock-up, the woman in the next cell returned weeping after she had made her one phone call and the recipient had refused to help her. Even as I spoke futile words of comfort and sat compassionately to hear her desperation, I experienced an incongruous apprehension of ultimate peace inherent in our human unity. I have known the same Sacred Listening Presence in service as a local church pastor, having been privileged to share the full moments of life with many different kinds of people.

As a minister in a small urban congregation, I ran across Orlando Patterson's work, *Slavery and Social Death*. It set off flashes of theological recognition for me about how much Christian theological language is embedded in the system of slavery. I entered doctoral studies with a desire to probe how the slave and family system of the Roman Empire influenced the early development of Christianity. My intellectual and theological quest was becoming part of my activist practice, as investigation into the origins of Christianity prompted questions about how to live it more fully in the present.

Active faith is a dangerous spiritual practice. For one thing, the danger to the practitioner is well-known. Following Jesus tends to threaten existing power structures and relationships. Jesus faced the consequences in the cross. Another danger of active faith is that we can never be entirely sure of what we are doing. None of us has a monopoly on the truth nor can we reliably predict the consequences of our actions. Yet passivity is also a response to the injustice of the world as it is. Whether acting or waiting, we act or wait in a hope not limited to our belief in the results our own actions. A greater transformative power is at work as well. These are some of the things I have learned in trying to live as a follower of Jesus.

Jesus

The original title of this essay was "Coming to Jesus." I had planned to trace how my work as a scholar brings me from awareness of an infinite God to meet Jesus at the center of my faith. While Jesus was not absent from my religious upbringing, God was always at the center. Jesus helped the covenant community understand God, but our relationship with God was the main thing. As I began to write, however, I was recognizing my process of maturation in the faith as a process of coming to Jesus. Again I was aware of the spiraling movement of faith. The wide and wonderful God of my childhood becomes more and more incarnate for me in the person of Jesus as I study his words and preach his life, death, and resurrection. At times I know myself more deeply alive as one of his followers. In difficult times

I have experienced the resurrection life as strength to stand up, strength from a source beyond my own personal resources. For me, coming to Jesus and coming through Jesus is a personal and covenantal choice to live the resurrection life.

Jesus has been socially constructed, deconstructed, and reconstructed in many ways to serve many purposes, as often as not in order to avoid his teaching's radical claims. The work of the Jesus Seminar reveals some of those radical claims for a new generation. My hope, however, is in the regenerative process that scholarly rediscovery of Christianity's origins can engender, rather than in scholarly efforts to reduce Christianity to a single source or a simple teaching. Trying to reduce this multi-dimensional Christian faith to its supposed "kernel" or "essence," as Adolf von Harnack attempted at the turn of the last century, risks what Alfred Loisy argued against him: the loss of the whole tree that has grown up from the seed(s). I stand with Loisy for the whole tree.

Now with the assistance of recent scholarship, including the work of the Westar Fellows, we glimpse an inclusive faith as a magnificent forest. The views of other early Christians reflected in the non-canonical texts are restoring parts of the forest that were lost through the years. I understand myself to be in a covenantal relationship with those lost voices from the past as well. I do not mean that I make an intellectual assent to every fantastic gnostic myth found in the Nag Hammadi texts, but I affirm such ancient people as engaged in a shared exploration of faith. For me the project of the faith community is not intellectual purification—that is, driving out those who are different—but rather it is an inclusiveness that accepts the diversity that enriches our understanding of faith.

The popular religious dimensions of Christian origins thus still have a claim on me as one of Jesus's followers. Only as a covenantal participant in the full humanity of Jesus's followers am I able to perceive his divinity. This participation takes place in ritual and bodily knowing, as well as in intellectual investigation. As a scholar of the various contexts of early Christianity, I see the gospels as popular religious texts, products as much of community ritual life as of lone writers composing texts. It is my judgment that in the passion narratives, particularly in Mark, we are reading elements of ritual re-enactments of the last days of Jesus' life, an experience early believers entered through baptism. Such ritual was similar to the function of the initiations into mystery cults in which participants entered the experience of a deity's story in a secret initiation ritual. Participants in the Christian ritual processed their own pain in recalling and sharing the experience of Jesus' crucifixion and thus were able to share the experience of his resurrection as well. Jesus' story functioned for Christians as the deity's story functioned for the mystery religions, and in this way Jesus became recognized as the divine Jesus Christ.

Jesus was also called "son of God." While the title has other implications, the other "son of God" of prime importance in the Roman Empire
was the Emperor. Using this title for Jesus proclaimed an alternative social
reality to that of the Empire and a counter-imperial perception of Jesus as
the real son of the real God and the ruler of the "kingdom" he proclaimed.
In their ritual and community life early Christians were creating alternative ways to relate to one another as family, and offering opportunities for
personal transformation and maintaining dignity by inclusion in Christ.
The early Christian response to Empire is similar to the myriad forms of
resistance that powerless people use. (The work of James C. Scott has been
helpful in exploring the counter-imperial dimensions of the early Christian
movements.) In covenant, I commit myself with others to continue promoting the creative alternatives they sought, alternatives we find through
entry into the transformative experience of Jesus' crucifixion and resurrection by means of ritual experience and in life. The Sacred Presence thus
becomes known among those who know suffering. Jesus Christ has come
to embody that sacred reality. Whatever process may bring it about, the
Sacred Presence is no less real for those who enter through incorporation
into Jesus' experience.

As I consider the crucifixion and resurrection experience, however, I am
bothered anew by a question from feminist discussions in my young adult
years: Does accepting the crucifixion-resurrection paradigm as a way of life
mean accepting abuse? How does this crucifixion-resurrection paradigm
connect to the dynamics of shame in the families of the first century and
in the lives of families and churches today? I continue to question how
atonement theology works and why so many find it so powerful to say that
"Jesus died for our sins"—an idea that is still puzzling to me. Currently I
am returning to the issue of connecting to the Sacred Listening Presence
only in silence and setting aside the crucifixion-resurrection paradigm for
now. Joy and a new awareness of wisdom emerge in the "fruits" of a life
connected with the Sacred Listening Presence.

Fruits

The "kingdom of God" is not only something for which we work in the
struggle for justice and peace, but also something we allow to work in
us, most profoundly as forgiving and healing power. Active faith is more
than activism. Daily fruits are its real indicators. For me, the core of the
work for human transformation is in a life of forgiveness, gratitude, and
compassion. These "fruits" of sharing the Sacred Presence are topics in
themselves, but I name them as features of the life that I believe is worth
living. Forgiveness seems to be difficult to think about and to practice
precisely because it requires acknowledgement of realities we would rather

not face, and because it brings about unsettling change. As a spiritual text, Flora Slosson Wuellner's slim volume continues to provide me with insights into forgiveness. The basic life choice of gratitude rather than resentment is both self-perpetuating and joy-giving. Compassion unites all these and is a sign of the Sacred Presence at work in our relationships. All of these fruits and others as well are rooted in the "life that really is life." I have come to recognize the life that reflects these realities as the resurrection life and the life that I believe endures beyond death—though in what form, we are unable to know. I only know that gratefully living in forgiveness and compassion the life I have been given is the essence of life itself. This kind of life is worth living in the same way that the alternative social reality Jesus proclaimed in the first century as the "imperial rule of God" is the social reality worth living. That is the covenant I experience being kept with me and all of us by a creative Sacred Presence in the universe.

Works Consulted

Courlander, Harold. *The Fourth World of the Hopis: The Epic Story of the Hopi Indians as Preserved in Their Legends*. New York: Crown, 1972.

de Saint-Exupéry, Antoine. *Citadelle*. [Paris]: Gallimard, 1948.

Eiseley, Loren C. *The Immense Journey*. New York: Time, [c. 1962].

Freire, Paulo. *Pedagogy of the Oppressed*. Trans. Myra Bergman Ramos. New York: Seabury, 1973.

Lakoff, George. *Moral Politics: How Liberals and Conservatives Think*. 2nd. ed. Chicago and London: University of Chicago Press, 2002.

Loisy, Alfred. *The Gospel and the Church*. Trans. Christopher Home. Lives of Jesus Series. Philadelphia: Fortress, 1976.

Neruda, Pablo. *Extravagaria*. Trans. Alistair Reid. New York: Farrar, Straus and Giroux, 1974.

Patterson, Orlando. *Slavery and Social Death: A Comparative Study*. Cambridge, MA: Harvard University Press, 1982.

Piercy, Marge. *To Be of Use*. Garden City, NJ and New York: Doubleday, 1969.

Rossetti, Christina Georgina. "Who Has Seen the Wind?" in *Sing-Song: A Nursery Rhyme Book*. London and New York: MacMillan, 1893.

Scott, James C. *Domination and the Arts of Resistance: Hidden Transcripts*. New Haven and London: Yale University Press, 1990.

Teilhard de Chardin, Pierre. *The Phenomenon of Man*. Trans. Bernard Wall. New York: Harper & Row, 1959.

von Harnack, Alfred. *What is Christianity?* Trans. Thomas B. Saunders. Harper Torchbook. New York: Harper & Row, 1957.

Ware, Corinne. *Discover Your Spiritual Type: A Guide to Individual and Congregational Growth*. Hernondon, VA: Alban Institute, 1995.

Wuellner, Flora Slosson. *Forgiveness, the Passionate Journey: Nine Steps of Forgiving Through Jesus' Beatitudes*. Nashville, TN: Upper Room, 2001.

Disparate Presence

Hal Taussig

When modern thinkers dare speak of meaning, they usually speak impersonally, analytically, and with pretense of objectivity. As one who has been trained in this same tradition of impersonal and supposedly objective analysis, I find it important to undercut some of its arrogance and pretense that still has a hold on me. So I begin this earnest and brief effort at trying to make sense of life and belief with an explicitly personal and subjective experience. What follows is a description of a regular spiritual exercise of mine. The exercise fits into a broader spiritual and theological practice that includes analytical approaches and that I will sketch out later in this essay:

I find myself staring intensely at something beautiful: a tulip in the moonlight, patterns of sunlight on my office wall, a tree. Not something necessarily breath-taking, like the Sawtooth Mountains in Idaho or the Maine coastline, although they would work equally well. Usually, however, I stare at something somewhat more prosaic, like flowers in a garden, clouds in the sky, or spider webs in the sunlight. Almost always it is something natural, but occasionally I focus on abstract colors or attractive lines in a building.

Then I chant a prayer to the object at which I am staring intently. Often my chanted prayer is one by composer John Bell of the Iona community:

Take, oh, take me as I am.
Summon out what I shall be.
Set your seal upon my heart,
And live in me.

These words—when I sing them—are meant as an explicit request of the particular tulip, sunlight, tree, mountains, coastline, clouds, or spider web. I treat the object as a personal presence. I don't just imagine that it *could* be a person. I relate to it honestly and directly as I would to a person who is listening to me and can respond, even though I know that the object isn't a person.

Here are several examples. I ask the mountain to "take me as I am." As I say these words, I remember who I am in my complex, incomplete, powerful, and inconsistent self. I expect the mountain to accept me and to let me know that it does. I address it as a real presence that hears my chant. Of course just as with a person, I never know for sure whether the mountain has really responded or not.

I ask the tree (or whatever) to "summon out what I shall be." As I chant these words, I call forth the potentials, incompletenesses, hopes, and urges within me and request that the tree bring them together into what I can become. I am aware that it may take the tree time to do this, but my request is serious, for I am convinced of the tree's power to call forth something new in me.

I ask the intricate veins of a plant's leaf to set their seal upon my heart. As I chant, I open myself to the veins of the plant (or the brilliant colors of the tulip or the abstract forms in a painting) that they may enter and infuse my being with their own. I expect the leaf's veins to soak into my inner life and thereby make a difference in the way I act, think, and feel.

I ask the sunlight on the wall to "live in me." My song invites the sunlight inside me, not just as some kind of metaphorical experience, but as an actual penetration into my body by the sunlight at which I am staring at that very moment. I anticipate and subsequently confirm that this sunlit pattern on the wall does in fact reside in me partly because I have invited it in and partly because I expect it to do so. In that moment I experience disparate presence—delicate, untriumphant, yet persistent, full of beauty and goodness.

God?

One might say that I treat these various objects before me as God. I would not disagree, but would hasten also to clarify. I do not conceive a collective consciousness behind these particulars. There is no ensemble making up a single whole. My relationship to the flower, abstract painting, or sunlight on the wall is a particular one, each engaging me in and of itself. Each presence has its own quality. Inasmuch as I encounter presence in various relationships of this kind, it is disparate presence, with similarity and distinctness. Since I usually sing the "prayer" while staring at one particular moss-colored boulder, dandelion blossom, or abstract painting, I expect each particular reality to take me, summon forth from me, set its seal upon me, and live within me. Indeed I experience them doing that regularly. In short, I relate to each of them as presence, a quality similar to what many people call God.

Although I have great affection for the Bell prayer/song, I could say any number of relatively "traditional" prayers to these beautiful objects. For instance, using *The Complete Book of Christian Prayer*, I could say Augustine's prayer to the ocean, the spider web, and the tree:

Fill us with holy love,
And open to us the treasures of your wisdom.

All our desire is known to you,
And therefore perfect what you have begun. . . . (p. 4)

Or, using the prayer of William Laud, a seventeenth century poet, I could say to a pattern of mosaic tile, or a flock of geese circling overhead:

I give and offer up unto thee myself and all that is mine, actions and words, repose and silence; only do thou preserve and guide me, and direct my hand and mind and tongue to things. . . . (p. 55)

Or, I could say the prayer of St. Francis of Assisi to the green emerald wave of water:

You are love, you are wisdom
You are humility, you are endurance.
You are rest, you are peace.
You are joy and gladness, you are justice. . . . (p. 20)

Let me make this as pointed as possible. While I address these particular objects of beauty as if they in their discreteness and particularity were God, I am not addressing some abstraction or transcendence beyond them. I make my request, or praise, to the particular object itself. As fully as I can, I enter into a personal relationship with the tulip in the moonlight, the rock glistening on the beach, the spider's web, or the pattern on the wing of the dragonfly.

In other words, my meditation or prayer arises from beliefs that both contrast and coincide in some ways to traditional Christian doctrine. My convictions are these:

- The term "God" is a decent approximation of a powerful experience by human beings. Whatever one might mean by the word, "God" is not simply a matter of belief and perception, but of participation in a central dynamic in the universe. I reject a depersonalized notion of the universe, and propose that the universe is diffusely entwined with what one might call spirit or divinity.
- God does not exist outside the particular. There is no being out there somewhere who hears prayers, creates other beings, and directs history. Whatever one might mean by "God," the word cannot indicate an abstract reality. I reject the theism of conventional Christianity, Judaism, and Islam, and claim instead a reconstructed notion of divinity that is immanent, embodied in the world, and yet similar to many dimensions of the classic spiritualities and theologies of those same religions.
- God is limited. "God" is not the totality of existence but a particular and creative dimension of existence. I reject the idea of omnipotence and the notions of an Almighty God, and throw myself into a love for a limited God of goodness and beauty. This notion of God as limited and particular power does not serve only as a critique of traditional beliefs.

It also stands in opposition to the trendy and New Age notion of God as "everything."

- There are other ways to talk about the reality, power, and particularity of a disparate presence than with God-language. I reject all institutionalized passwords for relating to such presence, and celebrate its anachronistic availability.
- Although my own personal tastes have drawn me toward everyday objects of muted beauty in nature, this disparate presence is not limited to nature. Indeed, it would be the blandest of religious romanticism to propose a spirituality that claimed "nature" as its authority. Both my own practice and the history of spirituality in a variety of religions affirm that this presence cannot be limited to what is romantically and inaccurately labeled "nature." Occasionally I find myself doing similar meditations on the New York subway. Muslims pray in direct relationship to abstract drawings. Many Christians meditate on everything from wafers to mandalas.

Although my spiritual exercise of praying to beautiful objects does entwine itself with some beliefs, I regard the exercise itself as much more important than the related beliefs; that is, I suspect that my beliefs have not generated the practice as much as the practice and personal experience have helped shape the beliefs. This statement reflects a deeper conviction that spiritual practice is more reliable than articulated religious beliefs. In this regard I subscribe to the affirmation that C. G. Jung once enunciated during a television interview: "I do not believe in God. I see God."

A Personalized Universe

The universe in which I live is completely sufficient for an expansive, empowered, and vital life without recourse to a theological abstract transcendence. The universe's quotients of beauty, goodness, and truth (although neither ubiquitous nor triumphant) present us with an unending potential for a limitless creative unfolding. For me, if there is something beyond our universe, it is a subject completely beyond my capacity of knowing and therefore is irrelevant to the task of this essay—that of characterizing my belief and spiritual practice.

The universe is personal. By this I do not (as noted above) mean that there is a Person somewhere who exists and rules the universe. Rather, as cosmologists Brian Swimme and Thomas Berry propose, I mean that the universe is inherently connected, full of feeling, and differentiating; that is, particularities within the universe feel, actively relate to one another, and encourage one another to be different. The universe, then, carries within its unending particularities personal and relational dynamics far beyond the human sphere.

I recognize that the personal character of the universe leads some to believe in a Being who is a personal God. But I think that when such conviction is elaborated into a system of belief and practice, it inevitably runs aground and fails to answer important theoretical questions. Therefore, while I can understand the evocative power and partial benefit of belief in a personal God, I can neither commend it as an adequate belief nor recommend the practice that attends it.

Derived primarily from the disciplines of the physical and biological sciences, the universe of Berry and Swimme contains three fundamental characteristics:

"The evolution of the universe will be characterized by *differentiation, autopoiesis,* and *communion* throughout time and space and at every level of reality. These three terms . . . refer to the governing themes and the basal intentionality of all existence. . . . (73)

The first of these characteristics is differentiation (that is, a sorting out into distinct particularities):

> There has never been a time when the universe did not seek further differentiation. . . . Not only is each thing new and different from all other structures; the dynamics of the new structures are quantitatively new as well. The interactions governing the elementary particles are qualitatively and quantitatively distinct from those involving atoms, which are again different from the dynamics involved with stars and galaxies. . . . In the universe to be is to be different. To be is to be a unique manifestation of existence. . . . The seemingly infinite power for transfiguration in every region of the universe speaks of an inexhaustible fecundity at the root of reality. . . . The creativity of each place and time differs from that of every other place and time. The universe comes to us, each being and each moment announcing its thrilling news: I am fresh. To understand the universe you must understand me. (73–75)

Swimme and Berry describe the second characteristic by the Greek word *autopoiesis*, which they define as "the inner dimension of things":

> From living bodies to galaxies, we find a universe filled with structures exhibiting self-organizing dynamics. The self that is referred to by (this) autopoiesis is not visible to the eye. Only its effects can be discerned. . . .
>
> Living beings and such ecosystems as the tropical forests or the coral reefs are the chief exemplars of self-organizing dynamics. . . . Autopoiesis refers to the power each thing has to participate in the cosmos-creating endeavor. For instance we have spoken of the autopoiesis of a star. The star organizes hydrogen and helium and produces elements and light. This ordering is the central activity of the star itself. That is, the star has a functioning self, a dynamic of organization centered within itself. That which organizes this vast entity of elements and action is precisely what we mean by the star's power of self-articulation. . . . Autopoiesis points to the interior dimension of things. Even the simplest atom cannot be understood by considering

only its physical structure or the outer world of external relationships with other things. Things emerge with an inner capacity for self-manifestation. (75–76)

Berry and Swimme's third basic principle of the universe is that of communion, which they describe in the following manner:

"To be is to be related, for relationship is the essence of existence. In the very first instant when the primitive particles rushed forth, every one of them was connected to every other one in the entire universe. At no time in the future existence of the universe would they ever arrive at a point of disconnection. Alienation for a particle is a theoretical impossibility. . . .

Nothing is itself without everything else. Our Sun emerged into being out of the creativity of so many millions of former beings. The elements of the floating presolar cloud had been created by former stars and by the primeval fireball. . . . The universe advances into community. . . . (77–78)

Swimme and Berry's understanding of the universe's three basic characteristics working together goes like this: "The universe advances into community—into a differentiated web of relationships among sentient centers of creativity" (77). The deep relationality and inner-quality of everything in the Swimme and Berry scheme makes the universe deeply personal without necessarily pointing to the existence of a personal God. In their portrait of the behaviors of rocks, atoms, dragonflies, and other aspects of the universe, a sentient web of differentiated being emerges. Disparate presence is observed, described, and celebrated.

It is important to notice both the similarities and differences between this presence and the traditional Christian understanding of God. The same values of differentiation, inner life, and connectedness are affirmed in both. In traditional Christian self-understanding this differentiation, subjectivity, and communion come together in the personal God. Berry and Swimme affirm these three basic dynamics of existence, but do not posit a personal God. The universe is indeed deeply personal, since everything—from atoms to zebras—has an inner life. And the hypothesized unity of existence can be compared to the notion of God. If one will grant that "God" can be understood in terms of the three basic characteristics of the universe as described by Swimme and Berry, then I can speak of God and describe my relationship to God as a way of talking about the thoroughgoing differentiation, innerness, and connectedness of the universe in which I live. Conversely, inasmuch as I relate to the universe as always differentiating, inner, and connected (as I do in the prayer exercise outlined at the beginning of this essay), I do not necessarily need to postulate a mythical personal God, since I am connected personally to the universe.

My affirmation of a "personal God" in terms of a personal universe—or better, perhaps, a godless personal universe—depends on my personal involvement in the universe's dynamics of differentiation, inner life, and communion. In other words, my affirmation comes not primarily from my (or Berry/Swimme's) intellectual analysis, but from my own ability to respect and participate in the dynamics of differentness, innerness, and connectedness as found in the universe and in others in the human family. Again, as C. G. Jung said: "I do not believe in God. I see God."

Embracing the De-Centered Postmodern

When cosmologist Brian Swimme is asked to locate the center of the universe, he states clearly that it is multi-centered, by which he means that Newtonian perspectives cannot do justice to the notion of the big bang or the "flaming forth" at the beginning of the universe. There is no one center where the big bang began, Swimme states. Rather there are many centers. Although this is not understandable from conventional perspectives, it is standard in the physics of the past 75 years and basic to the larger set of discoveries that include the relativity of time and space discovered by Albert Einstein and the uncertainty principle postulated by Werner Heisenberg. In other words, science posits that a completely objective knowledge is no longer possible. Therefore when people of a more philosophical or religious inclination explore the contingencies of knowing, they are not necessarily being "unscientific."

Until very recently, however, Western thought and its child, Christian theology, have assumed an objectivist lens, and assumed it was the task of theology and all Western thought to describe objective reality. Postmodern thought, however, has challenged this as both impossible and arrogant. Postmodernists like Michel Foucault and Jacques Derrida assert—properly I think—that every articulation about what is true or objective has an inherent power interest and social location: that is to say, no one can be objective, because the individual's own power interests and social influences prevent it. For some postmodernists this rules out any discussion of a common knowledge, but for most (including myself) a limited possibility of a common knowing exists. To be sure, such knowing is somewhat less than completely objective, but is nevertheless helpful to those who wish to describe their common awareness of a disparate presence.

Creeds within Christian tradition are perhaps the best example of this arrogant and naive assertion of objective knowledge because they claim to represent the eternal truth for Christian belief. Yet looking back from our present point in time, it is evident that these creeds use terms belonging to a time different from ours, and therefore they are unable to render any kind of statement of objective truth for our time. Similarly, an historical analysis of the process of making creeds has made it clear that while engaged in formulating these documents, the creed-makers had many personal power-interests at heart.

The postmodern challenge to the creeds frees contemporary thinking from pretense and arrogance. Those of us willing to risk it are now able to propose what we regard as of significant value on the basis of an admitted particularity that claims no final objective perspective. Rooting oneself in a particular relationality with the universe makes it clear that one cannot speak for everyone. Facing the particular trees, spiders, and dancing lights in one's own situation in life, and describing the resulting experience humbly, allows for one's own provisional truth to be expressed in a way that avoids arrogance, but permits innerness, differentiation, and connectedness. As Swimme and Berry propose, no one final objective center exists from which to speak with authority. We must admit our power interests and affirm the social locations that both relativize us and create in us partial authority for a particular time and place.

Jesus and the Basileia of God

The core teachings of Jesus as described in the work of the Jesus Seminar have facilitated my active relationship to the disparate presence that I have encountered in mediation/prayer and clarified by the cosmological analysis of Swimme and Berry.

Jesus' proclamation of the "*basileia* of God" (traditionally translated as "kingdom of God," but of late often referred to and translated as "the domain of God," "the realm of God," "the reign of God," or the "kindom of God") is at the heart of his teachings. In the core red and pink sayings, those identified as authentic by the Jesus Seminar, one finds a focus on God's *basileia* as a dynamic presence in a wide range of experiences in the world. These experiences, according to Jesus' teachings, do not tend to be obvious "mountain-top" experiences. Rather, they are encounters with aspects of life often deemed ordinary or even mundane.

Jesus says that the *basileia* of God is like a mustard seed that grows into a common bush often considered a weed in Jesus' world (Mark 4:30–32), or a woman baking bread (Luke 13:20–21), or a Samaritan—a member of a despised ethnic minority (Luke 10:30–35). Like the other parables of Jesus, these images appeal to specific everyday experiences in order to describe an encounter with God's *basileia*. It is a disparate encounter, a surprising way to experience something divine, and a challenge to see the world differently. The Gospel of Thomas describes the *basileia* as "spread out upon all the earth, and people just don't see it" (113).

A striking correspondence exists between the disparate presence I experienced in my prayer/meditation exercises; the differentiating, inner, and connected dimensions of the universe; and Jesus' teachings about the *basileia* of God:

- In all three there is a shyness about God-talk. The kind of prayer/meditation exercise I am recommending can be related to God, but God-talk is not essential to engage disparate presence. Both Swimme and Berry describe the dynamics of the universe in language akin to traditional attributions of God, but never use the term "God." Jesus did not teach about an experience of God directly, but rather used the circumlocution of the *basileia* of God.
- In all three cases the location of the experience is particular and ordinary, rather than grandiose and metaphysical. The presence intimated is disparate and diffuse. The character of what might be called divine is implicit, not triumphal.
- Each of these ways of considering disparate presence is open-ended. The many objects with which I can pray/meditate are not limited to a prescribed list, nor is a set procedure demanded. For Berry and Swimme the universe is expanding and the kinds of interactions limitless. The *basileia* of God keeps cropping up where one least expects it.

By invoking the disparate presence of the *basileia* of God that emerges in the teachings of Jesus, I do not mean to privilege those teachings. I am sure this presence is accessible without reference to Jesus. But it is through the teaching of Jesus that I often arrive at a consciousness of the disparate presence. The teachings of Jesus are also the primary modality for many others within Christian tradition who seek a more integrated, humble, and grounded encounter with this same presence.

Evil, Pain, and Suffering

The provisional but persistent power of differentiation, innerness, and connectedness in the universe calls me into particular relationships with persons, flowers, rocks, and buildings. In my connectedness to them, I ground myself in my own particularity ("take, oh take me as I am"), and ask for my own and the rock's (or person's or flower's) innerness to interact and call forth from me ("summon out what I shall be") so that both the connectedness and differentiation elaborate themselves by extension into me ("set your seal upon my heart and live in me"). This encounter with the particularity of the universe's character, as noted above, parallels Jesus' teaching about the *basileia* of God. Facing into the specific being of a mustard plant or sunlight on a wall greets a disparate presence in unlikely places and hails it as that which can draw us and all being out into a whole of goodness and wholeness.

But how can such a delicate and fragile relationship to women baking bread or other experiences of *basileia* be an adequate address to the enormous violence, cruelty, pain, and destruction so evident in life? How can the characteristics of differentiation, innerness, and connectedness in all things effectively counter evil? No position on the meaning of life and the significance of belief and thought can be taken in our day without addressing the power of cruelty, damage, and chaos throughout the universe.

My position is neither triumphal nor skeptical. Rather I think that the future is yet held in the balance. It is clear to me that connectedness, innerness, and differentiation can help enormously in bringing forth goodness, truth, and beauty. But it is not clear to me whether that is enough to overrule the disintegrative and chaotic components of the universe. It is not clear whether the deepening of human differentiation, innerness, and connectedness to all that is can affect the future of the universe, but I do think that more innerness, connectedness, and differentiation overall can counteract some disintegration and chaos in human relationships. One can make very similar and relatively provisional affirmations about the *basileia* of God. I simply do not know whether the *basileia* of God can continue to counteract entropy, disintegration, and chaos. It seems possible, but not inevitable. When I pray to a leaf, I place myself in the same creative tension relative to the ultimate outcome that is found within the universe itself—and in Jesus' teachings. I attach myself to a fragile and unfolding possibility, unsure of the final chapter.

As poet Mary Oliver writes,

How many mysteries have you seen in your
    lifetime? How many nets pulled
full over the boat's side, each silver body
    ready or not falling into
submission? How many roses in early summer
    uncurling above the pale sands then
falling back in unfathomable
    willingness? And what can you say? Glory
to the rose and the leaf, to the seed, to the
    silver fish. Glory to time and the wild fields,
and to joy. And to grief's shock and torpor, its near swoon.

A Postscript from Inside Biblical Scholarship

Biblical scholars grew timid and brittle in the twentieth century. The collision of worldwide tragedy, rationality, and galloping change led the field of biblical scholarship as a whole to retreat from trying to make sense of life's big questions. Therefore most biblical scholars retreated into the safety of technical scholarship on small questions, leaving the big questions to the ambitions of science, the hubris of politicians, and the folly of poets. This present volume, then, is a breath of fresh air, an opportunity to embrace the possibility of saying how we make sense of life. The reader will measure us as to whether we have been honest and bold enough.

The rigors of analysis inherent in post-enlightenment biblical scholarship can be of help in keeping us honest. The bold deconstruction of Christian triumphalism in biblical scholarship of the last 200 years provides an important grounding in critical perspectives. The broad scope of the Bible itself can act as expansive companion to the analytical and critical tendencies of scholarship. The imaginative character of much of the biblical language can beckon toward bold and expressive statements.

The assembling of the Jesus Seminar and the deliberations of its scholars also constituted a courageous event. It energized the making of meaning out of the old traditions and was willing to go public with its findings. One of the early keynotes of the seminar was its auspicious blending of humility and imagination. Robert Funk's inaugural address to the Seminar in March of 1985 contained just such a call to imaginative discourse about important questions of meaning, tempered with the humility of perspective. He said: "What we need is a new fiction . . . a new story that reaches beyond old beginnings and endings. . . . Not any fiction will do . . . . We require a new, liberating fiction, one that squares with the best knowledge we can now accumulate and one that transcends self-serving ideologies. And we need a fiction that we recognize to be fictive."

Because of occasional lapses into rationalism and rehearsing the virtues of the so-called Enlightenment of the eighteenth century, it is not clear to me that the Seminar has always remembered that its work had to do with fictional constructs. What is clear to me, however, is that the call for a new fiction integrating the figure of Jesus into a more comprehensive framework lives on in this volume. A sense of fictional construct remains alive within the particulars while the whole succeeds in maintaining a semi-consciousness of the quest for meaning of its readers. Fiction was, of course, the main craft of the historical Jesus as he spun out invented stories from life experience. His fictions are also the place where the persistence of differentiation, innerness, and connectedness gain subtle expression. His parables announce a disparate presence—tenuous, honest, bold, and imaginative.

Works Consulted

Bell, John. "Take, Oh Take Me as I Am" in the record album: *Come All You People: Shorter Songs for Worship.* Iona Community: Wild Goose Worship Group, 1994.

The Complete Book of Christian Prayer. New York: Continuum, 1998.

Einstein, Albert. *Relativity: The Special and General Theory.* New York: Three Rivers Press, 1961.

Funk, Robert. "Inaugural Address: Jesus Seminar." *Foundations and Facets Forum* 1.1 (1985) 14–15.

Heisenberg, Werner. *Philosphical Problems of Quantum Physics*. Woodbridge, Connecticut: Ox Bow Press, 1979.

Jung, Carl Gustav. "Face to Face." Interview by John Freeman, BBC Interview Program. Interview with Carl Gustav Jung. October 22, 1959.

Newton, Isaac. *The Principia: Mathematical Principles of Natural Philosophy*. Berkeley: University of California, 1999.

Oliver, Mary. *Thirst*. Boston: Beacon Press, 2006.

Swimme, Brian, and Thomas Berry. *The Universe Story: From the Primordial Flaring Forth to the Ecozoic Era*. New York: HarperCollins, 1992.

Ancient Texts and Authors

Other Texts And Authors

Modern Authors

LaVergne, TN USA
04 October 2009
159834LV00004B/2/P